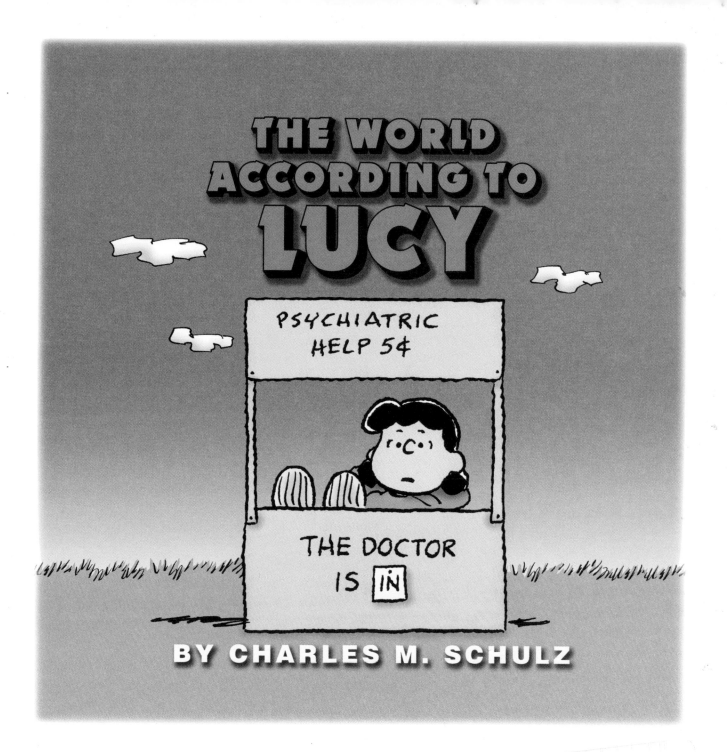

THE WORLD ACCORDING TO LUCY

PSYCHIATRIC
HELP 5¢
THE DOCTOR
IS IN

BY CHARLES M. SCHULZ

Ballantine Books * New York

A Ballantine Book
Published by The Ballantine Publishing Group
Copyright © 2002 by United Feature Syndicate, Inc.

www.ballantinebooks.com
www.snoopy.com

Library of Congress Catalog Card Number: 2001118649

ISBN 0-345-44271-7

Cover design by Paige Braddock, Charles M. Schulz Creative Associates

Manufactured in the United States of America

First Edition: April 2002

10 9 8 7 6 5 4 3 2 1

The World According to Lucy

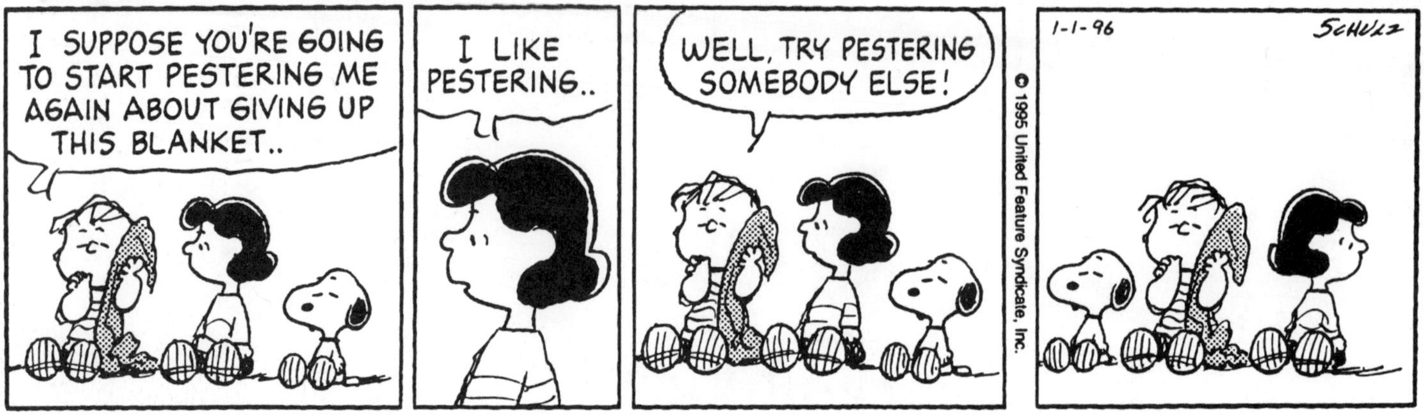
I SUPPOSE YOU'RE GOING TO START PESTERING ME AGAIN ABOUT GIVING UP THIS BLANKET..
I LIKE PESTERING..
WELL, TRY PESTERING SOMEBODY ELSE!
© 1995 United Feature Syndicate, Inc.
1-1-96
SCHULZ

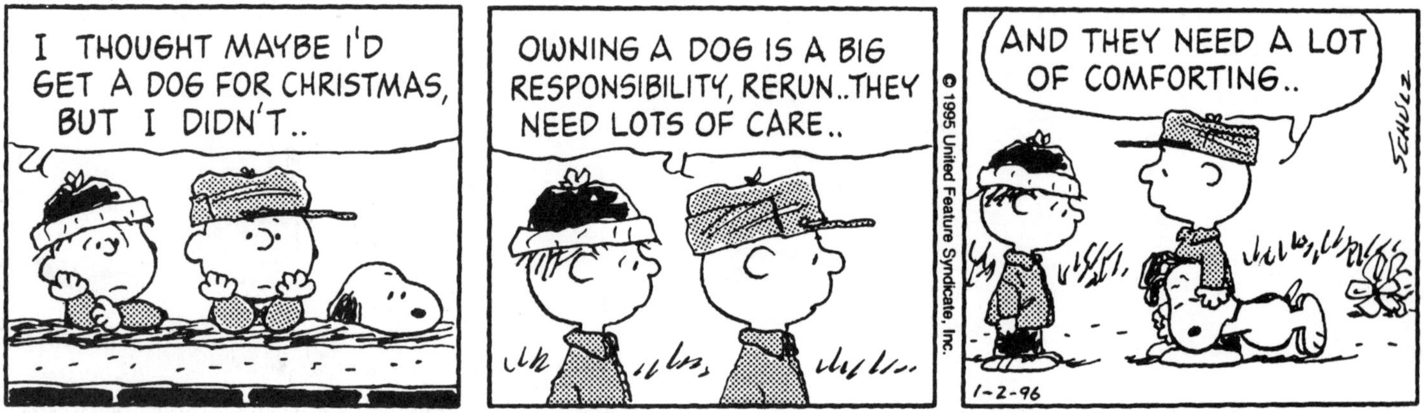
I THOUGHT MAYBE I'D GET A DOG FOR CHRISTMAS, BUT I DIDN'T..
OWNING A DOG IS A BIG RESPONSIBILITY, RERUN..THEY NEED LOTS OF CARE..
© 1995 United Feature Syndicate, Inc.
AND THEY NEED A LOT OF COMFORTING..
SCHULZ
1-2-96

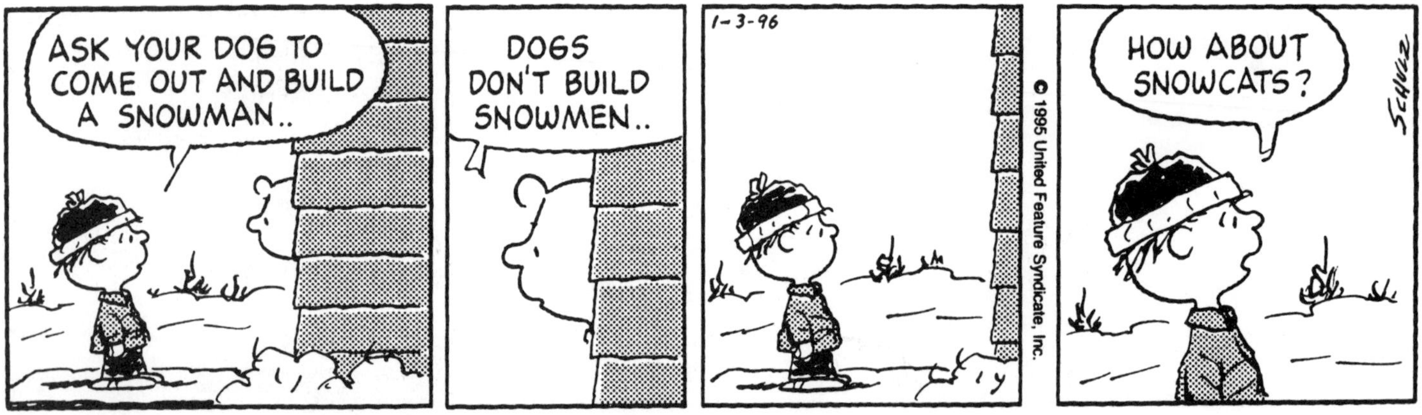
ASK YOUR DOG TO COME OUT AND BUILD A SNOWMAN..
DOGS DON'T BUILD SNOWMEN..
1-3-96
© 1995 United Feature Syndicate, Inc.
HOW ABOUT SNOWCATS?
SCHULZ

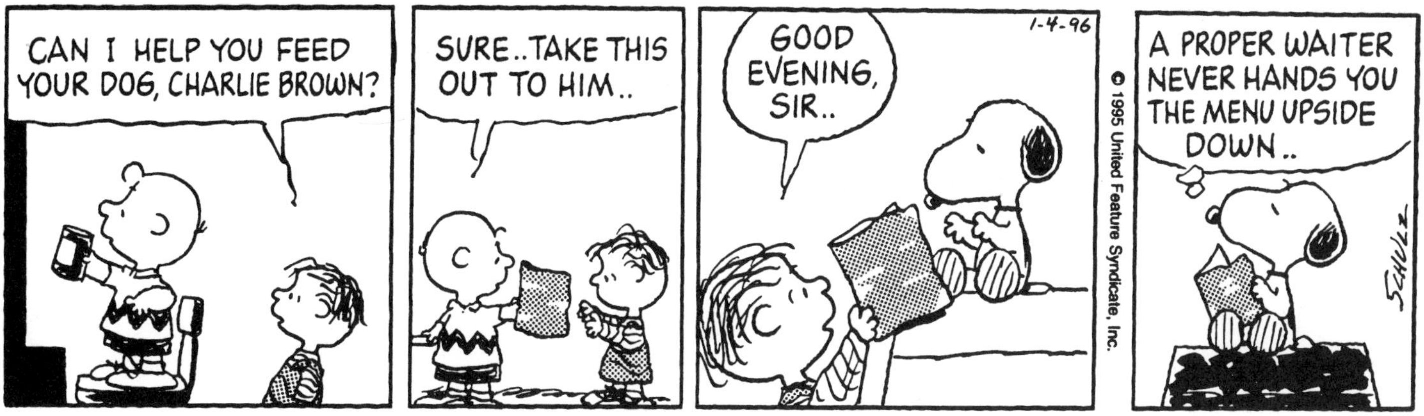
CAN I HELP YOU FEED YOUR DOG, CHARLIE BROWN?
SURE..TAKE THIS OUT TO HIM..
GOOD EVENING, SIR..
1-4-96
© 1995 United Feature Syndicate, Inc.
A PROPER WAITER NEVER HANDS YOU THE MENU UPSIDE DOWN..
SCHULZ

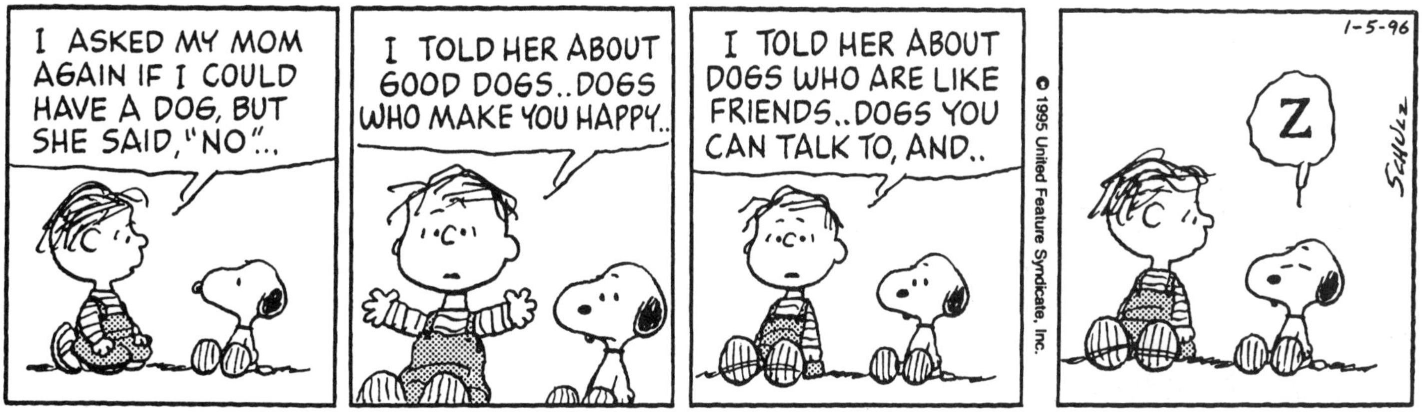
I ASKED MY MOM AGAIN IF I COULD HAVE A DOG, BUT SHE SAID, "NO"..
I TOLD HER ABOUT GOOD DOGS..DOGS WHO MAKE YOU HAPPY..
I TOLD HER ABOUT DOGS WHO ARE LIKE FRIENDS..DOGS YOU CAN TALK TO, AND..
© 1995 United Feature Syndicate, Inc.
1-5-96
Z
SCHULZ

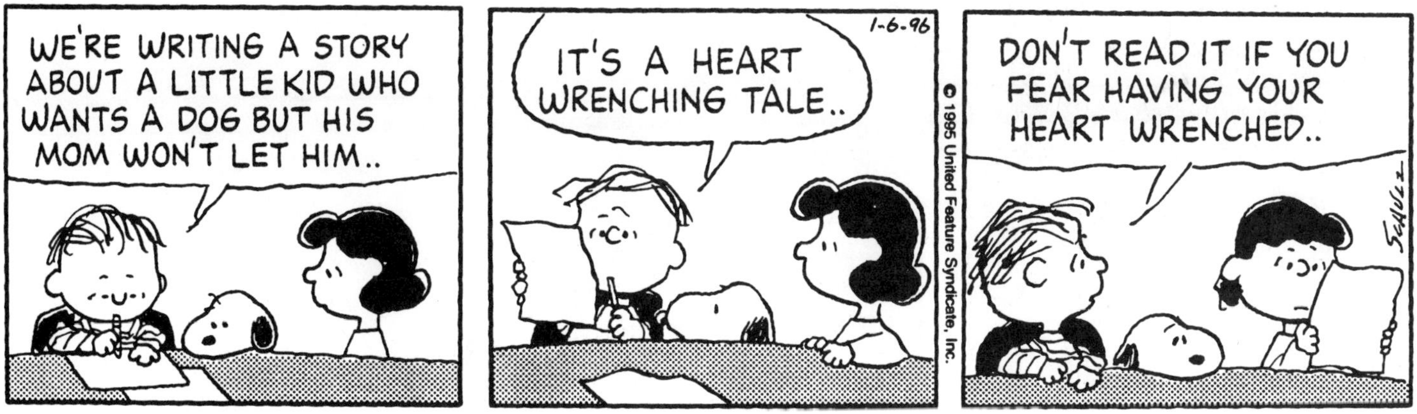
WE'RE WRITING A STORY ABOUT A LITTLE KID WHO WANTS A DOG BUT HIS MOM WON'T LET HIM..
1-6-96
IT'S A HEART WRENCHING TALE..
© 1995 United Feature Syndicate, Inc.
DON'T READ IT IF YOU FEAR HAVING YOUR HEART WRENCHED..
SCHULZ

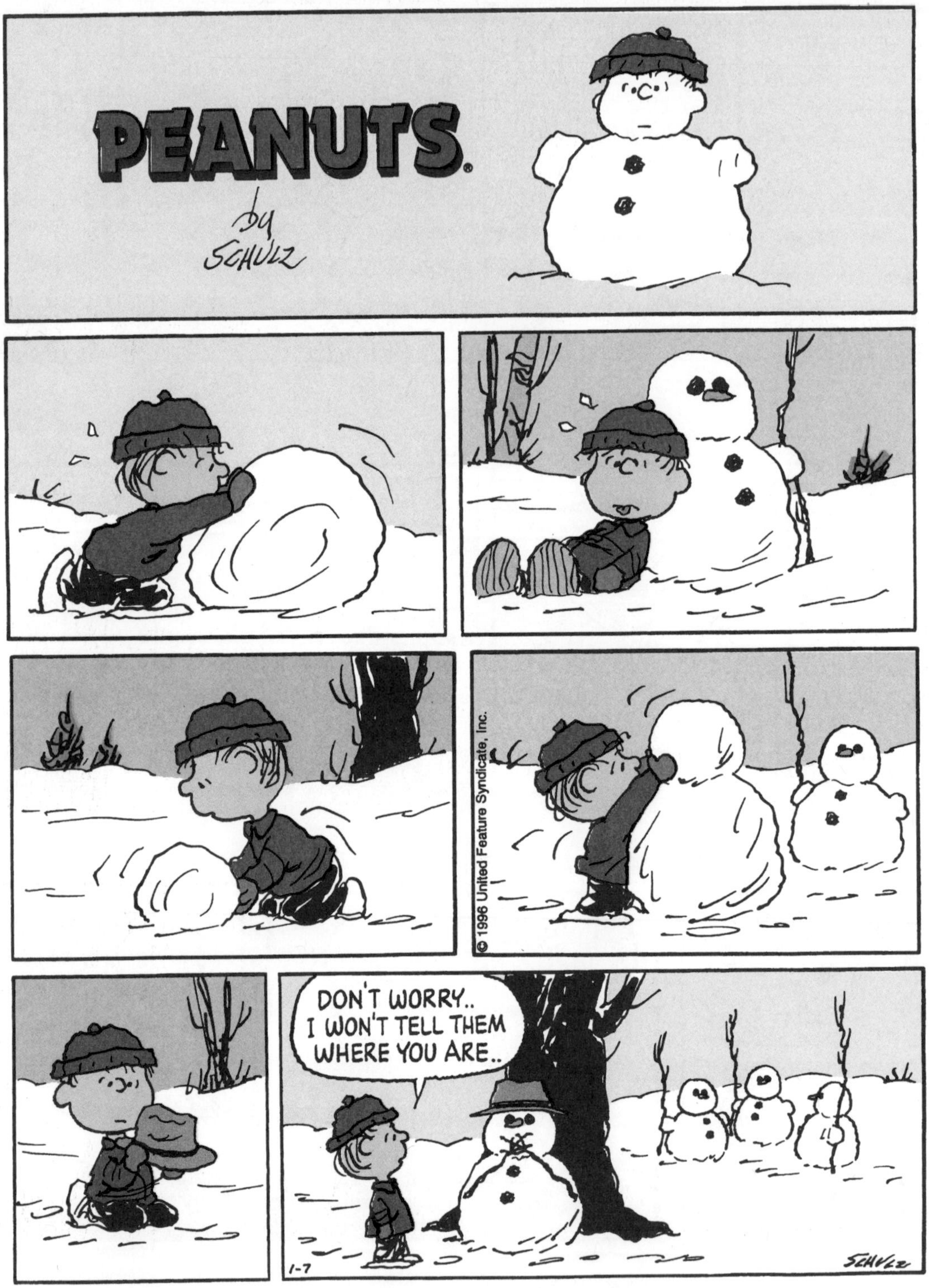
PEANUTS.
by SCHULZ
© 1996 United Feature Syndicate, Inc.
DON'T WORRY..
I WON'T TELL THEM
WHERE YOU ARE..
1-7
SCHULZ

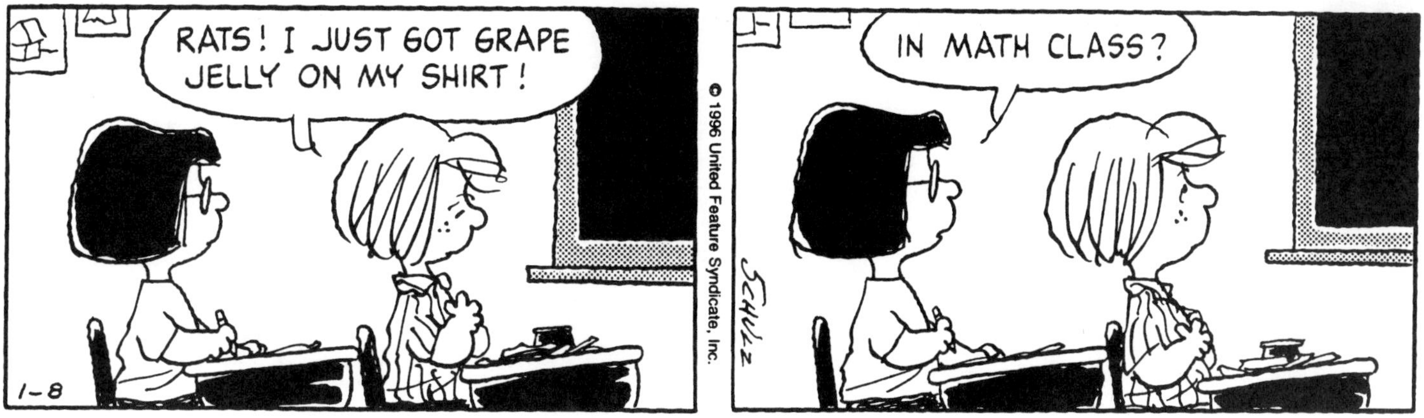
RATS! I JUST GOT GRAPE JELLY ON MY SHIRT!
IN MATH CLASS?
© 1996 United Feature Syndicate, Inc.
SCHULZ
1-8

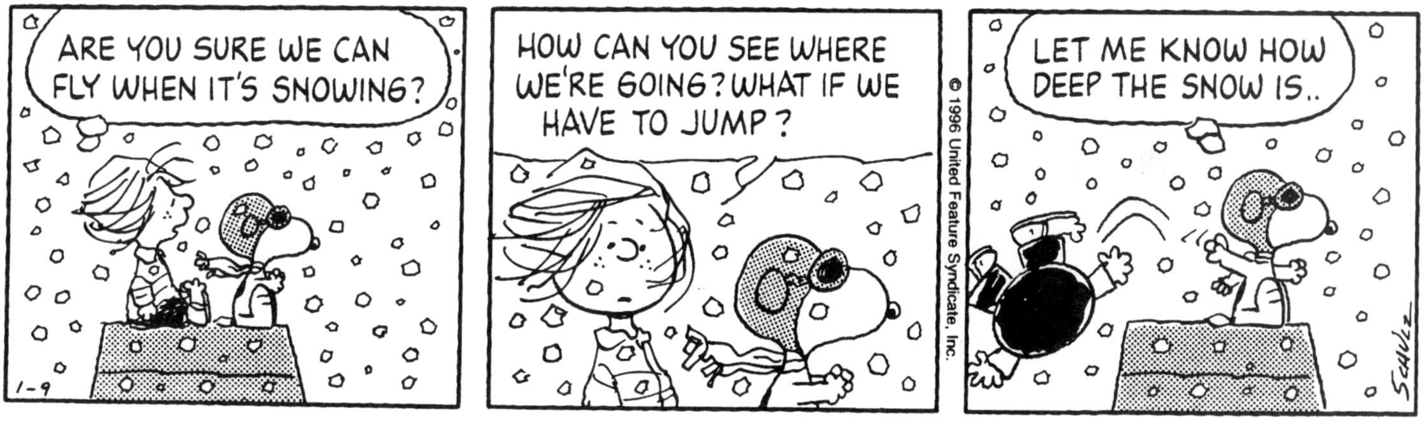
ARE YOU SURE WE CAN FLY WHEN IT'S SNOWING?
HOW CAN YOU SEE WHERE WE'RE GOING? WHAT IF WE HAVE TO JUMP?
LET ME KNOW HOW DEEP THE SNOW IS..
© 1996 United Feature Syndicate, Inc.
SCHULZ
1-9

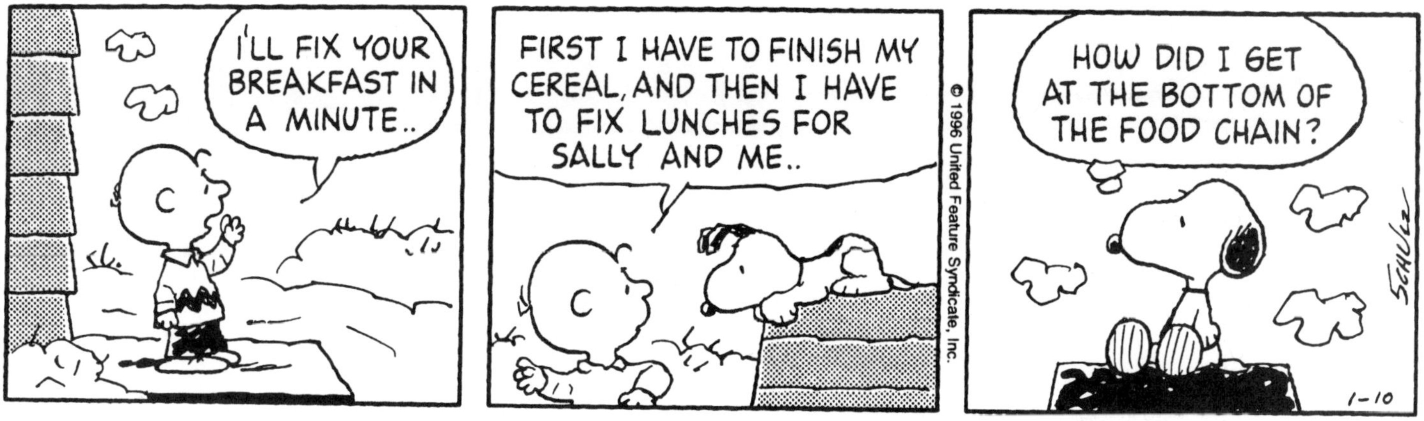
I'LL FIX YOUR BREAKFAST IN A MINUTE..
FIRST I HAVE TO FINISH MY CEREAL, AND THEN I HAVE TO FIX LUNCHES FOR SALLY AND ME..
HOW DID I GET AT THE BOTTOM OF THE FOOD CHAIN?
© 1996 United Feature Syndicate, Inc.
SCHULZ
1-10

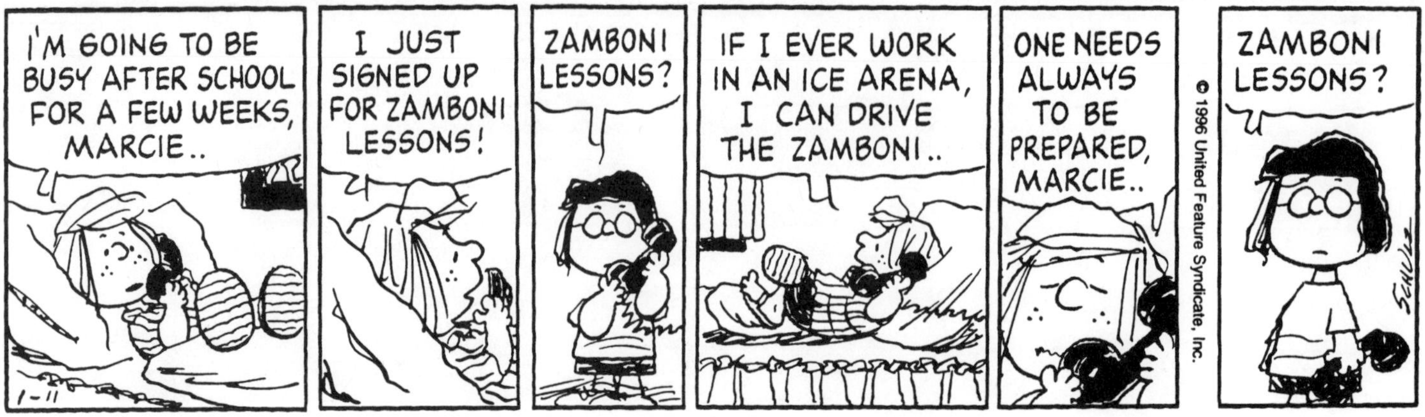
I'M GOING TO BE BUSY AFTER SCHOOL FOR A FEW WEEKS, MARCIE..
I JUST SIGNED UP FOR ZAMBONI LESSONS!
ZAMBONI LESSONS?
IF I EVER WORK IN AN ICE ARENA, I CAN DRIVE THE ZAMBONI..
ONE NEEDS ALWAYS TO BE PREPARED, MARCIE..
ZAMBONI LESSONS?
© 1996 United Feature Syndicate, Inc.

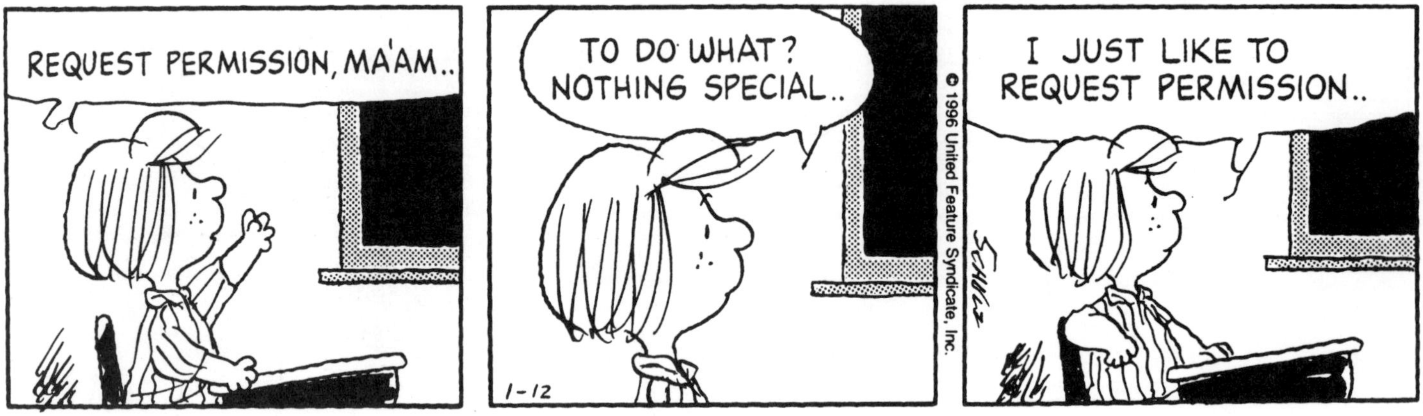
REQUEST PERMISSION, MA'AM..
TO DO WHAT? NOTHING SPECIAL..
I JUST LIKE TO REQUEST PERMISSION..
© 1996 United Feature Syndicate, Inc.

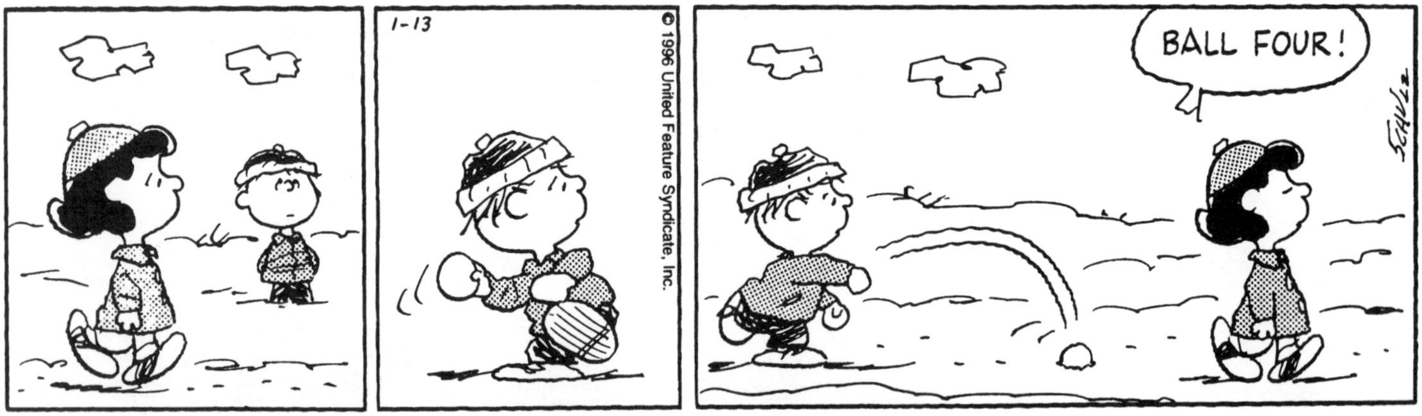
BALL FOUR!
© 1996 United Feature Syndicate, Inc.

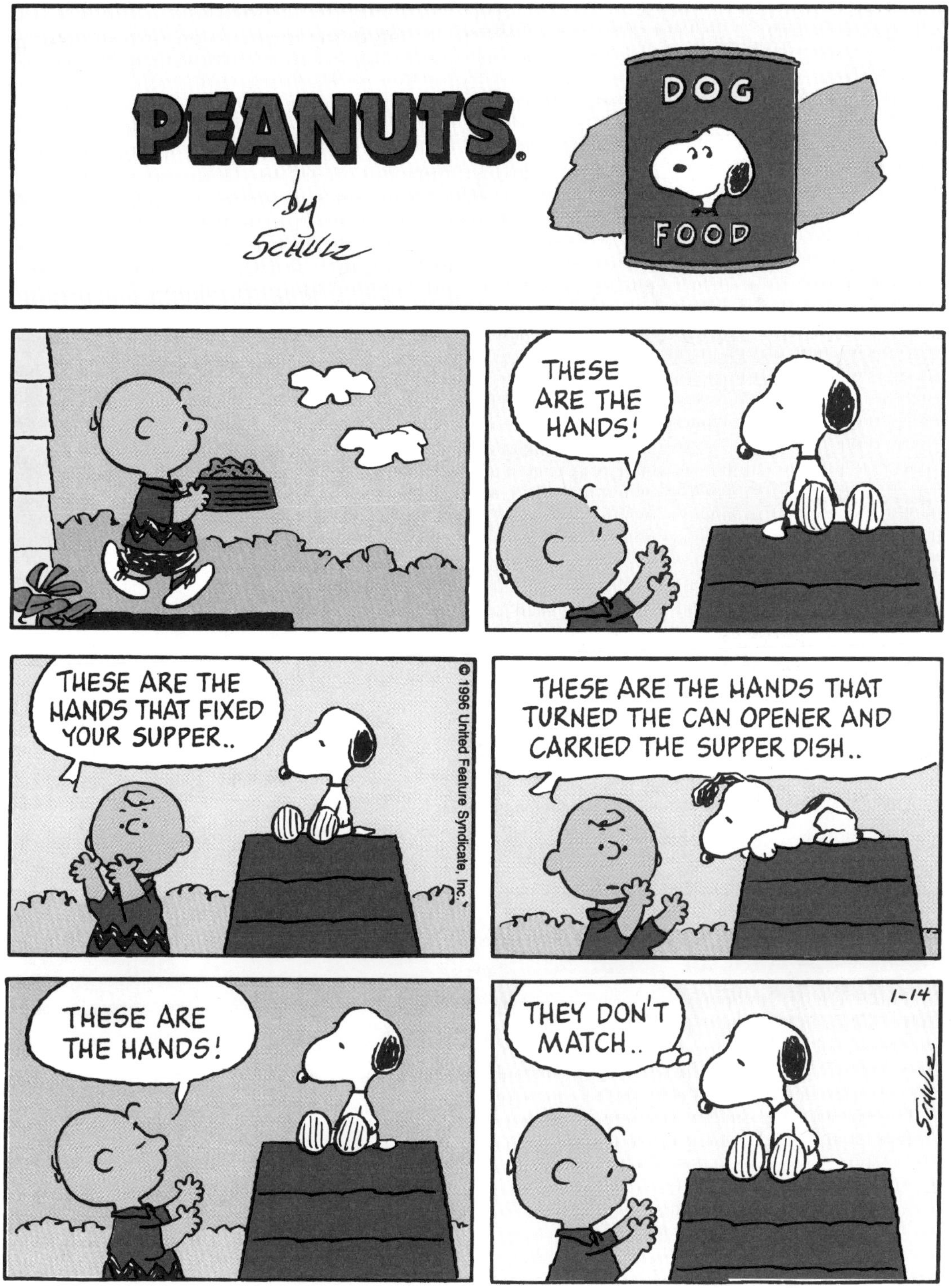
PEANUTS
by SCHULZ
DOG
FOOD
THESE ARE THE HANDS!
THESE ARE THE HANDS THAT FIXED YOUR SUPPER..
© 1996 United Feature Syndicate, Inc.
THESE ARE THE HANDS THAT TURNED THE CAN OPENER AND CARRIED THE SUPPER DISH..
THESE ARE THE HANDS!
1-14
THEY DON'T MATCH..
SCHULZ

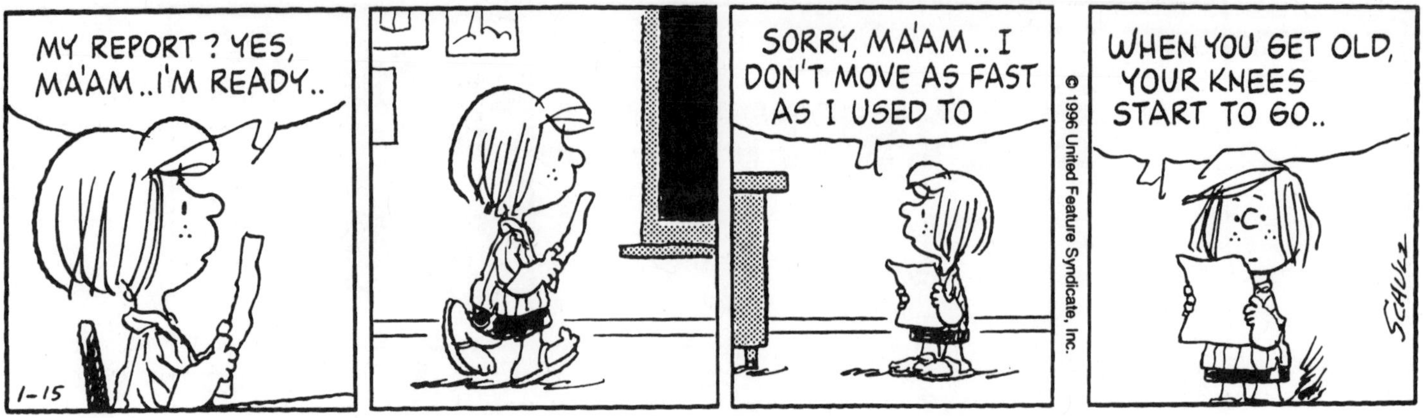
MY REPORT ? YES, MA'AM .. I'M READY ..
SORRY, MA'AM .. I DON'T MOVE AS FAST AS I USED TO
WHEN YOU GET OLD, YOUR KNEES START TO GO ..
© 1996 United Feature Syndicate, Inc.
1-15
SCHULZ

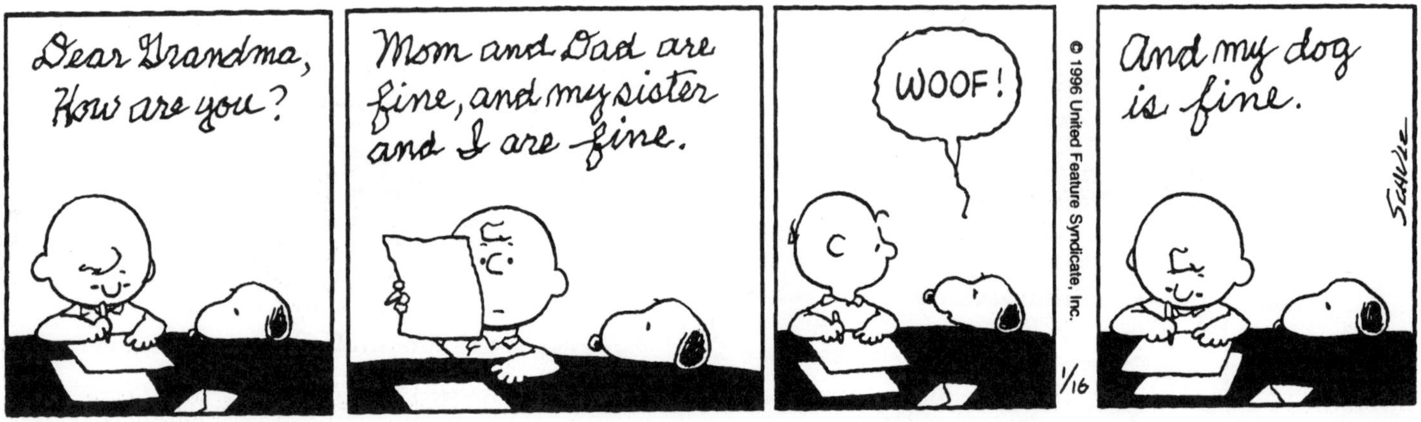
Dear Grandma, How are you?
Mom and Dad are fine, and my sister and I are fine.
WOOF!
And my dog is fine.
© 1996 United Feature Syndicate, Inc.
1/16
SCHULZ

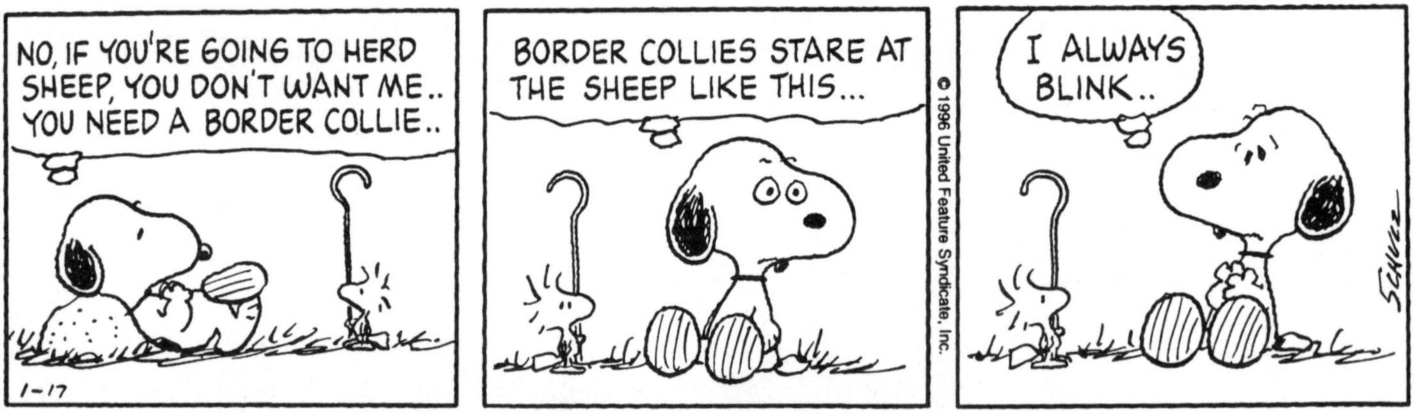
NO, IF YOU'RE GOING TO HERD SHEEP, YOU DON'T WANT ME .. YOU NEED A BORDER COLLIE ..
BORDER COLLIES STARE AT THE SHEEP LIKE THIS ...
I ALWAYS BLINK ..
© 1996 United Feature Syndicate, Inc.
1-17
SCHULZ

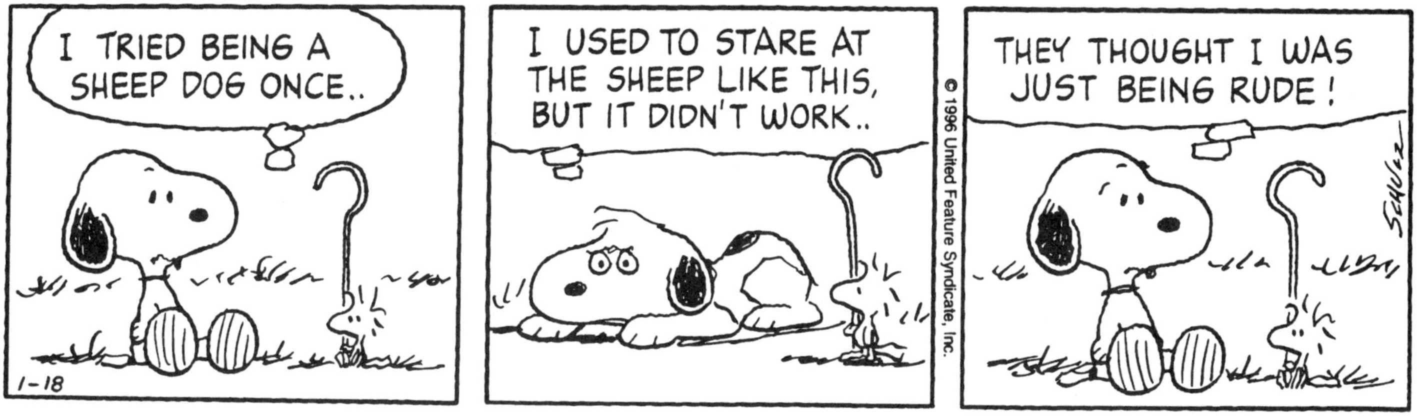
I TRIED BEING A SHEEP DOG ONCE..
I USED TO STARE AT THE SHEEP LIKE THIS, BUT IT DIDN'T WORK..
THEY THOUGHT I WAS JUST BEING RUDE!
1-18
© 1996 United Feature Syndicate, Inc.
SCHULZ

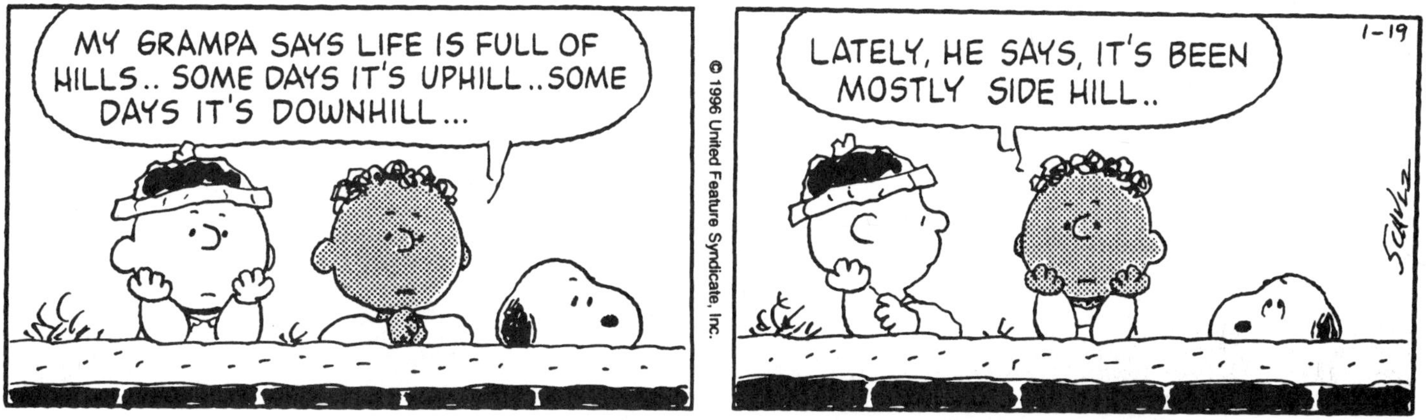
MY GRAMPA SAYS LIFE IS FULL OF HILLS.. SOME DAYS IT'S UPHILL..SOME DAYS IT'S DOWNHILL...
LATELY, HE SAYS, IT'S BEEN MOSTLY SIDE HILL..
1-19
© 1996 United Feature Syndicate, Inc.
SCHULZ

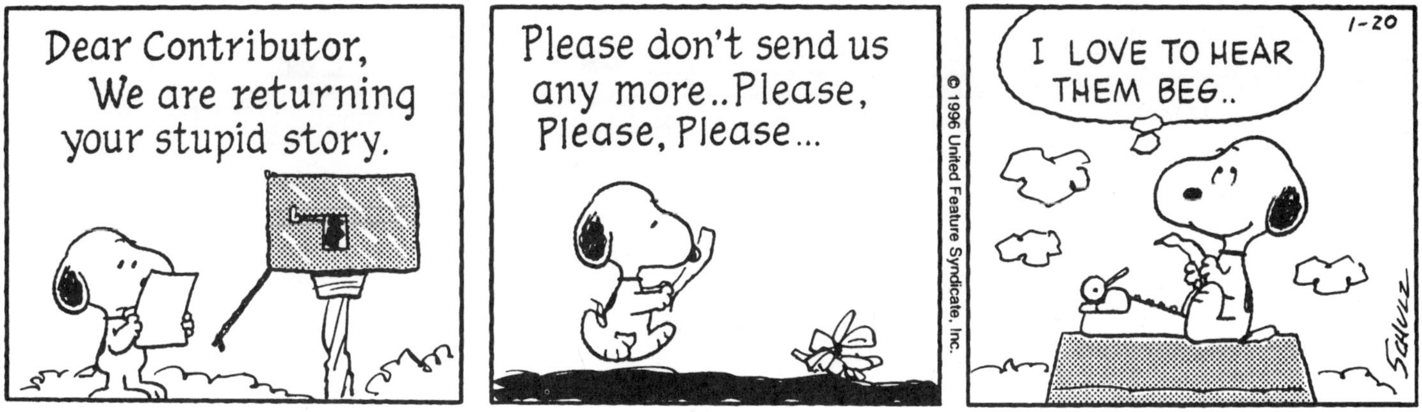
Dear Contributor,
We are returning your stupid story.
Please don't send us any more..Please, Please, Please...
I LOVE TO HEAR THEM BEG..
1-20
© 1996 United Feature Syndicate, Inc.
SCHULZ

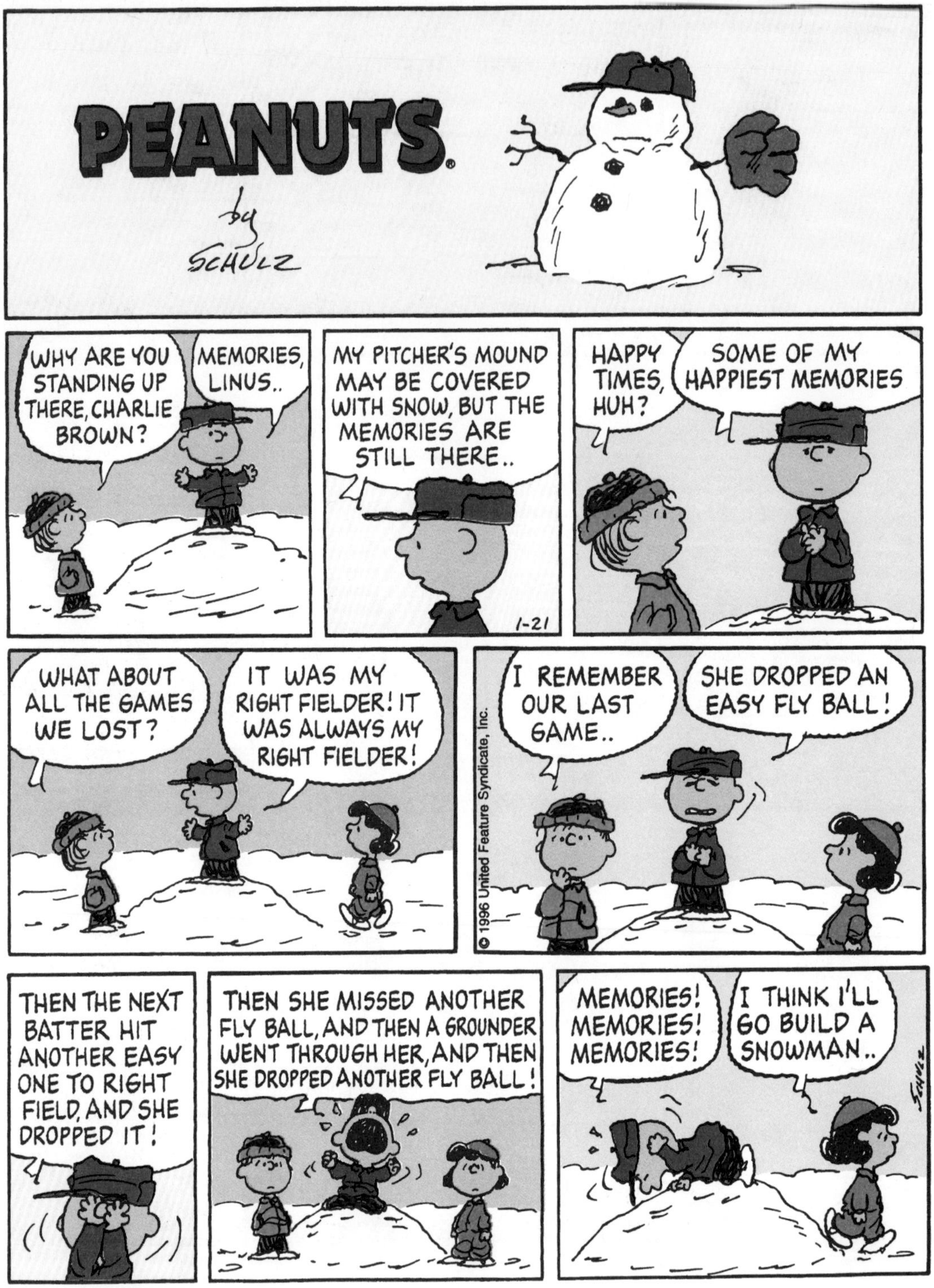
PEANUTS
by SCHULZ
WHY ARE YOU STANDING UP THERE, CHARLIE BROWN?
MEMORIES, LINUS..
MY PITCHER'S MOUND MAY BE COVERED WITH SNOW, BUT THE MEMORIES ARE STILL THERE..
1-21
HAPPY TIMES, HUH?
SOME OF MY HAPPIEST MEMORIES
WHAT ABOUT ALL THE GAMES WE LOST?
IT WAS MY RIGHT FIELDER! IT WAS ALWAYS MY RIGHT FIELDER!
© 1996 United Feature Syndicate, Inc.
I REMEMBER OUR LAST GAME..
SHE DROPPED AN EASY FLY BALL!
THEN THE NEXT BATTER HIT ANOTHER EASY ONE TO RIGHT FIELD, AND SHE DROPPED IT!
THEN SHE MISSED ANOTHER FLY BALL, AND THEN A GROUNDER WENT THROUGH HER, AND THEN SHE DROPPED ANOTHER FLY BALL!
MEMORIES! MEMORIES! MEMORIES!
I THINK I'LL GO BUILD A SNOWMAN..
SCHULZ

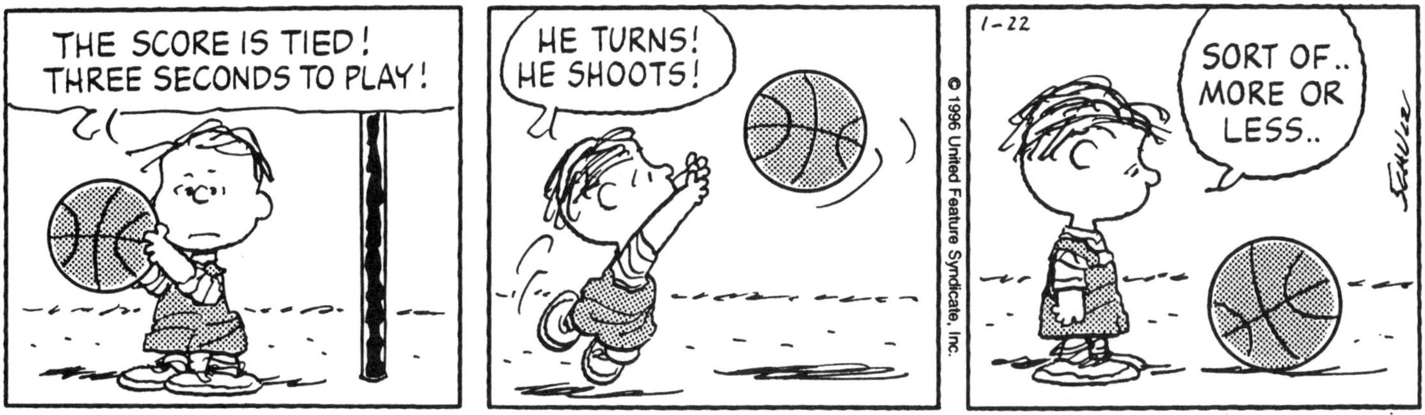
THE SCORE IS TIED! THREE SECONDS TO PLAY!
HE TURNS! HE SHOOTS!
© 1996 United Feature Syndicate, Inc.
1-22
SORT OF.. MORE OR LESS..

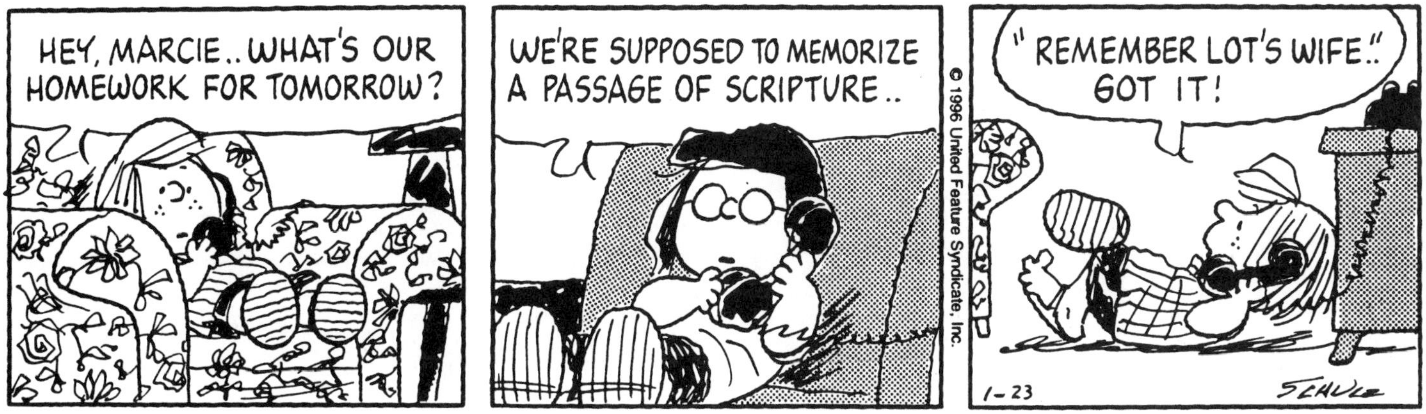
HEY, MARCIE.. WHAT'S OUR HOMEWORK FOR TOMORROW?
WE'RE SUPPOSED TO MEMORIZE A PASSAGE OF SCRIPTURE..
© 1996 United Feature Syndicate, Inc.
"REMEMBER LOT'S WIFE." GOT IT!
1-23

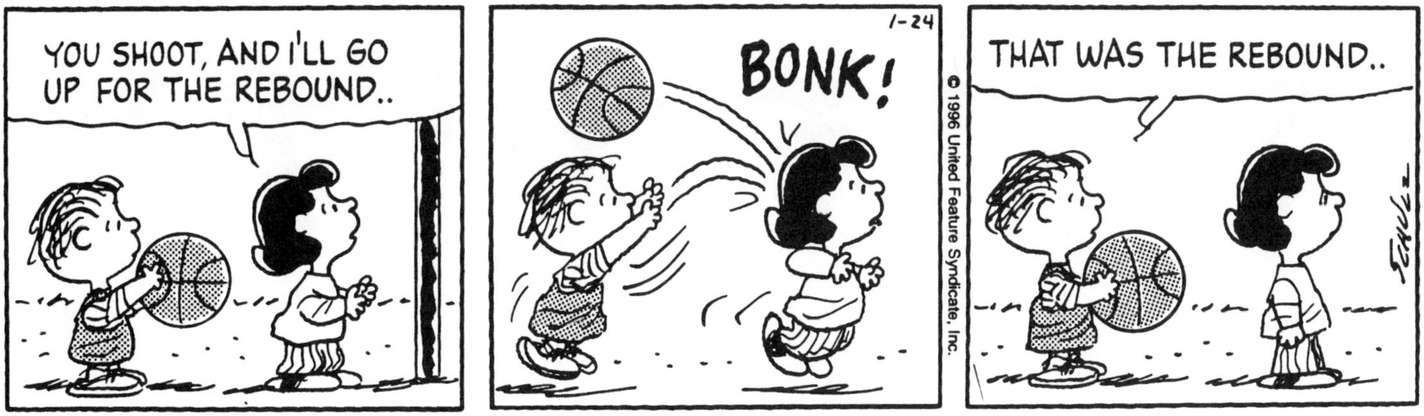
YOU SHOOT, AND I'LL GO UP FOR THE REBOUND..
1-24
BONK!
© 1996 United Feature Syndicate, Inc.
THAT WAS THE REBOUND..

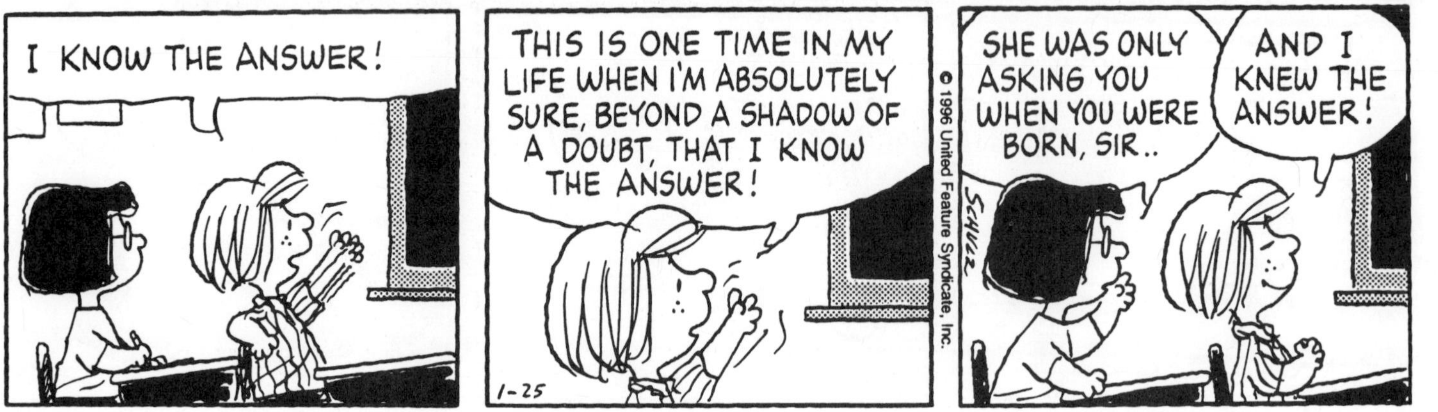
I KNOW THE ANSWER!
THIS IS ONE TIME IN MY LIFE WHEN I'M ABSOLUTELY SURE, BEYOND A SHADOW OF A DOUBT, THAT I KNOW THE ANSWER!
1-25
© 1996 United Feature Syndicate, Inc.
SHE WAS ONLY ASKING YOU WHEN YOU WERE BORN, SIR..
AND I KNEW THE ANSWER!
SCHULZ

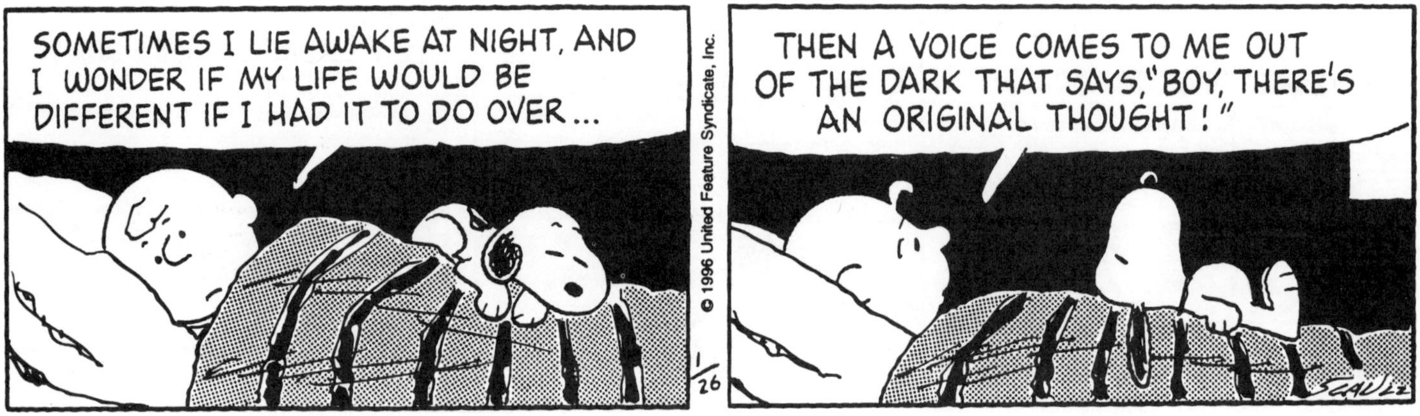
SOMETIMES I LIE AWAKE AT NIGHT, AND I WONDER IF MY LIFE WOULD BE DIFFERENT IF I HAD IT TO DO OVER...
1/26
© 1996 United Feature Syndicate, Inc.
THEN A VOICE COMES TO ME OUT OF THE DARK THAT SAYS, "BOY, THERE'S AN ORIGINAL THOUGHT!"
SCHULZ

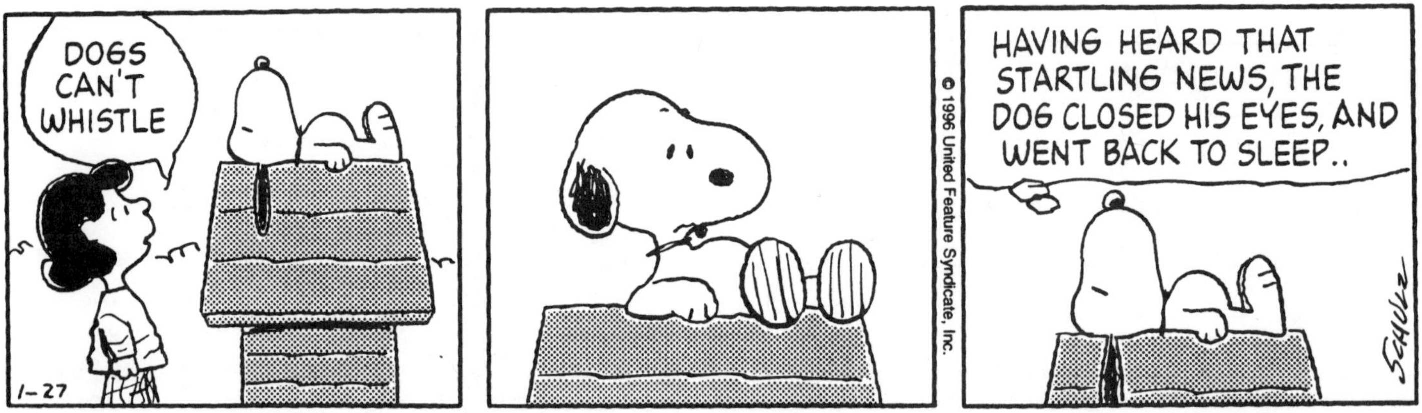
DOGS CAN'T WHISTLE
1-27
© 1996 United Feature Syndicate, Inc.
HAVING HEARD THAT STARTLING NEWS, THE DOG CLOSED HIS EYES, AND WENT BACK TO SLEEP..
SCHULZ

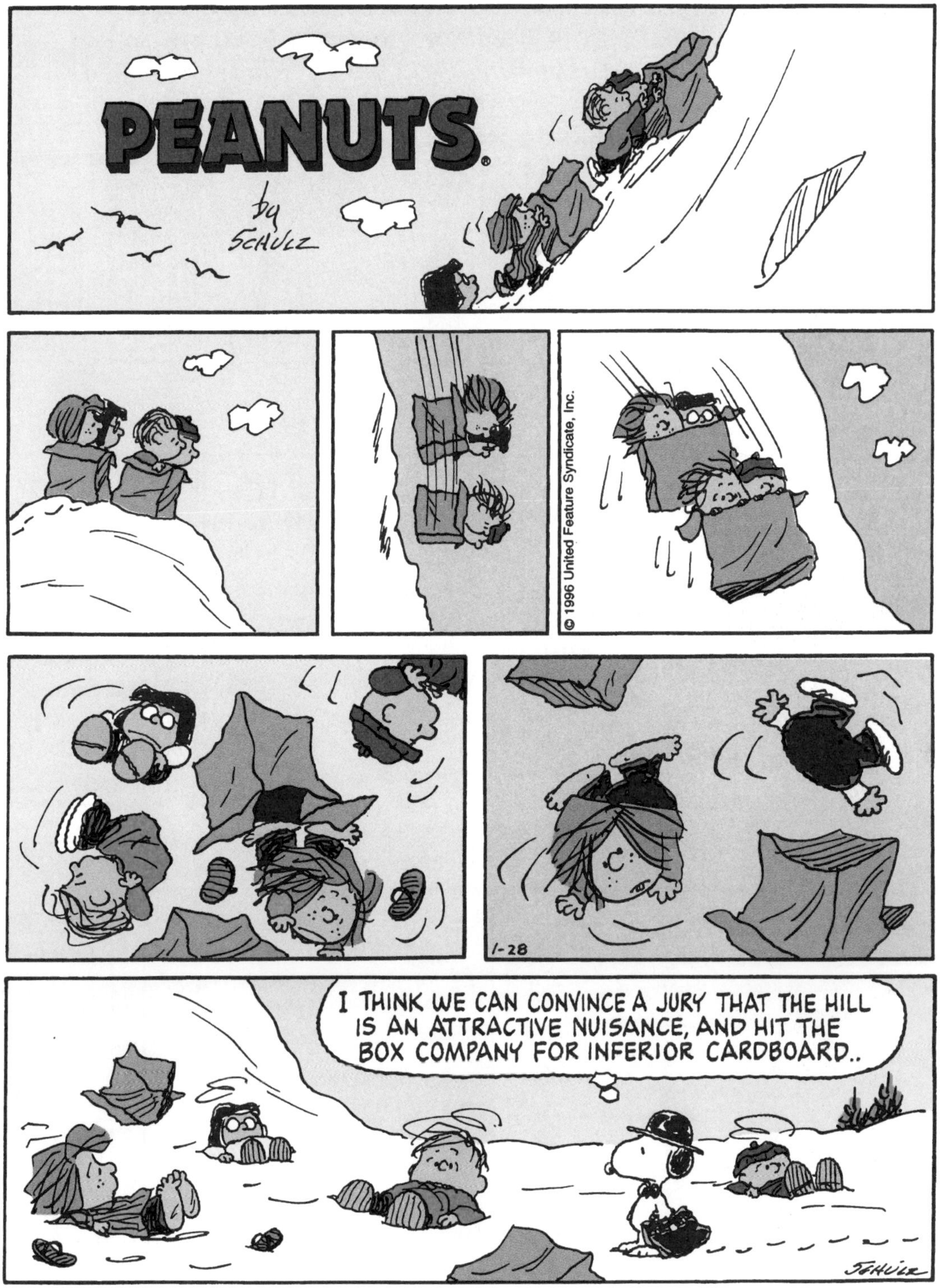
PEANUTS
by SCHULZ
© 1996 United Feature Syndicate, Inc.
1-28
I THINK WE CAN CONVINCE A JURY THAT THE HILL IS AN ATTRACTIVE NUISANCE, AND HIT THE BOX COMPANY FOR INFERIOR CARDBOARD..
SCHULZ

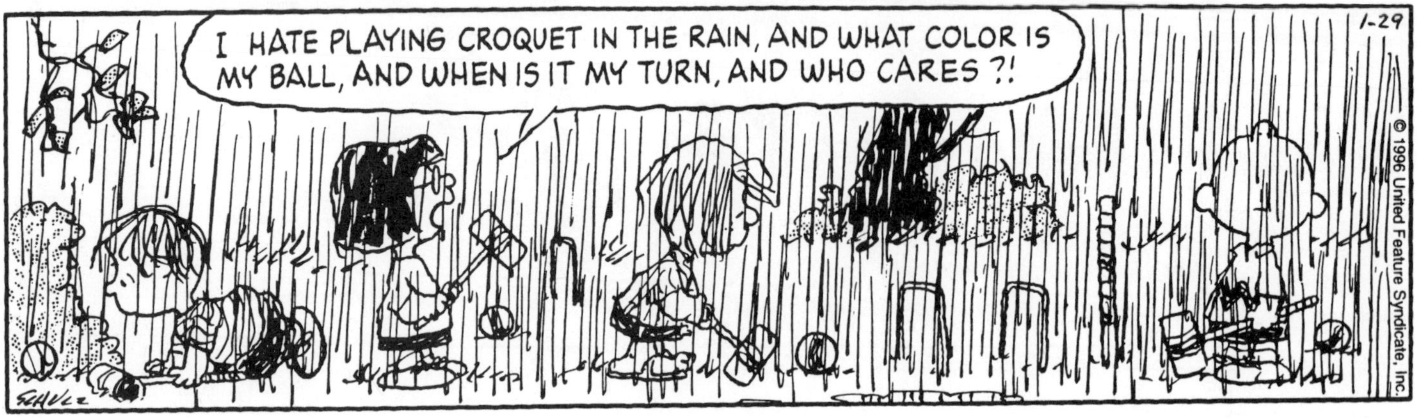
I HATE PLAYING CROQUET IN THE RAIN, AND WHAT COLOR IS MY BALL, AND WHEN IS IT MY TURN, AND WHO CARES ?!
1-29
© 1996 United Feature Syndicate, Inc.

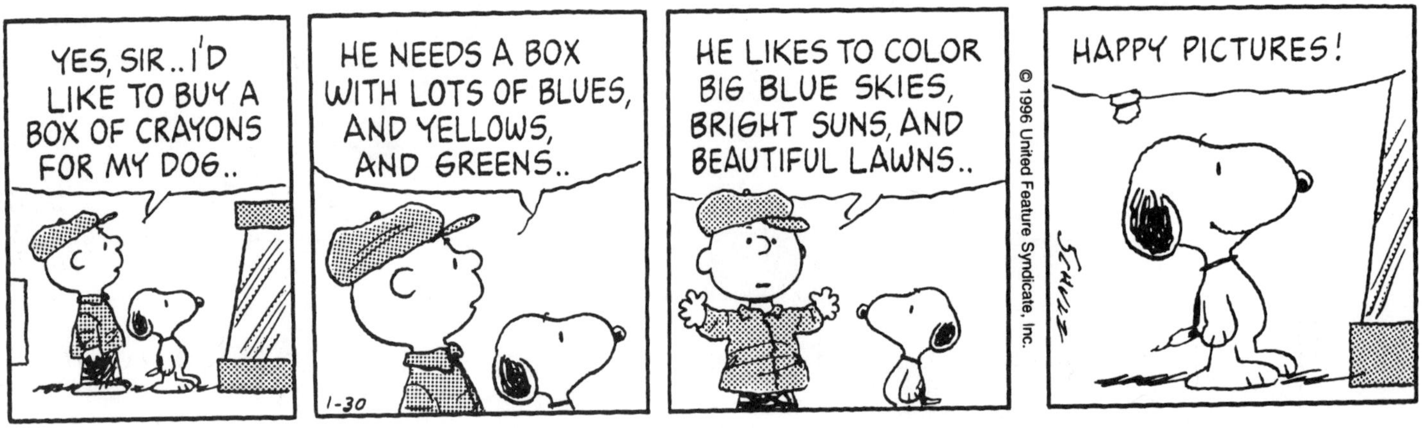
YES, SIR.. I'D LIKE TO BUY A BOX OF CRAYONS FOR MY DOG..
HE NEEDS A BOX WITH LOTS OF BLUES, AND YELLOWS, AND GREENS..
1-30
HE LIKES TO COLOR BIG BLUE SKIES, BRIGHT SUNS, AND BEAUTIFUL LAWNS..
© 1996 United Feature Syndicate, Inc.
HAPPY PICTURES!

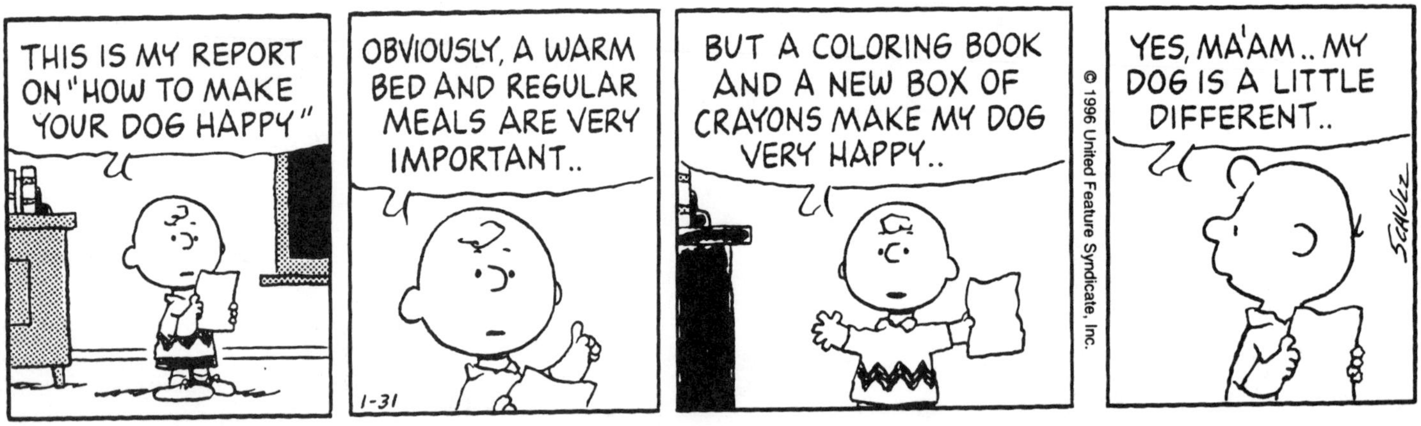
THIS IS MY REPORT ON "HOW TO MAKE YOUR DOG HAPPY"
OBVIOUSLY, A WARM BED AND REGULAR MEALS ARE VERY IMPORTANT..
1-31
BUT A COLORING BOOK AND A NEW BOX OF CRAYONS MAKE MY DOG VERY HAPPY..
© 1996 United Feature Syndicate, Inc.
YES, MA'AM.. MY DOG IS A LITTLE DIFFERENT..

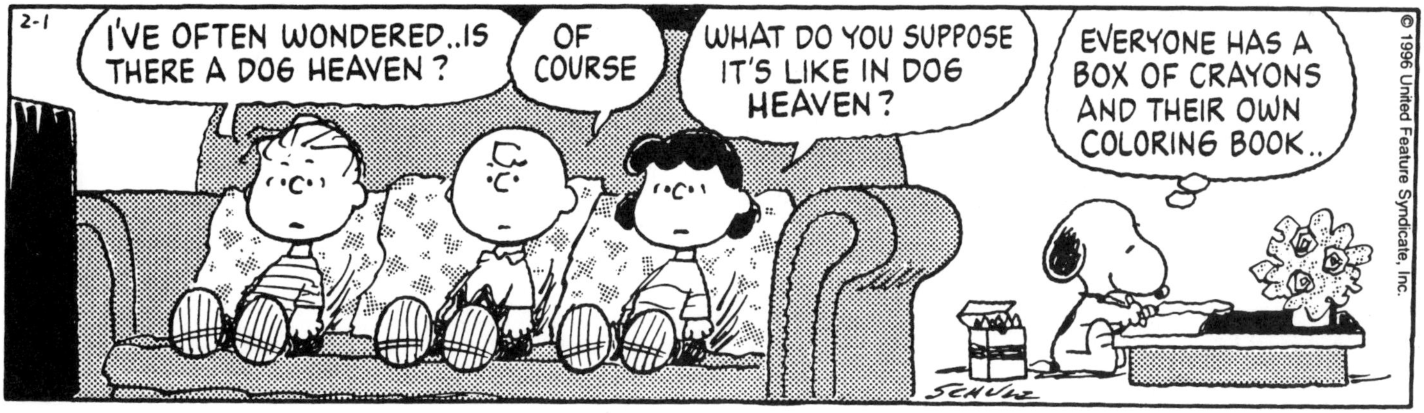
2-1
I'VE OFTEN WONDERED..IS THERE A DOG HEAVEN ?
OF COURSE
WHAT DO YOU SUPPOSE IT'S LIKE IN DOG HEAVEN ?
EVERYONE HAS A BOX OF CRAYONS AND THEIR OWN COLORING BOOK..
SCHULZ
© 1996 United Feature Syndicate, Inc.

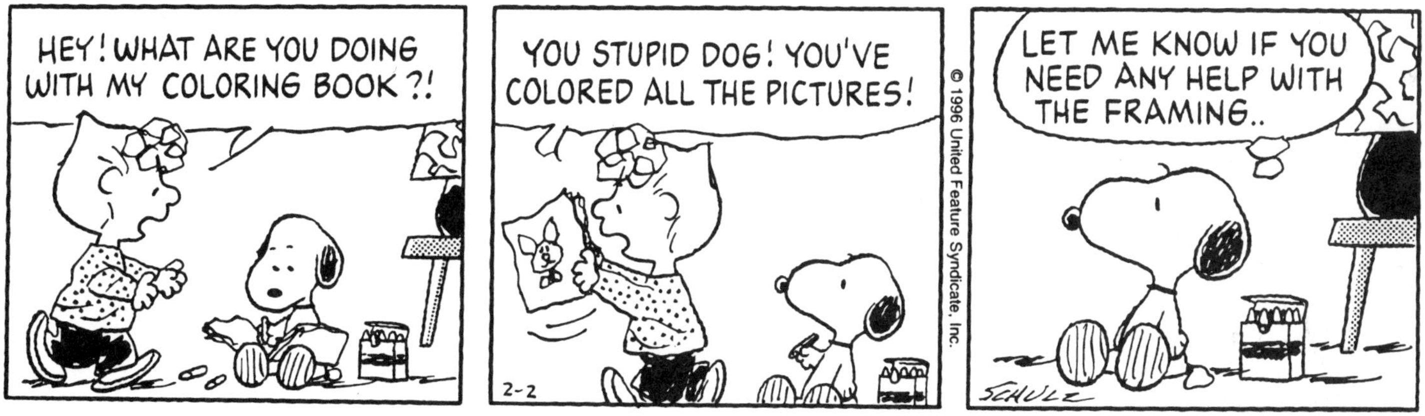
HEY! WHAT ARE YOU DOING WITH MY COLORING BOOK ?!
YOU STUPID DOG! YOU'VE COLORED ALL THE PICTURES!
2-2
© 1996 United Feature Syndicate, Inc.
LET ME KNOW IF YOU NEED ANY HELP WITH THE FRAMING..
SCHULZ

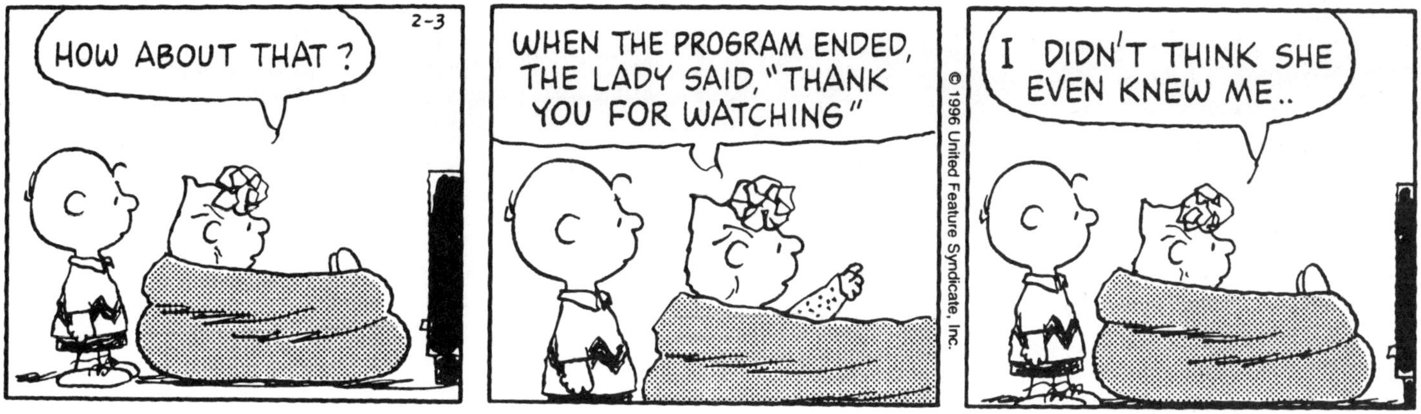
2-3
HOW ABOUT THAT ?
WHEN THE PROGRAM ENDED, THE LADY SAID, "THANK YOU FOR WATCHING"
© 1996 United Feature Syndicate, Inc.
I DIDN'T THINK SHE EVEN KNEW ME..

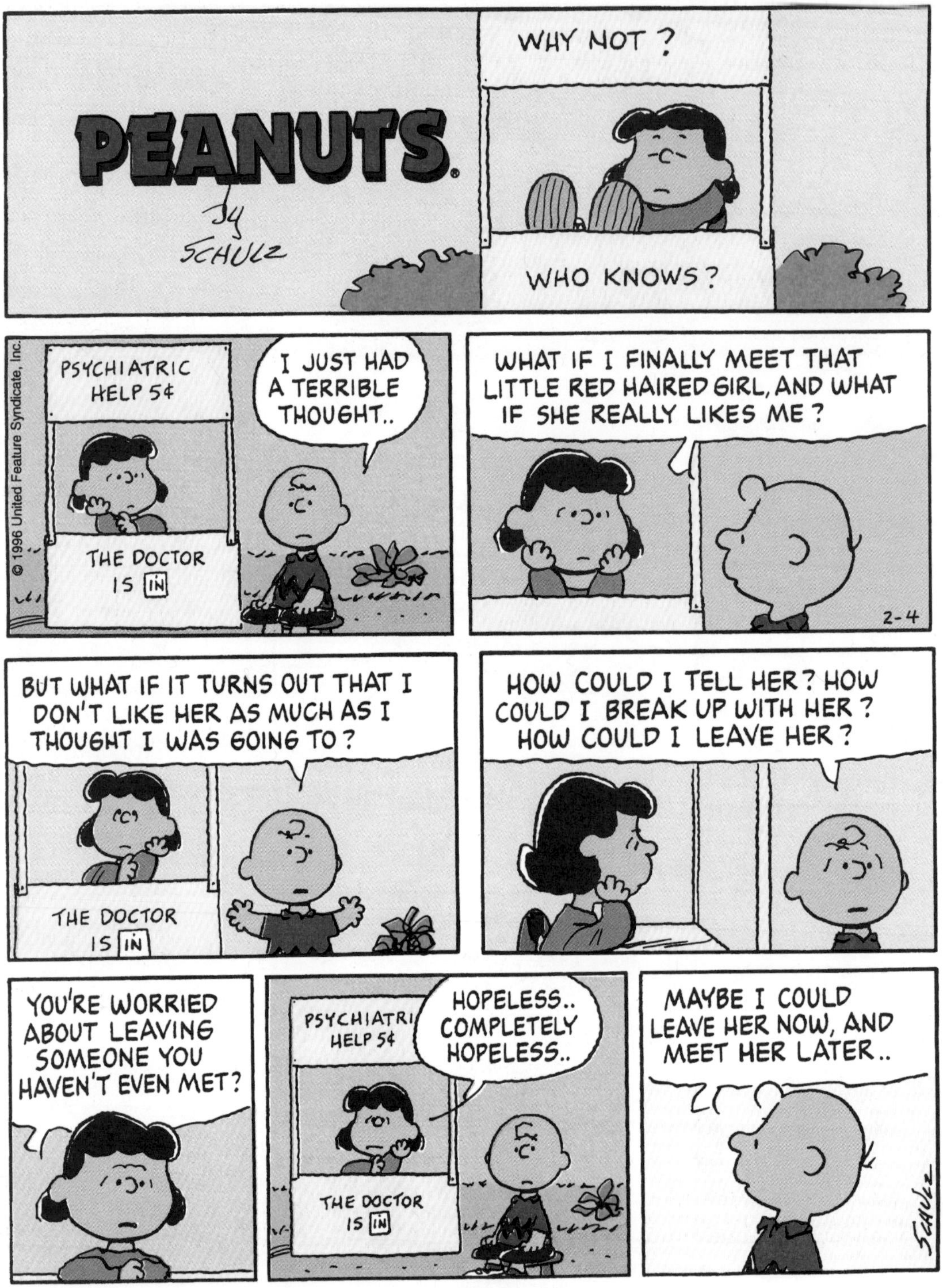
PEANUTS
SCHULZ
WHY NOT?
WHO KNOWS?
PSYCHIATRIC HELP 5¢
THE DOCTOR IS IN
© 1996 United Feature Syndicate, Inc.
I JUST HAD A TERRIBLE THOUGHT..
WHAT IF I FINALLY MEET THAT LITTLE RED HAIRED GIRL, AND WHAT IF SHE REALLY LIKES ME?
2-4
THE DOCTOR IS IN
BUT WHAT IF IT TURNS OUT THAT I DON'T LIKE HER AS MUCH AS I THOUGHT I WAS GOING TO?
HOW COULD I TELL HER? HOW COULD I BREAK UP WITH HER? HOW COULD I LEAVE HER?
YOU'RE WORRIED ABOUT LEAVING SOMEONE YOU HAVEN'T EVEN MET?
PSYCHIATRI HELP 5¢
THE DOCTOR IS IN
HOPELESS.. COMPLETELY HOPELESS..
MAYBE I COULD LEAVE HER NOW, AND MEET HER LATER..
SCHULZ

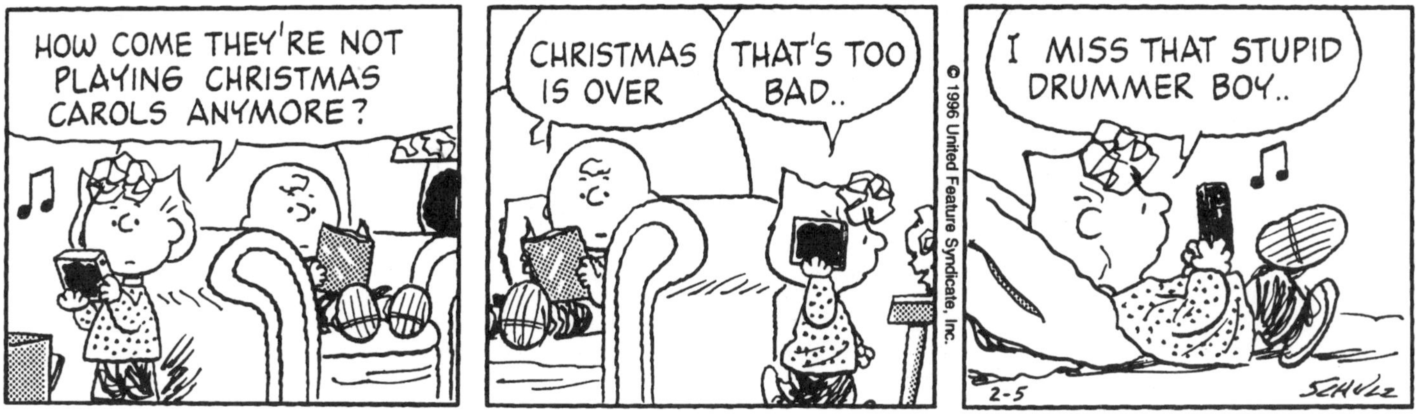
HOW COME THEY'RE NOT PLAYING CHRISTMAS CAROLS ANYMORE?
CHRISTMAS IS OVER
THAT'S TOO BAD..
I MISS THAT STUPID DRUMMER BOY..
© 1996 United Feature Syndicate, Inc.
2-5
SCHULZ

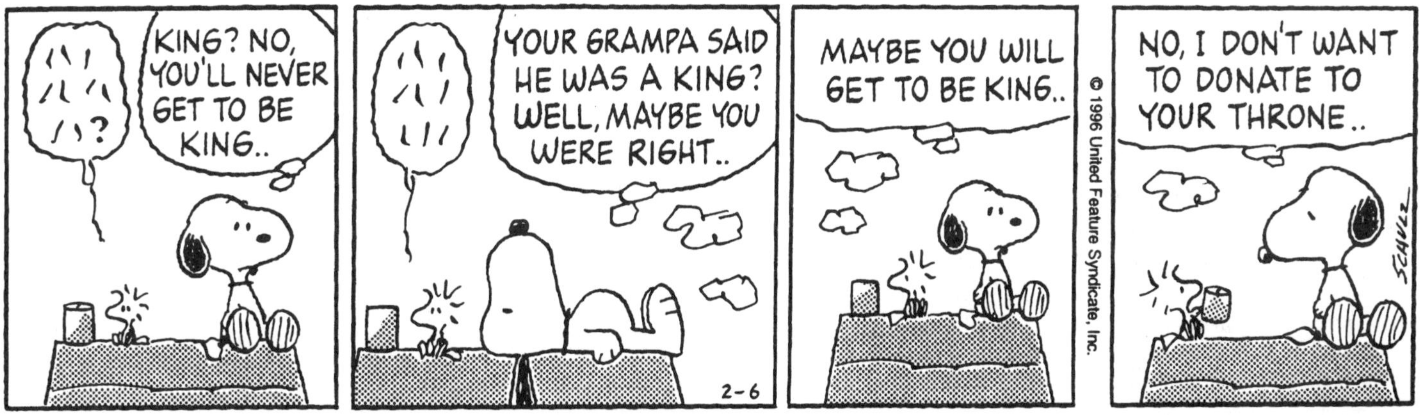
KING? NO, YOU'LL NEVER GET TO BE KING..
YOUR GRAMPA SAID HE WAS A KING? WELL, MAYBE YOU WERE RIGHT..
2-6
MAYBE YOU WILL GET TO BE KING..
© 1996 United Feature Syndicate, Inc.
NO, I DON'T WANT TO DONATE TO YOUR THRONE..
SCHULZ

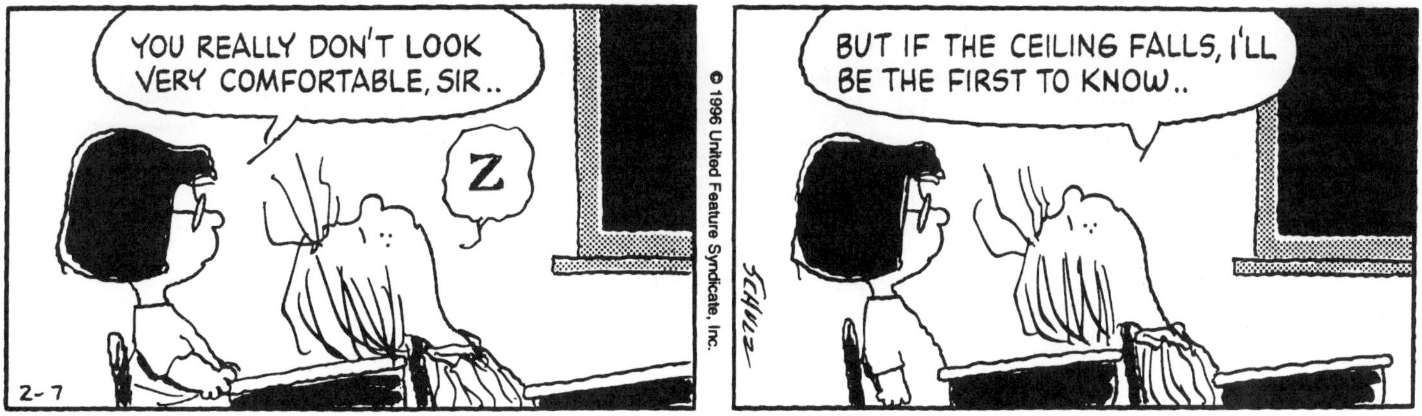
YOU REALLY DON'T LOOK VERY COMFORTABLE, SIR..
Z
2-7
© 1996 United Feature Syndicate, Inc.
SCHULZ
BUT IF THE CEILING FALLS, I'LL BE THE FIRST TO KNOW..

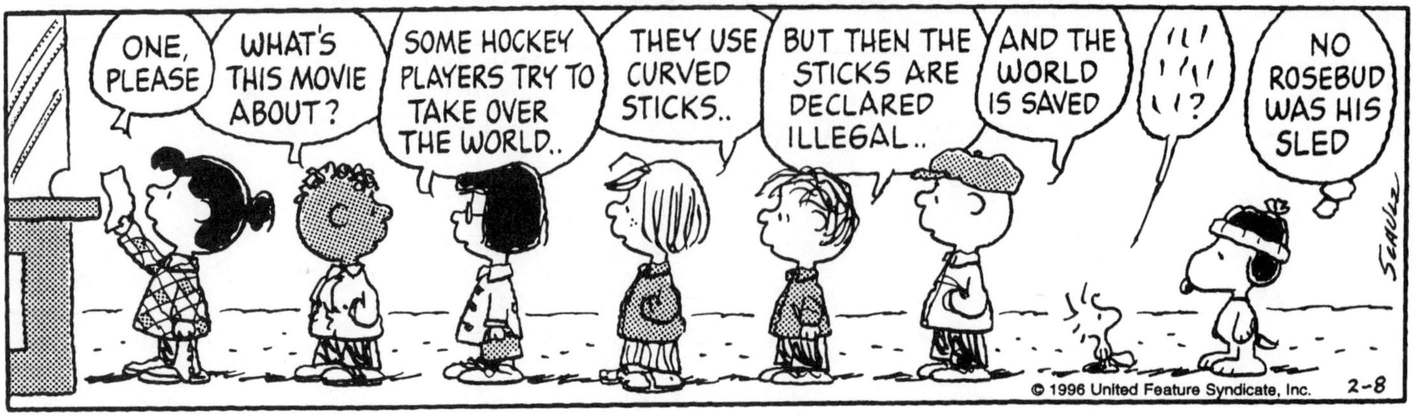
ONE, PLEASE
WHAT'S THIS MOVIE ABOUT?
SOME HOCKEY PLAYERS TRY TO TAKE OVER THE WORLD..
THEY USE CURVED STICKS..
BUT THEN THE STICKS ARE DECLARED ILLEGAL..
AND THE WORLD IS SAVED
NO ROSEBUD WAS HIS SLED
SCHULZ
© 1996 United Feature Syndicate, Inc.
2-8

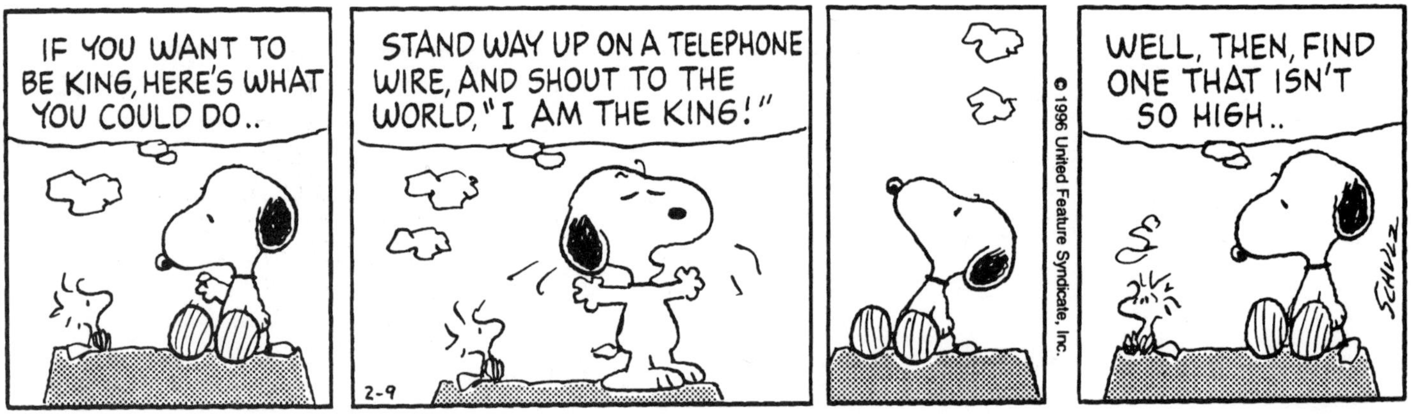
IF YOU WANT TO BE KING, HERE'S WHAT YOU COULD DO..
STAND WAY UP ON A TELEPHONE WIRE, AND SHOUT TO THE WORLD, "I AM THE KING!"
2-9
© 1996 United Feature Syndicate, Inc.
WELL, THEN, FIND ONE THAT ISN'T SO HIGH..
SCHULZ

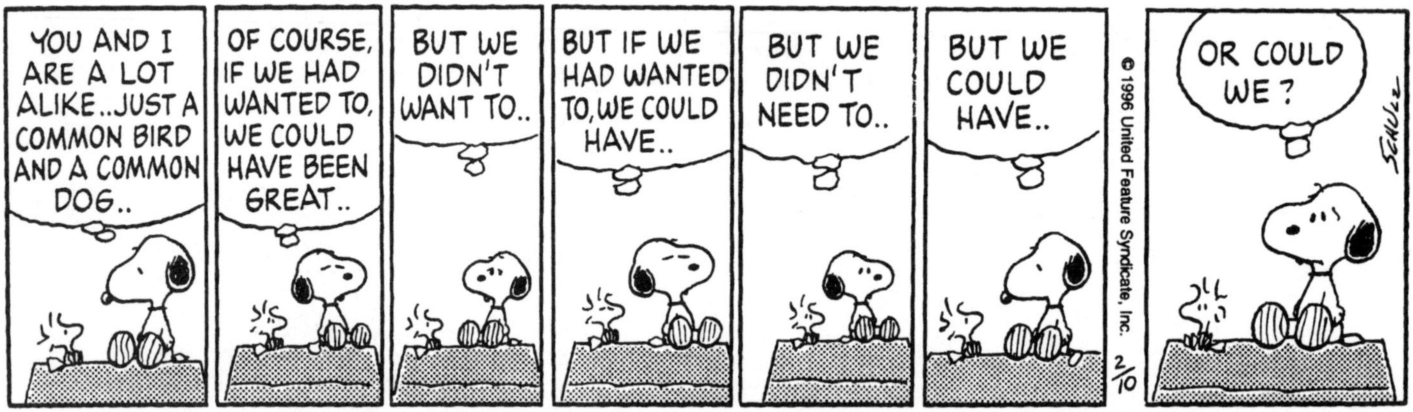
YOU AND I ARE A LOT ALIKE..JUST A COMMON BIRD AND A COMMON DOG..
OF COURSE, IF WE HAD WANTED TO, WE COULD HAVE BEEN GREAT..
BUT WE DIDN'T WANT TO..
BUT IF WE HAD WANTED TO, WE COULD HAVE..
BUT WE DIDN'T NEED TO..
BUT WE COULD HAVE..
© 1996 United Feature Syndicate, Inc.
2/10
OR COULD WE?
SCHULZ

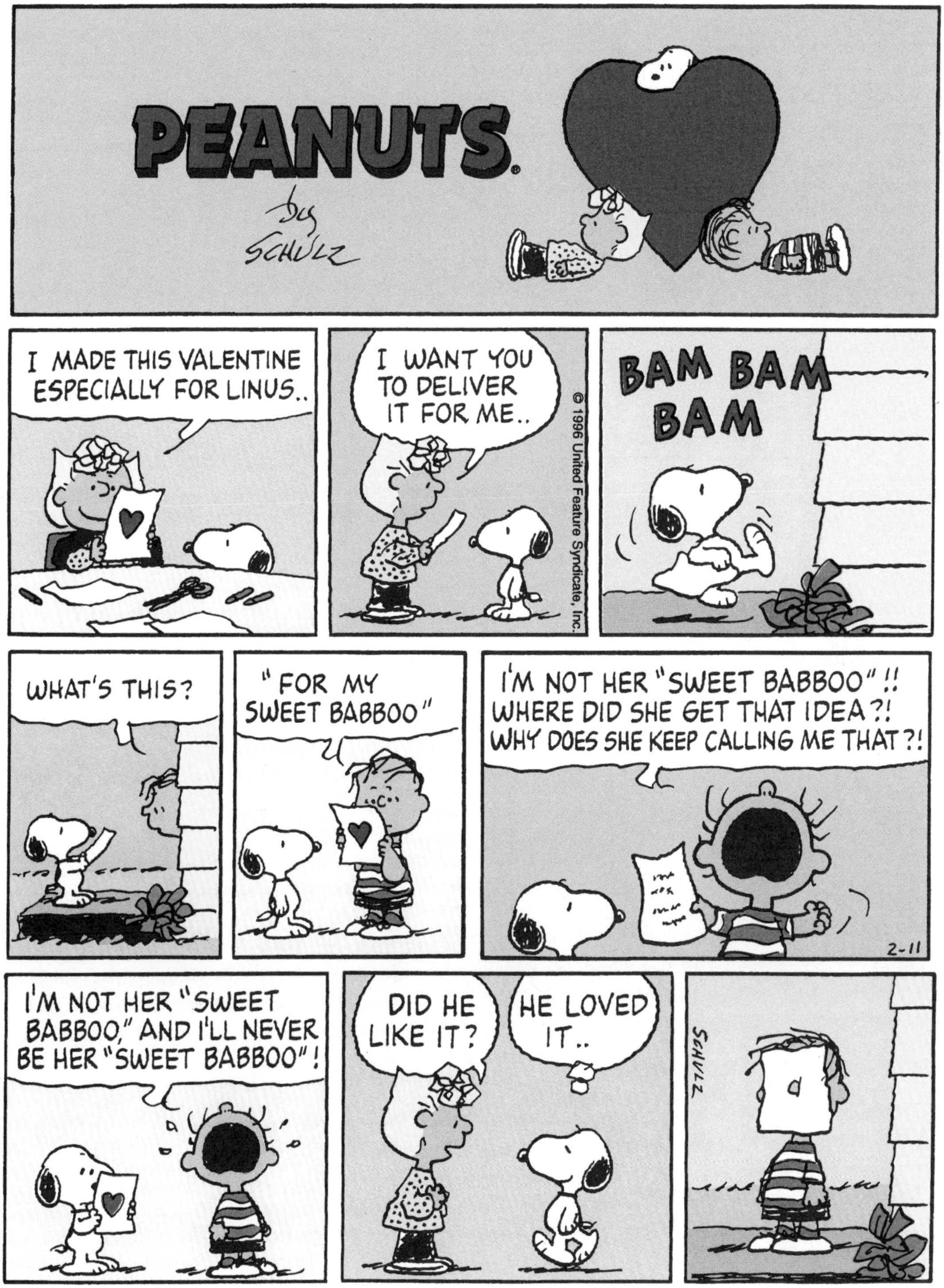
PEANUTS
by SCHULZ
I MADE THIS VALENTINE ESPECIALLY FOR LINUS..
I WANT YOU TO DELIVER IT FOR ME..
© 1996 United Feature Syndicate, Inc.
BAM BAM BAM
WHAT'S THIS?
"FOR MY SWEET BABBOO"
I'M NOT HER "SWEET BABBOO"!! WHERE DID SHE GET THAT IDEA?! WHY DOES SHE KEEP CALLING ME THAT?!
2-11
I'M NOT HER "SWEET BABBOO," AND I'LL NEVER BE HER "SWEET BABBOO"!
DID HE LIKE IT?
HE LOVED IT..
SCHULZ

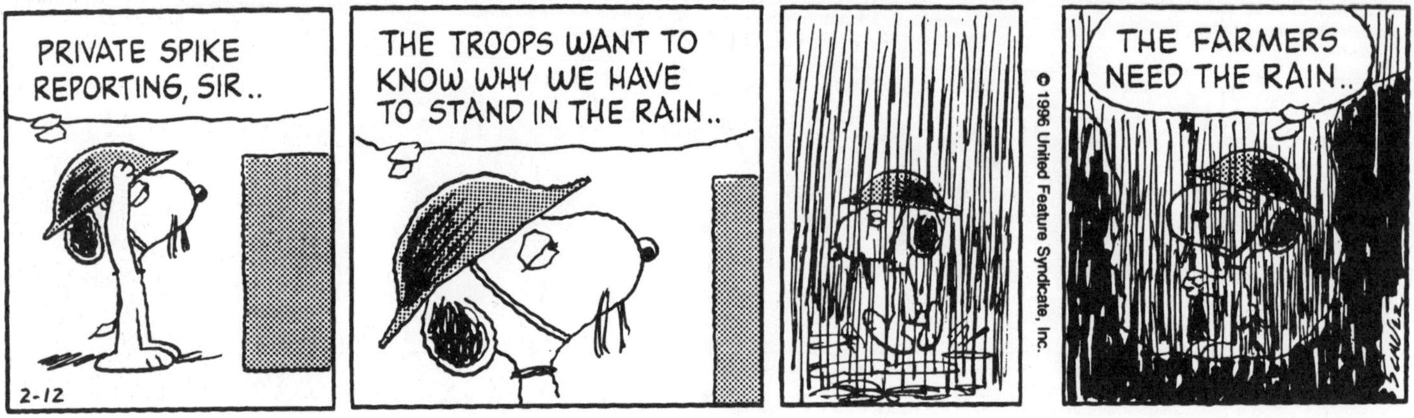
PRIVATE SPIKE REPORTING, SIR..
2-12
THE TROOPS WANT TO KNOW WHY WE HAVE TO STAND IN THE RAIN..
© 1996 United Feature Syndicate, Inc.
THE FARMERS NEED THE RAIN..

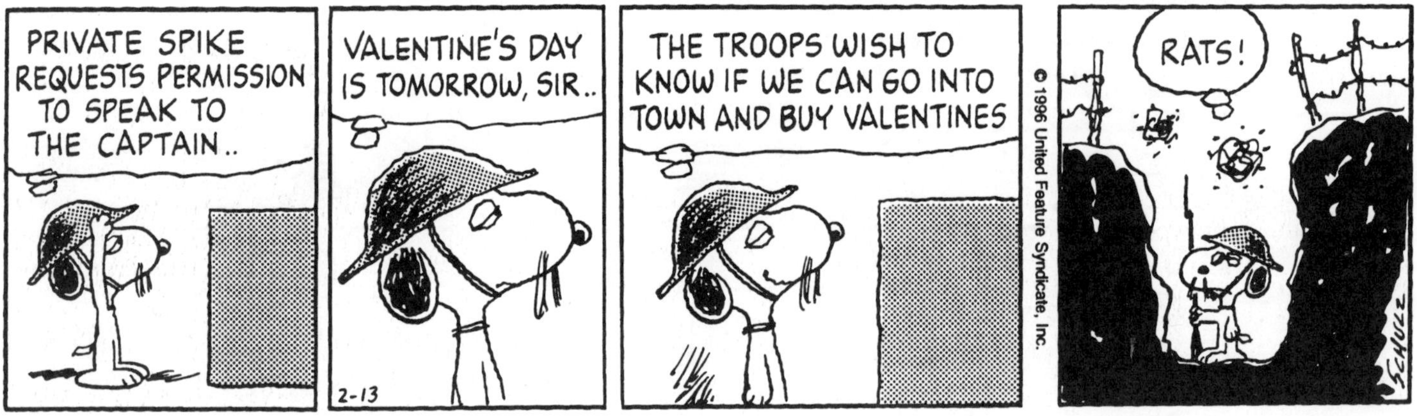
PRIVATE SPIKE REQUESTS PERMISSION TO SPEAK TO THE CAPTAIN..
VALENTINE'S DAY IS TOMORROW, SIR..
2-13
THE TROOPS WISH TO KNOW IF WE CAN GO INTO TOWN AND BUY VALENTINES
© 1996 United Feature Syndicate, Inc.
RATS!

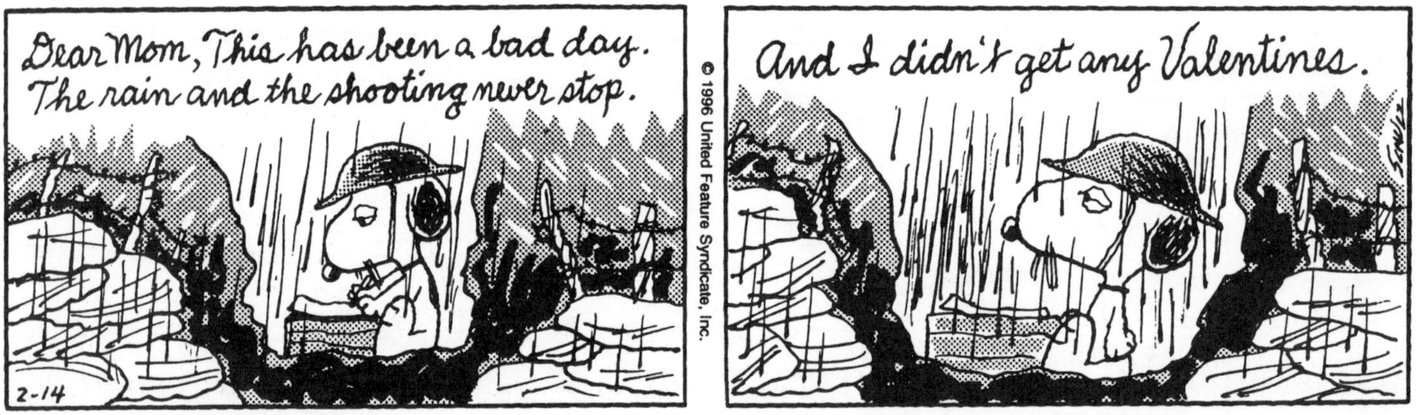
Dear Mom, This has been a bad day. The rain and the shooting never stop.
2-14
© 1996 United Feature Syndicate, Inc.
And I didn't get any Valentines.

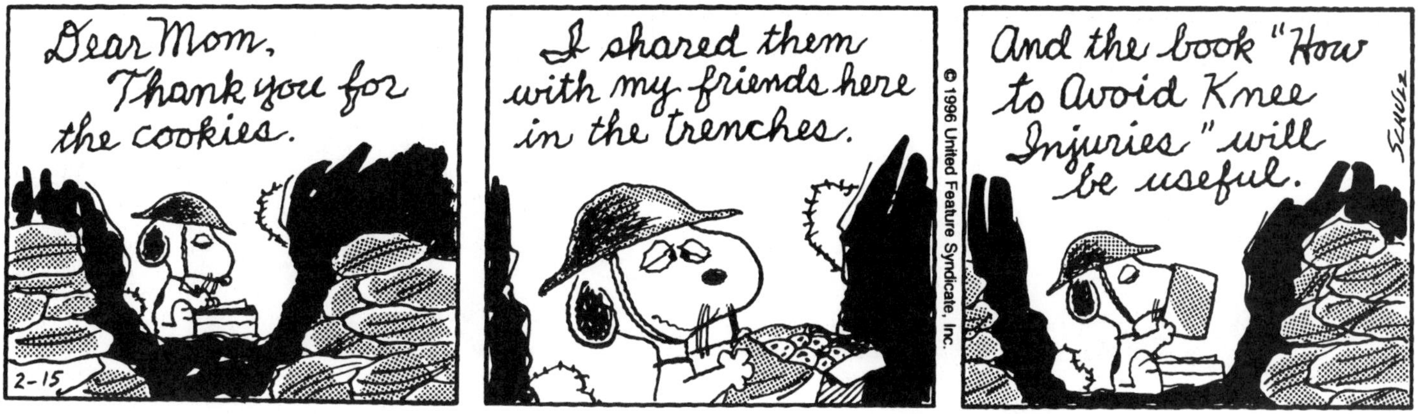
Dear Mom, Thank you for the cookies.
2-15
I shared them with my friends here in the trenches.
© 1996 United Feature Syndicate, Inc.
And the book "How to Avoid Knee Injuries" will be useful.
SCHULZ

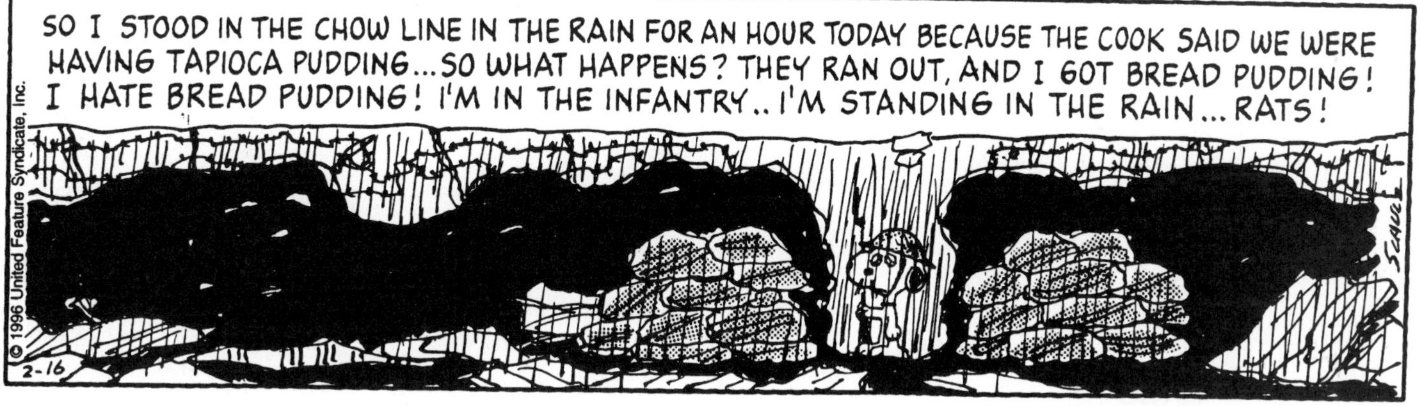
SO I STOOD IN THE CHOW LINE IN THE RAIN FOR AN HOUR TODAY BECAUSE THE COOK SAID WE WERE HAVING TAPIOCA PUDDING...SO WHAT HAPPENS? THEY RAN OUT, AND I GOT BREAD PUDDING! I HATE BREAD PUDDING! I'M IN THE INFANTRY.. I'M STANDING IN THE RAIN... RATS!
© 1996 United Feature Syndicate, Inc.
2-16
SCHULZ

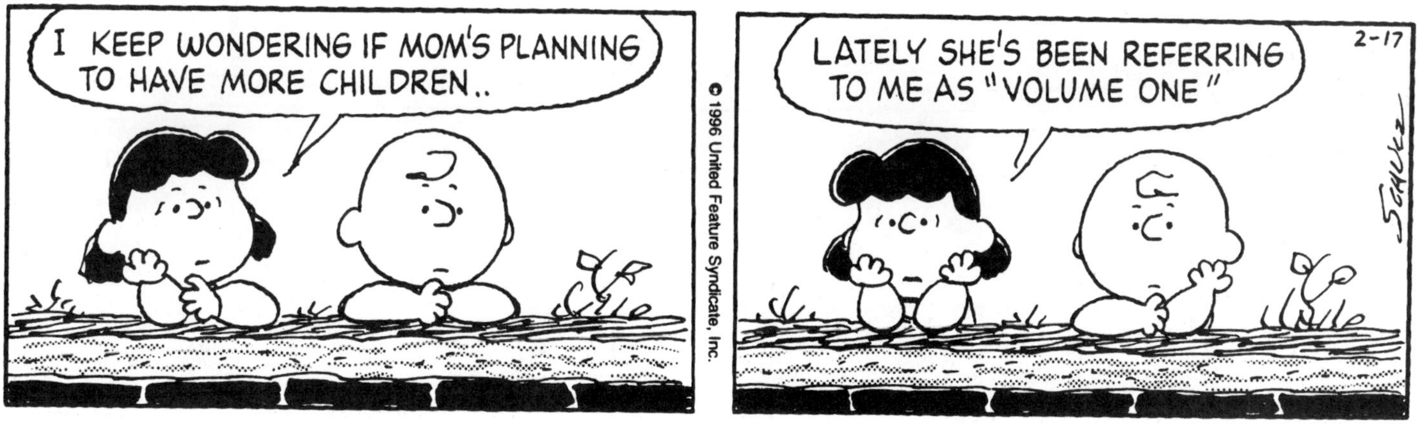
I KEEP WONDERING IF MOM'S PLANNING TO HAVE MORE CHILDREN..
© 1996 United Feature Syndicate, Inc.
LATELY SHE'S BEEN REFERRING TO ME AS "VOLUME ONE"
2-17
SCHULZ

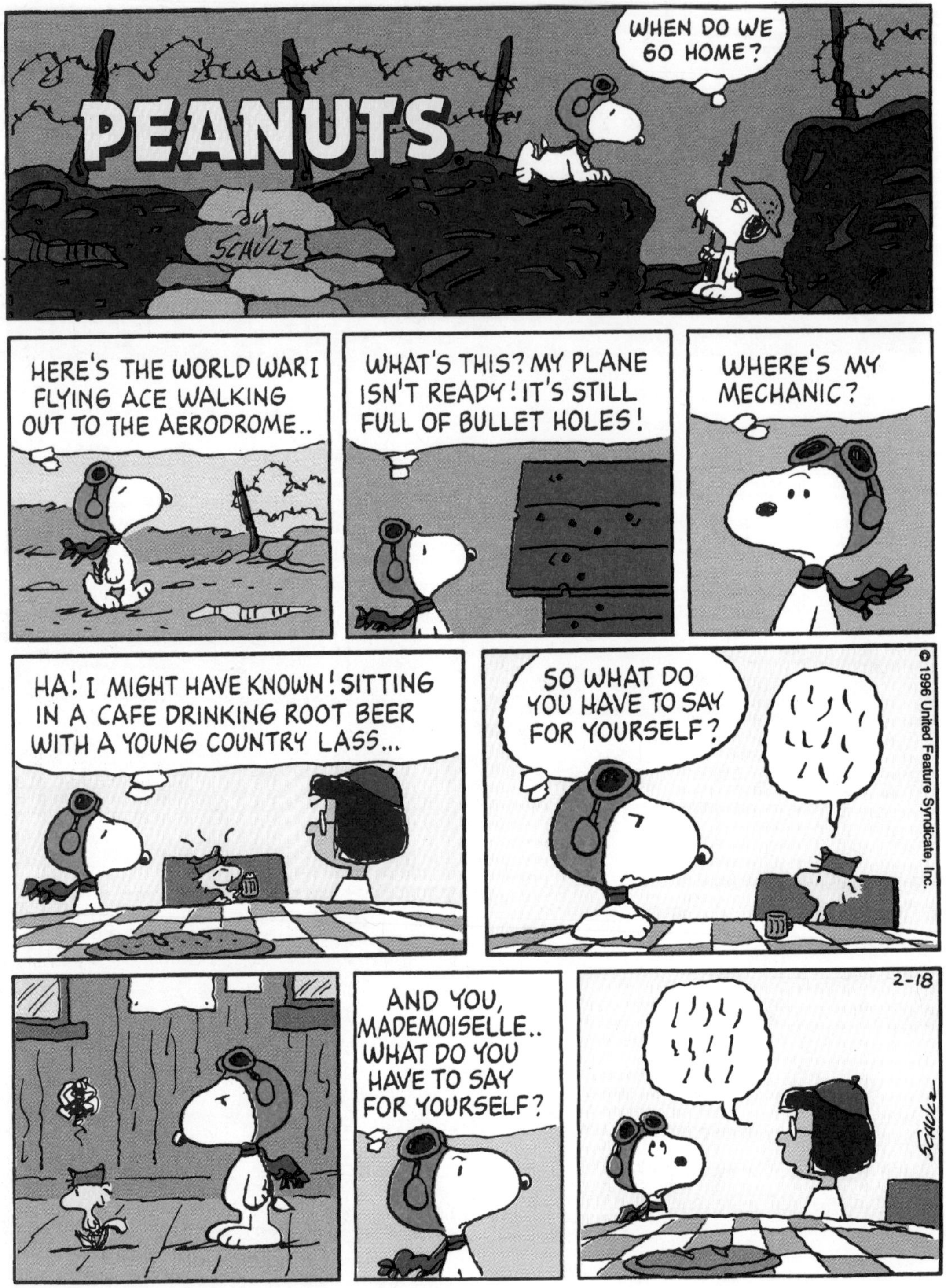
PEANUTS
by SCHULZ
WHEN DO WE GO HOME?
HERE'S THE WORLD WAR I FLYING ACE WALKING OUT TO THE AERODROME..
WHAT'S THIS? MY PLANE ISN'T READY! IT'S STILL FULL OF BULLET HOLES!
WHERE'S MY MECHANIC?
HA! I MIGHT HAVE KNOWN! SITTING IN A CAFE DRINKING ROOT BEER WITH A YOUNG COUNTRY LASS...
SO WHAT DO YOU HAVE TO SAY FOR YOURSELF?
© 1996 United Feature Syndicate, Inc.
2-18
AND YOU, MADEMOISELLE.. WHAT DO YOU HAVE TO SAY FOR YOURSELF?
SCHULZ

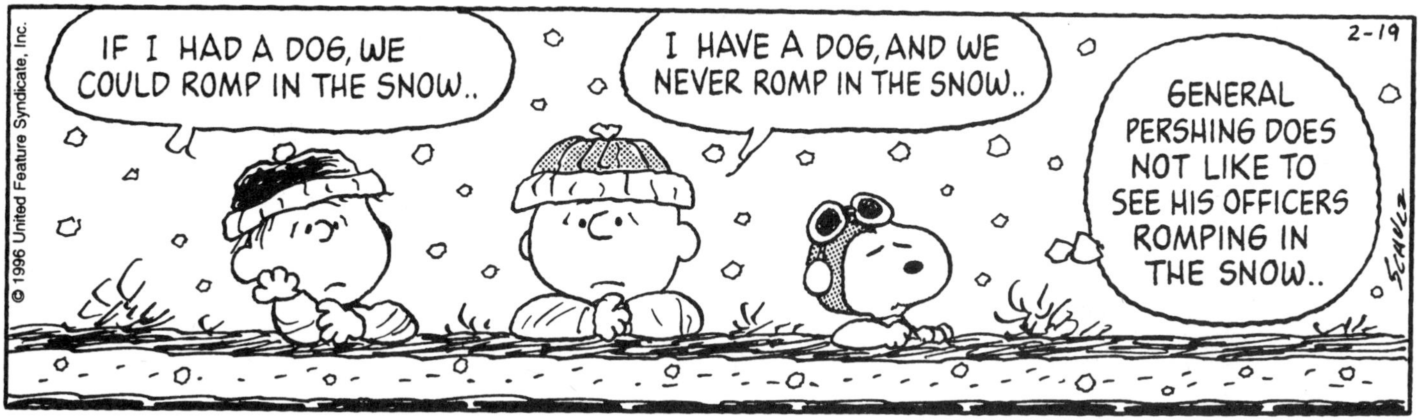
© 1996 United Feature Syndicate, Inc.
2-19
IF I HAD A DOG, WE COULD ROMP IN THE SNOW..
I HAVE A DOG, AND WE NEVER ROMP IN THE SNOW..
GENERAL PERSHING DOES NOT LIKE TO SEE HIS OFFICERS ROMPING IN THE SNOW..
SCHULZ

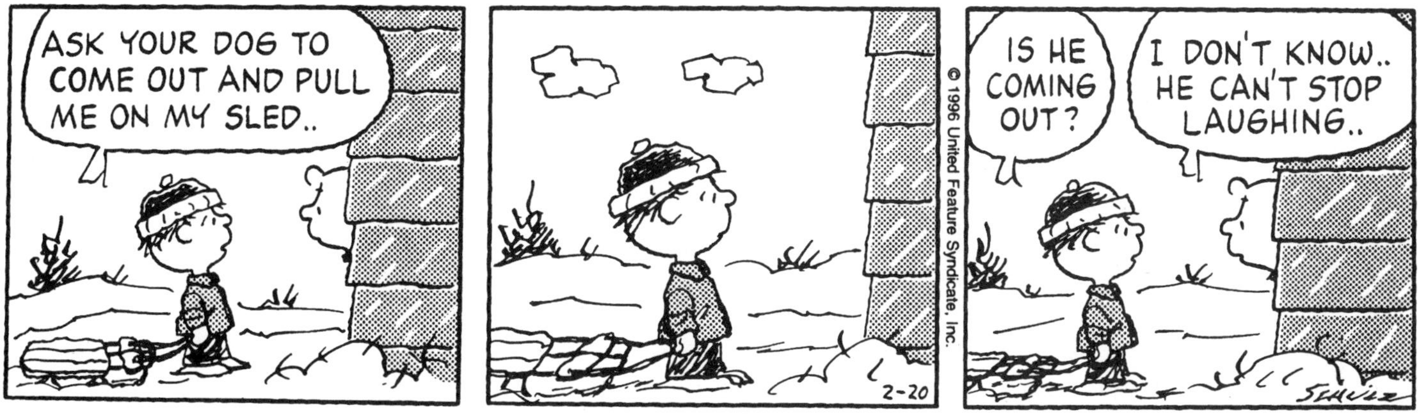
ASK YOUR DOG TO COME OUT AND PULL ME ON MY SLED..
2-20
© 1996 United Feature Syndicate, Inc.
IS HE COMING OUT?
I DON'T KNOW.. HE CAN'T STOP LAUGHING..
SCHULZ

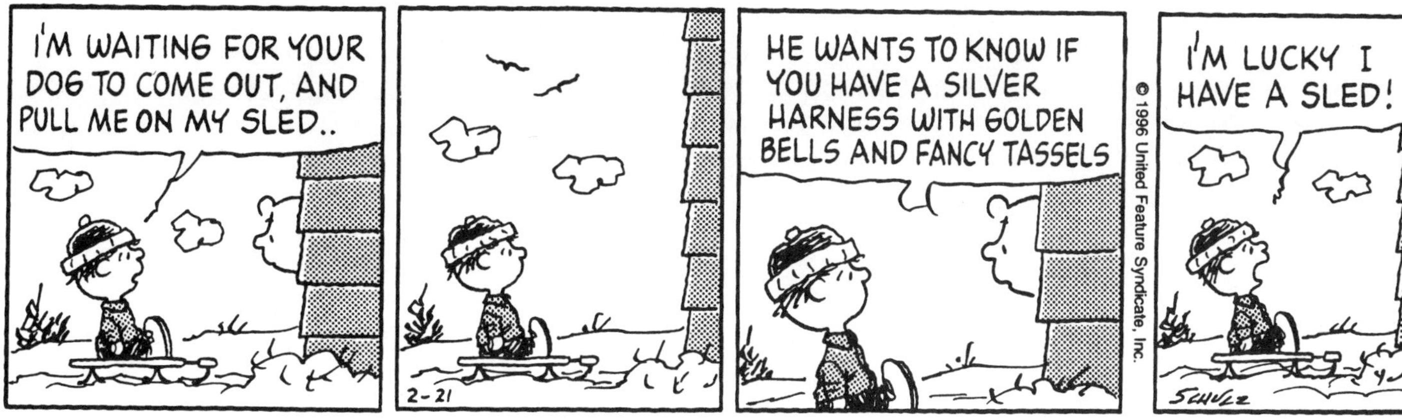
I'M WAITING FOR YOUR DOG TO COME OUT, AND PULL ME ON MY SLED..
2-21
HE WANTS TO KNOW IF YOU HAVE A SILVER HARNESS WITH GOLDEN BELLS AND FANCY TASSELS
© 1996 United Feature Syndicate, Inc.
I'M LUCKY I HAVE A SLED!
SCHULZ

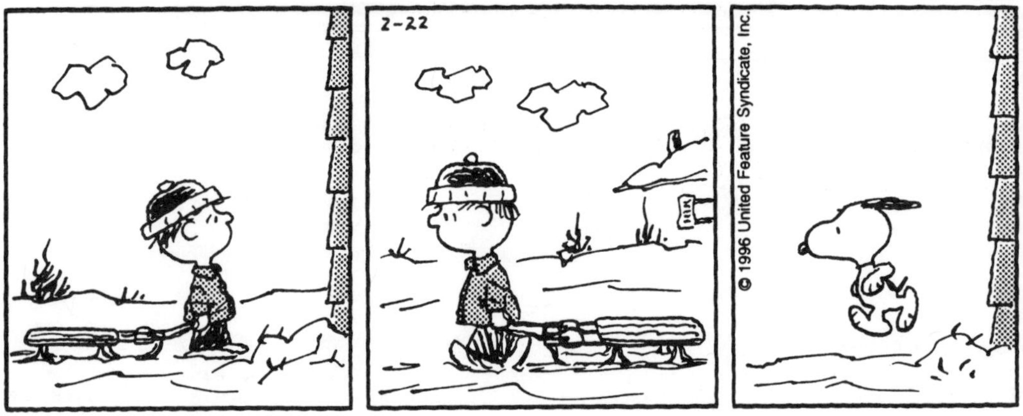
2-22
© 1996 United Feature Syndicate, Inc.
MUSH!
SCHULZ

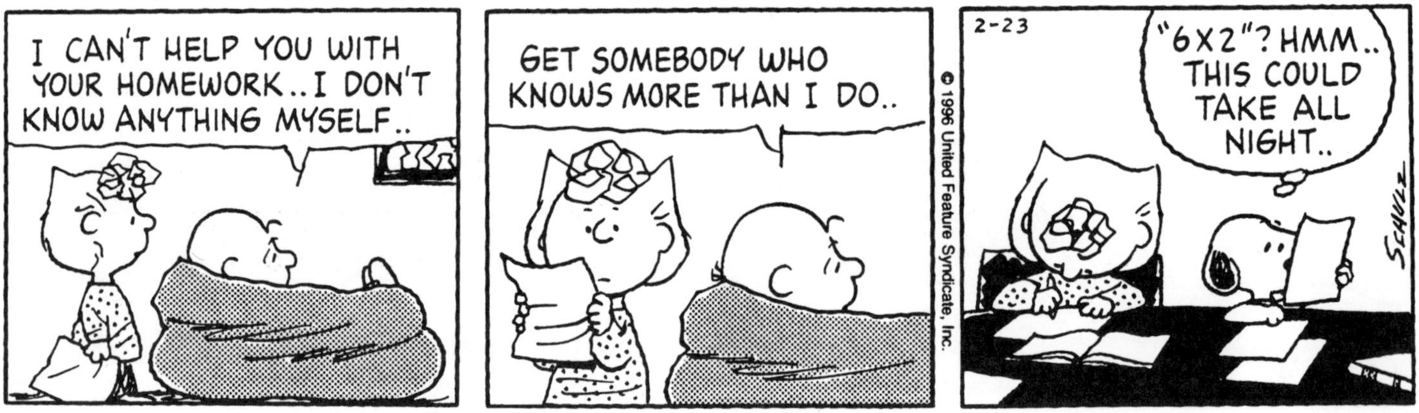
I CAN'T HELP YOU WITH YOUR HOMEWORK..I DON'T KNOW ANYTHING MYSELF..
GET SOMEBODY WHO KNOWS MORE THAN I DO..
© 1996 United Feature Syndicate, Inc.
2-23
"6X2"? HMM.. THIS COULD TAKE ALL NIGHT..
SCHULZ

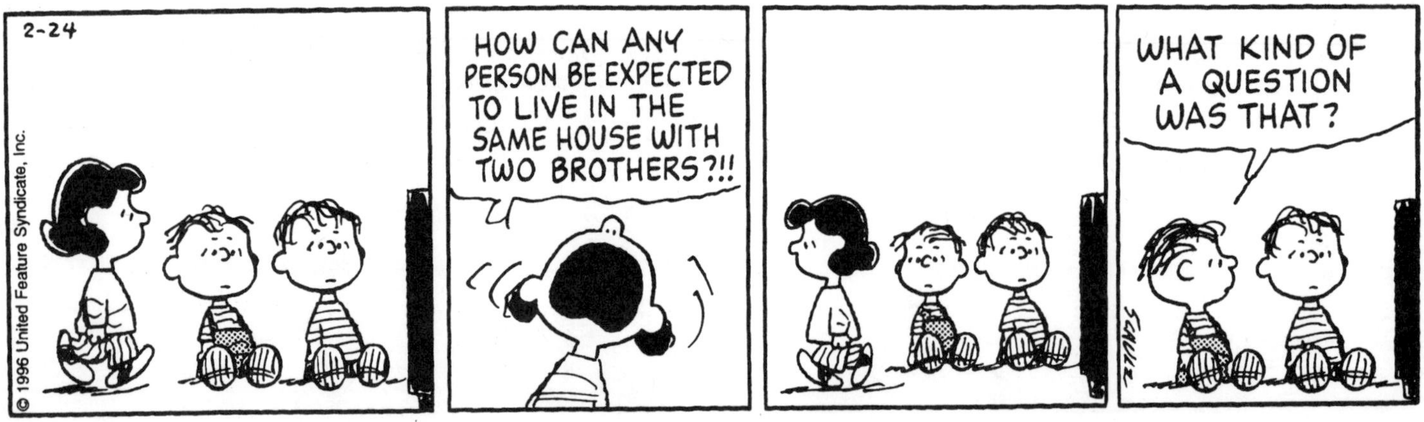
2-24
© 1996 United Feature Syndicate, Inc.
HOW CAN ANY PERSON BE EXPECTED TO LIVE IN THE SAME HOUSE WITH TWO BROTHERS?!!
WHAT KIND OF A QUESTION WAS THAT?
SCHULZ

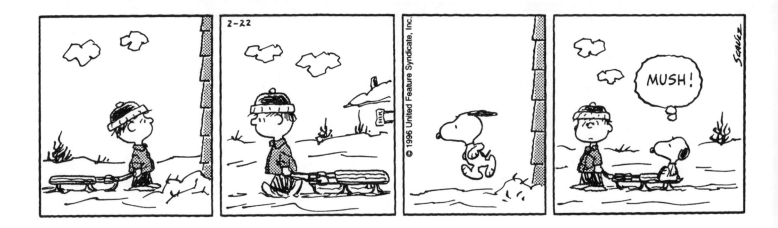

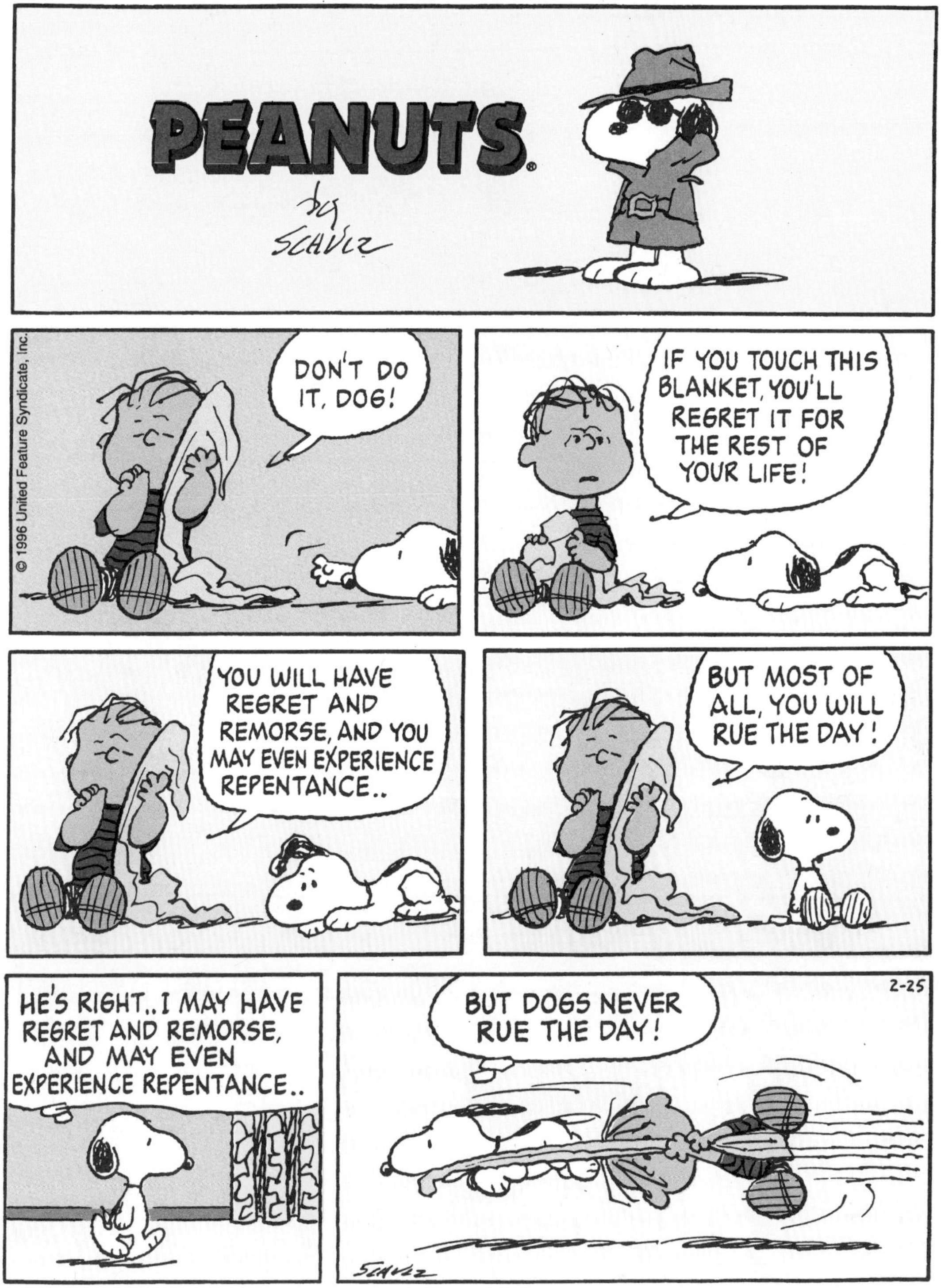
PEANUTS
by SCHULZ
© 1996 United Feature Syndicate, Inc.
DON'T DO IT, DOG!
IF YOU TOUCH THIS BLANKET, YOU'LL REGRET IT FOR THE REST OF YOUR LIFE!
YOU WILL HAVE REGRET AND REMORSE, AND YOU MAY EVEN EXPERIENCE REPENTANCE..
BUT MOST OF ALL, YOU WILL RUE THE DAY!
HE'S RIGHT.. I MAY HAVE REGRET AND REMORSE, AND MAY EVEN EXPERIENCE REPENTANCE..
2-25
BUT DOGS NEVER RUE THE DAY!
SCHULZ

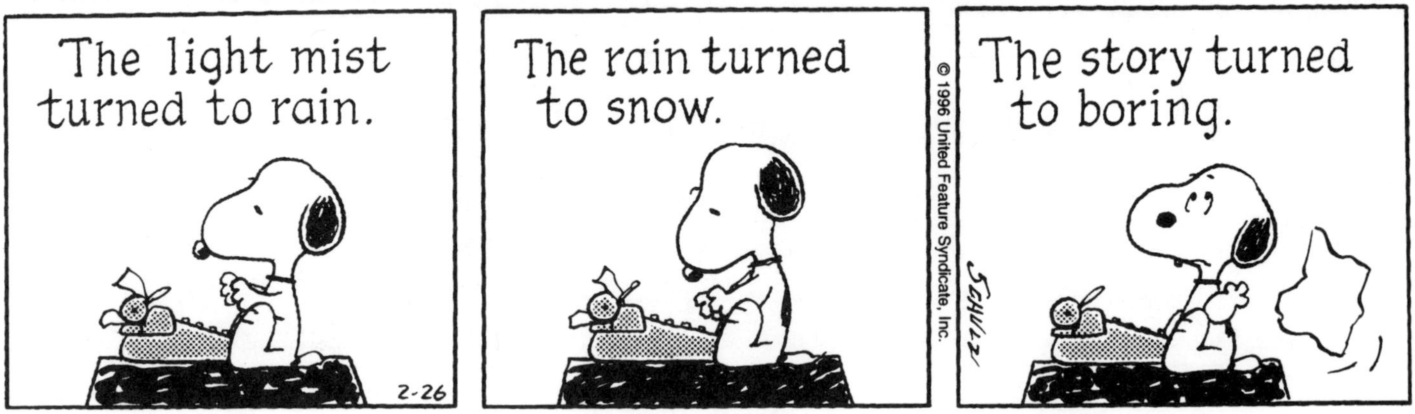
The light mist turned to rain.
2-26
The rain turned to snow.
© 1996 United Feature Syndicate, Inc.
The story turned to boring.
SCHULZ

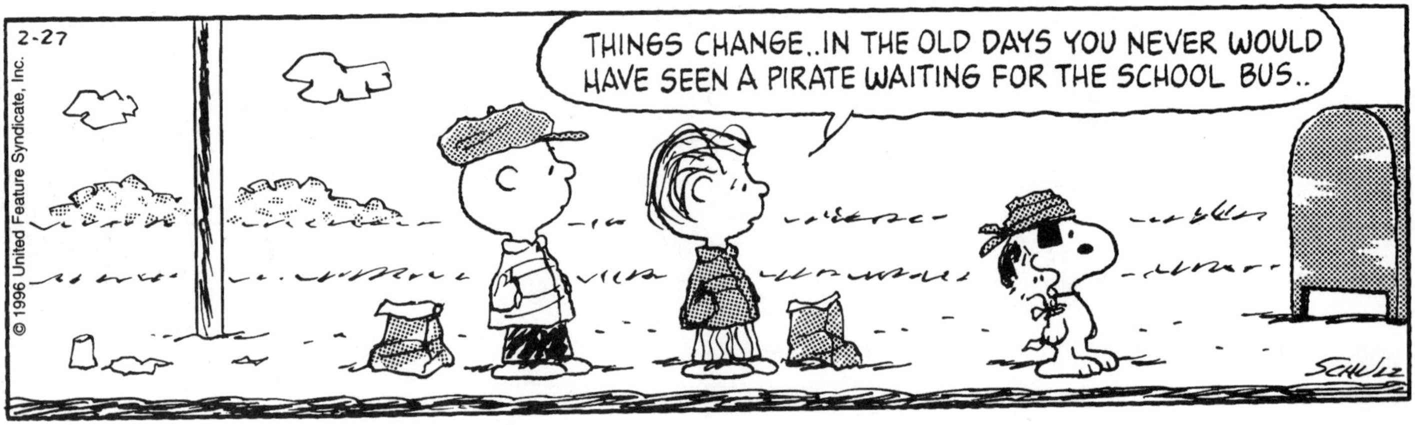
2-27
© 1996 United Feature Syndicate, Inc.
THINGS CHANGE..IN THE OLD DAYS YOU NEVER WOULD HAVE SEEN A PIRATE WAITING FOR THE SCHOOL BUS..
SCHULZ

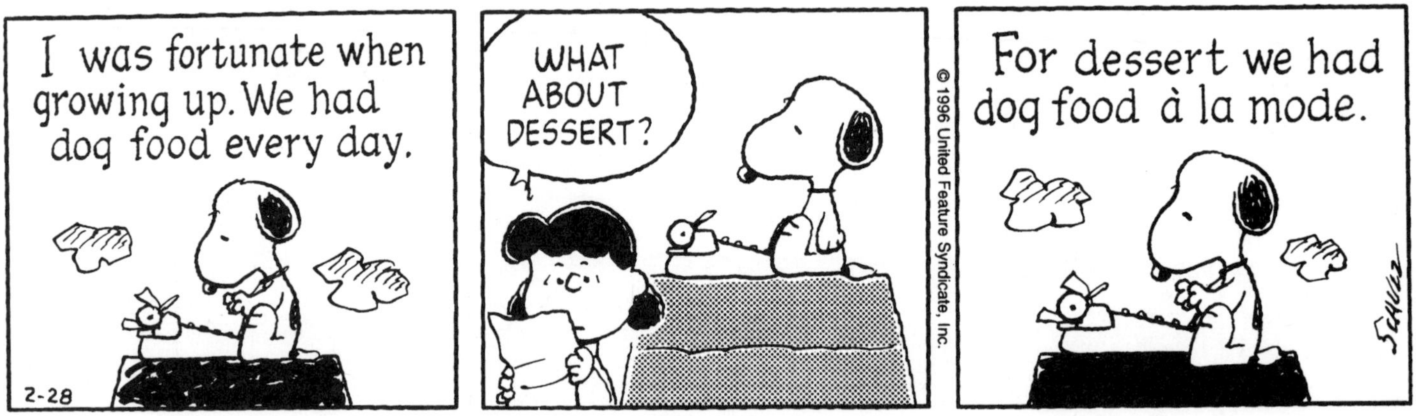
I was fortunate when growing up. We had dog food every day.
2-28
WHAT ABOUT DESSERT?
© 1996 United Feature Syndicate, Inc.
For dessert we had dog food à la mode.
SCHULZ

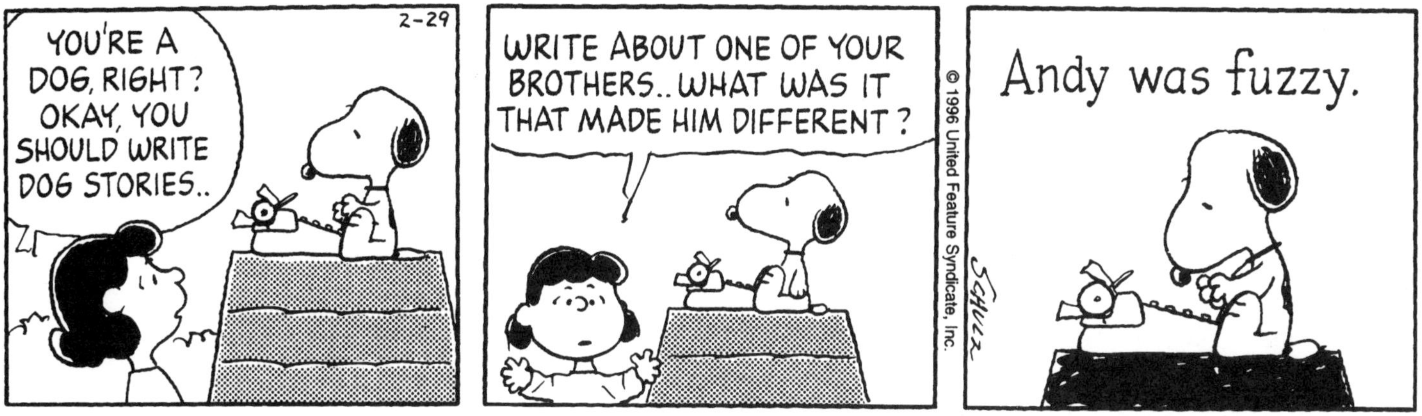
2-29
YOU'RE A DOG, RIGHT? OKAY, YOU SHOULD WRITE DOG STORIES..
WRITE ABOUT ONE OF YOUR BROTHERS..WHAT WAS IT THAT MADE HIM DIFFERENT?
© 1996 United Feature Syndicate, Inc.
Andy was fuzzy.

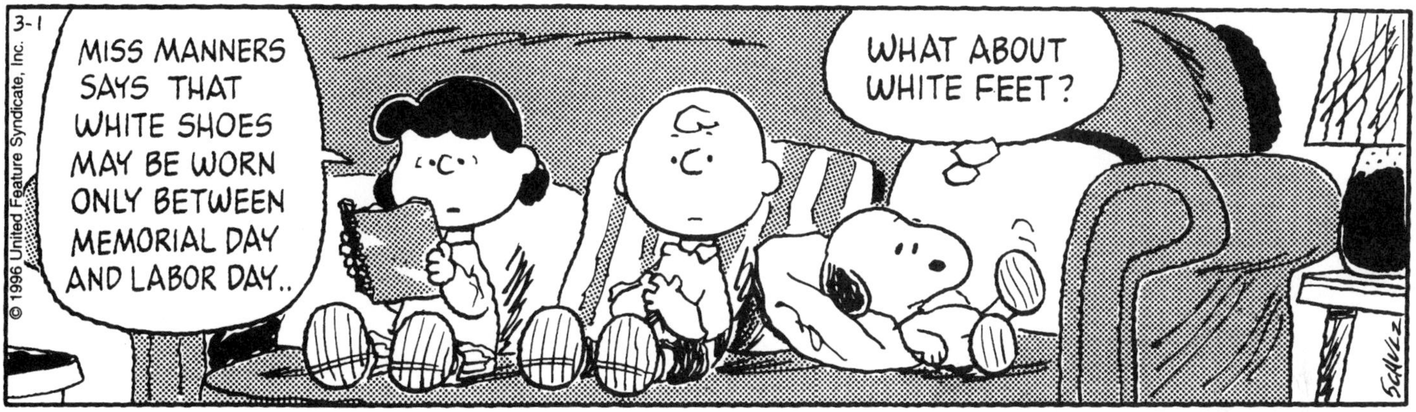
3-1
© 1996 United Feature Syndicate, Inc.
MISS MANNERS SAYS THAT WHITE SHOES MAY BE WORN ONLY BETWEEN MEMORIAL DAY AND LABOR DAY..
WHAT ABOUT WHITE FEET?

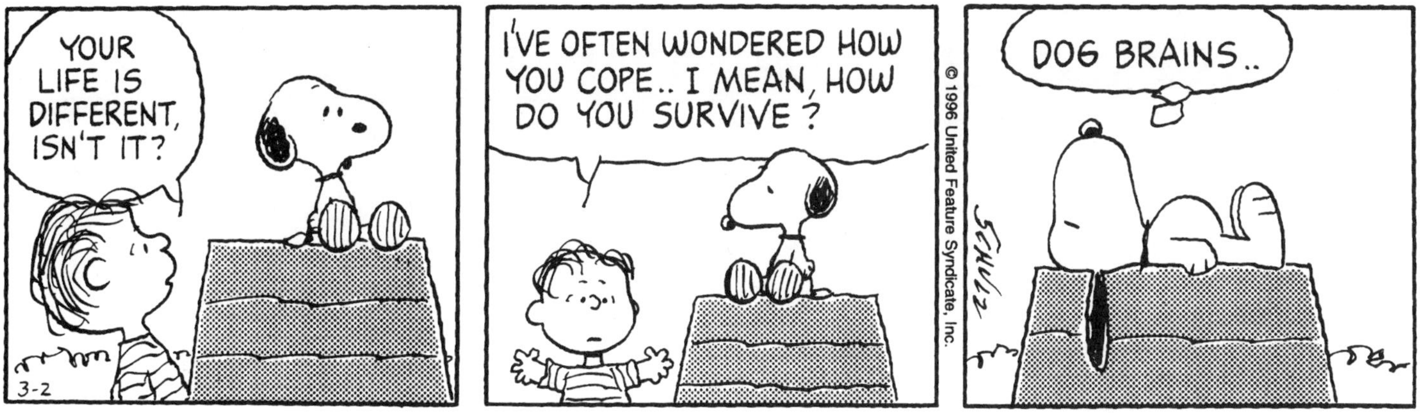
YOUR LIFE IS DIFFERENT, ISN'T IT?
3-2
I'VE OFTEN WONDERED HOW YOU COPE.. I MEAN, HOW DO YOU SURVIVE?
© 1996 United Feature Syndicate, Inc.
DOG BRAINS..

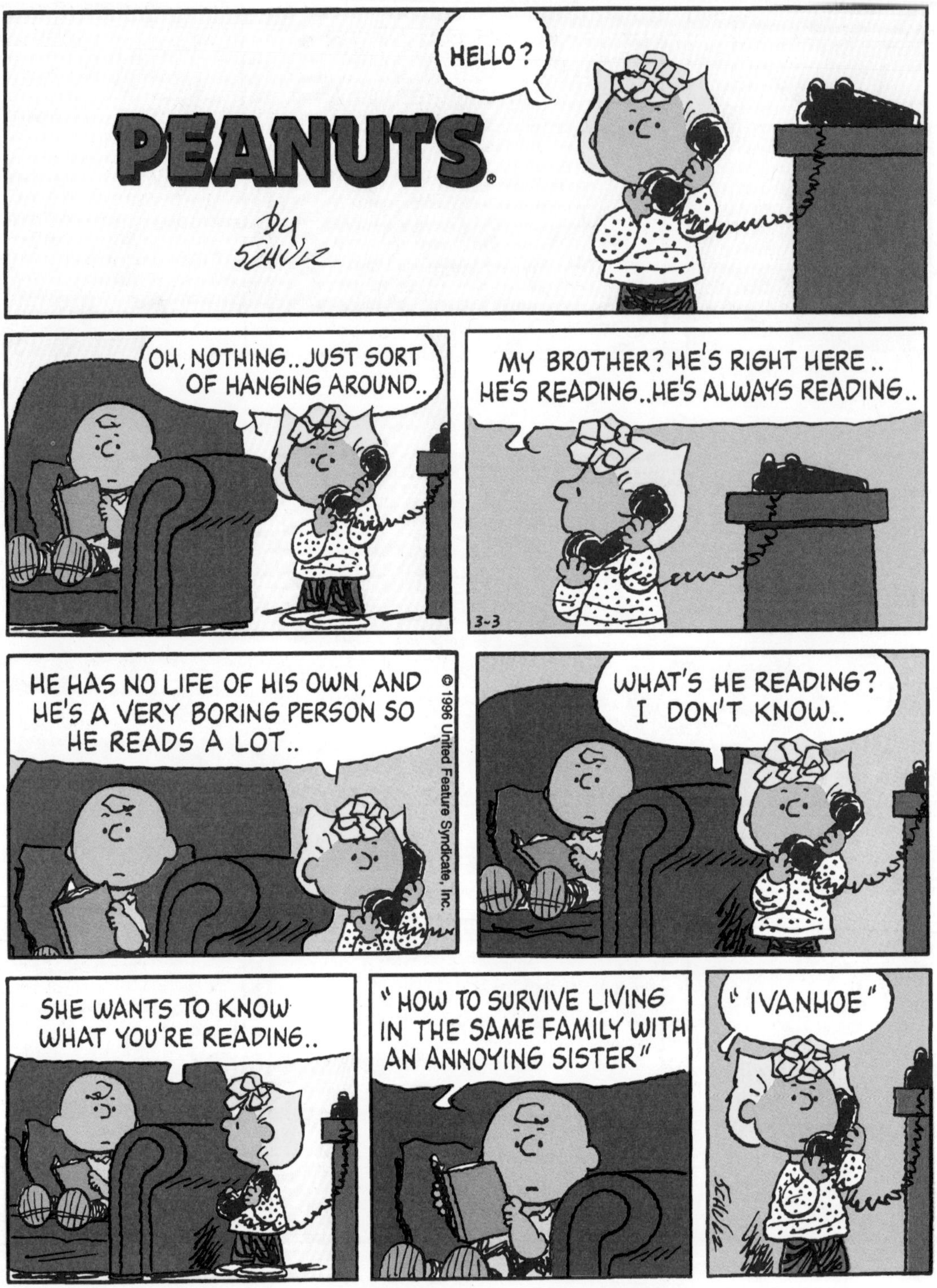
PEANUTS
by SCHULZ
HELLO?
OH, NOTHING.. JUST SORT OF HANGING AROUND..
MY BROTHER? HE'S RIGHT HERE.. HE'S READING.. HE'S ALWAYS READING..
3-3
HE HAS NO LIFE OF HIS OWN, AND HE'S A VERY BORING PERSON SO HE READS A LOT..
© 1996 United Feature Syndicate, Inc.
WHAT'S HE READING? I DON'T KNOW..
SHE WANTS TO KNOW WHAT YOU'RE READING..
"HOW TO SURVIVE LIVING IN THE SAME FAMILY WITH AN ANNOYING SISTER"
"IVANHOE"
SCHULZ

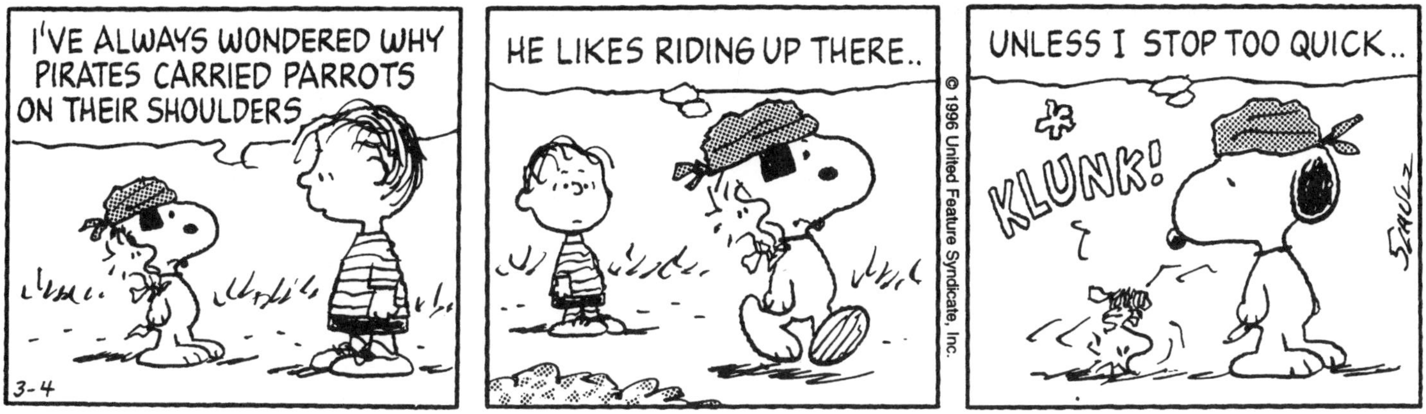
I'VE ALWAYS WONDERED WHY PIRATES CARRIED PARROTS ON THEIR SHOULDERS
3-4
HE LIKES RIDING UP THERE..
© 1996 United Feature Syndicate, Inc.
UNLESS I STOP TOO QUICK..
KLUNK!
SCHULZ

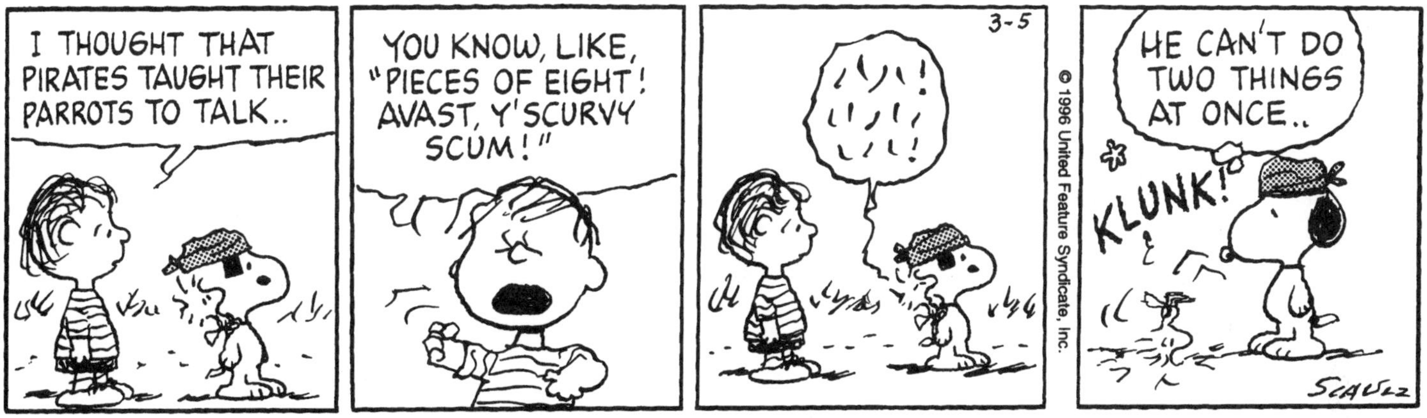
I THOUGHT THAT PIRATES TAUGHT THEIR PARROTS TO TALK..
YOU KNOW, LIKE, "PIECES OF EIGHT! AVAST, Y'SCURVY SCUM!"
3-5
© 1996 United Feature Syndicate, Inc.
HE CAN'T DO TWO THINGS AT ONCE..
KLUNK!
SCHULZ

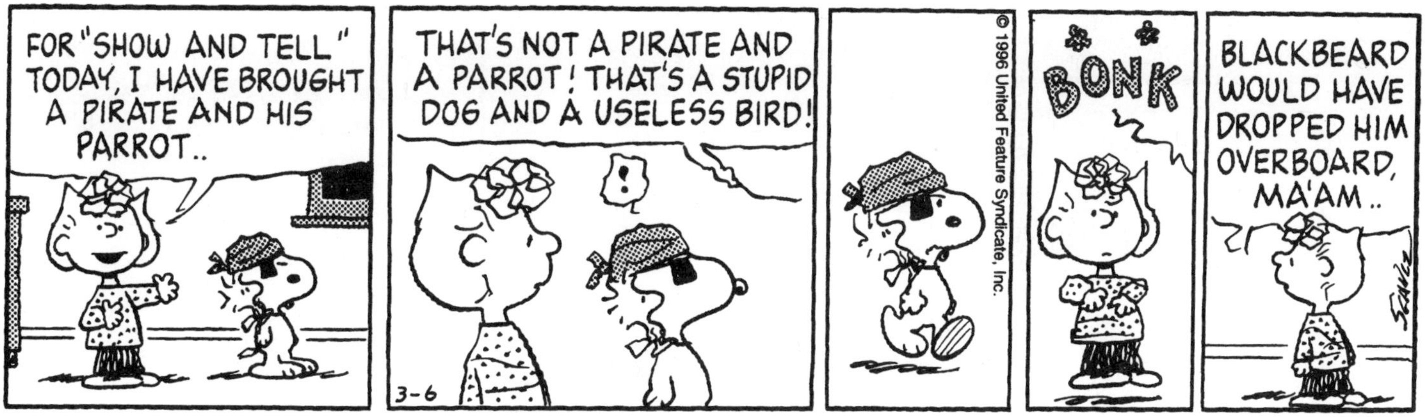
FOR "SHOW AND TELL" TODAY, I HAVE BROUGHT A PIRATE AND HIS PARROT..
THAT'S NOT A PIRATE AND A PARROT! THAT'S A STUPID DOG AND A USELESS BIRD!
!
3-6
© 1996 United Feature Syndicate, Inc.
BONK
BLACKBEARD WOULD HAVE DROPPED HIM OVERBOARD, MA'AM..
SCHULZ

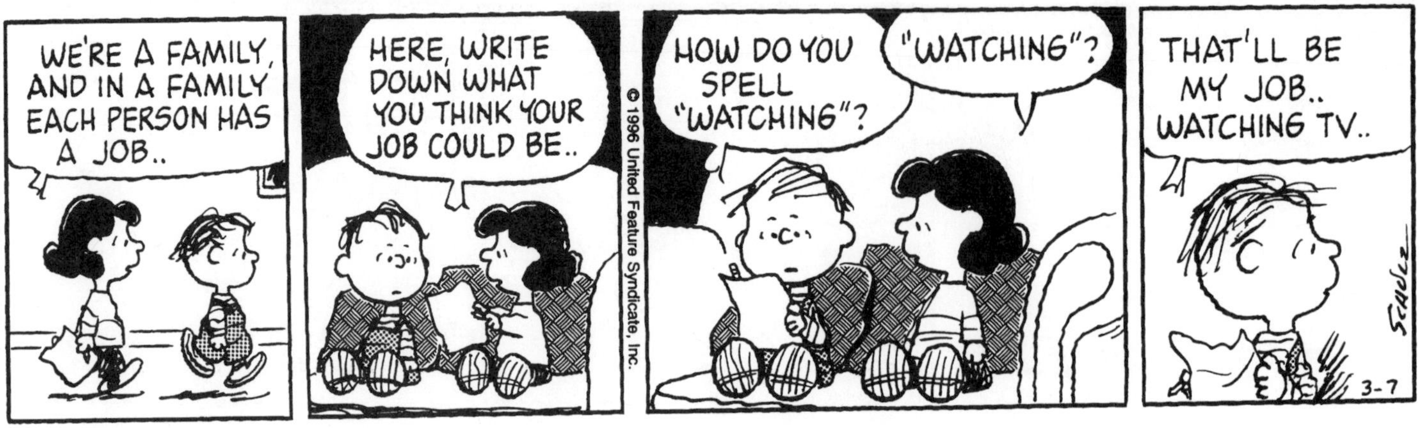
WE'RE A FAMILY, AND IN A FAMILY EACH PERSON HAS A JOB..
HERE, WRITE DOWN WHAT YOU THINK YOUR JOB COULD BE..
© 1996 United Feature Syndicate, Inc.
HOW DO YOU SPELL "WATCHING"?
"WATCHING"?
THAT'LL BE MY JOB.. WATCHING TV..
SCHULZ
3-7

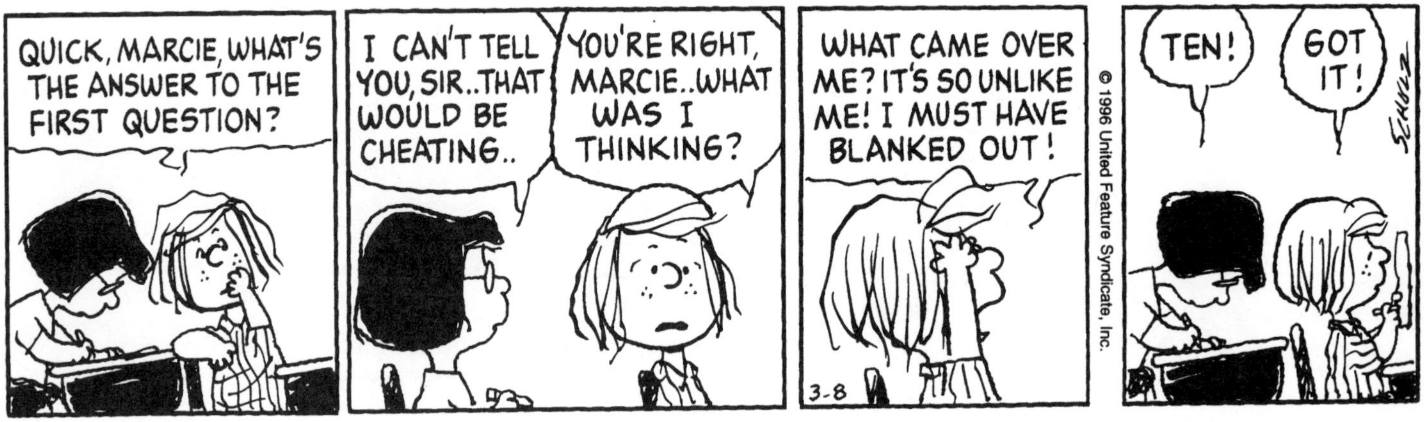
QUICK, MARCIE, WHAT'S THE ANSWER TO THE FIRST QUESTION?
I CAN'T TELL YOU, SIR..THAT WOULD BE CHEATING..
YOU'RE RIGHT, MARCIE..WHAT WAS I THINKING?
WHAT CAME OVER ME? IT'S SO UNLIKE ME! I MUST HAVE BLANKED OUT!
3-8
© 1996 United Feature Syndicate, Inc.
TEN!
GOT IT!
SCHULZ

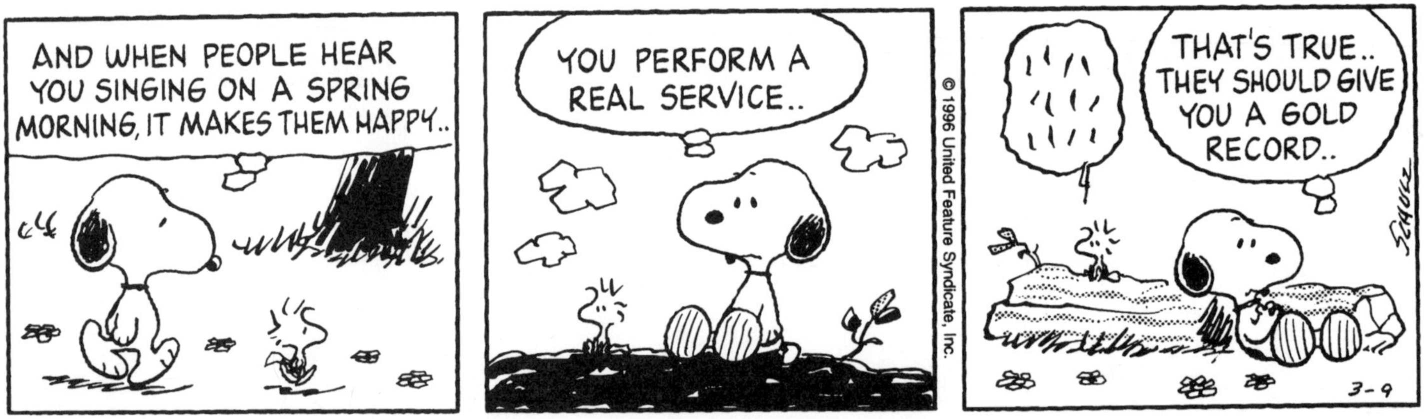
AND WHEN PEOPLE HEAR YOU SINGING ON A SPRING MORNING, IT MAKES THEM HAPPY..
YOU PERFORM A REAL SERVICE..
© 1996 United Feature Syndicate, Inc.
THAT'S TRUE.. THEY SHOULD GIVE YOU A GOLD RECORD..
SCHULZ
3-9

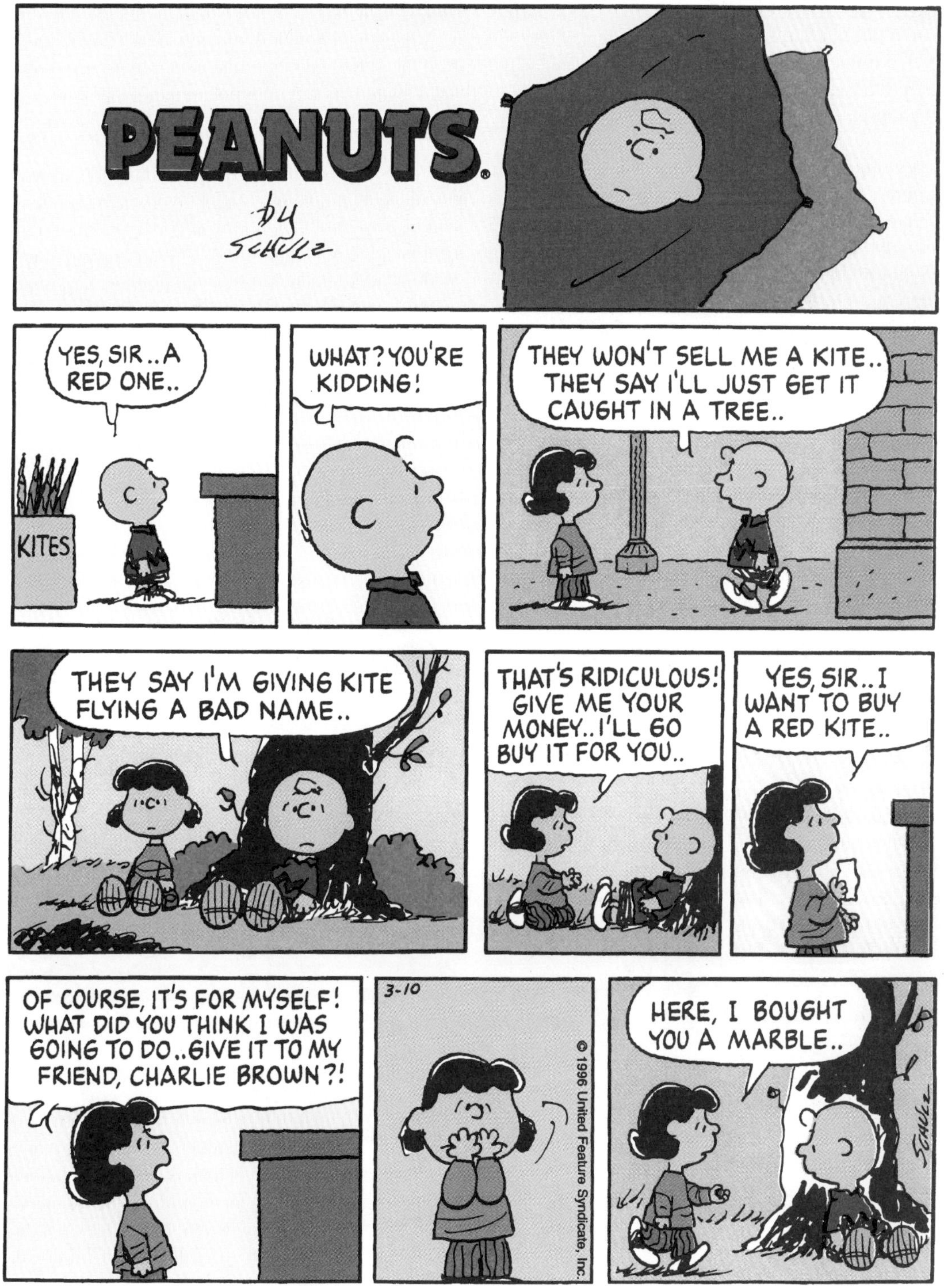
PEANUTS
by SCHULZ
YES, SIR..A RED ONE..
KITES
WHAT? YOU'RE KIDDING!
THEY WON'T SELL ME A KITE.. THEY SAY I'LL JUST GET IT CAUGHT IN A TREE..
THEY SAY I'M GIVING KITE FLYING A BAD NAME..
THAT'S RIDICULOUS! GIVE ME YOUR MONEY..I'LL GO BUY IT FOR YOU..
YES, SIR..I WANT TO BUY A RED KITE..
OF COURSE, IT'S FOR MYSELF! WHAT DID YOU THINK I WAS GOING TO DO..GIVE IT TO MY FRIEND, CHARLIE BROWN?!
3-10
© 1996 United Feature Syndicate, Inc.
HERE, I BOUGHT YOU A MARBLE..
SCHULZ

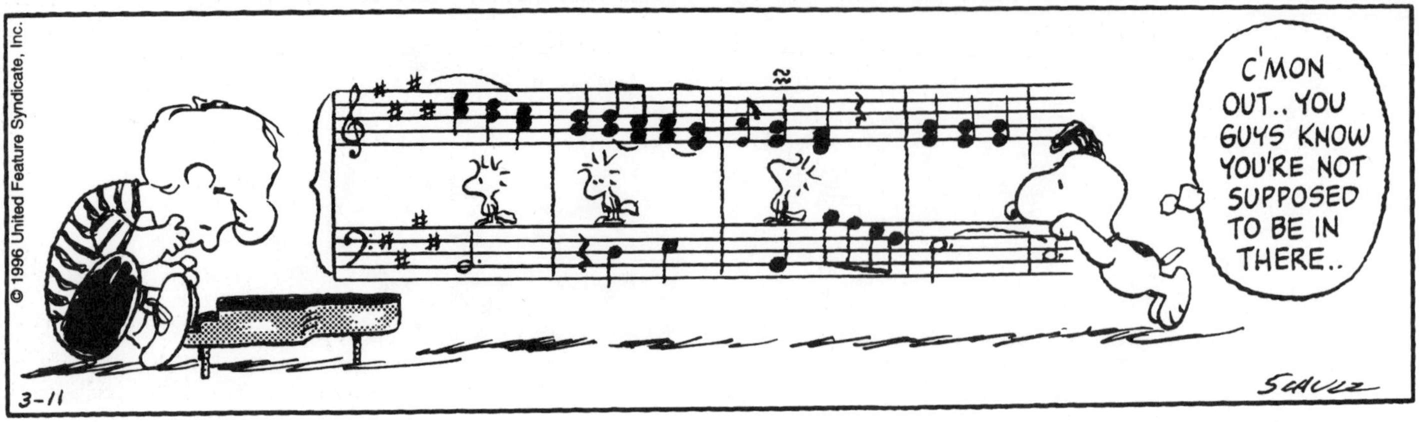
© 1996 United Feature Syndicate, Inc.
C'MON OUT.. YOU GUYS KNOW YOU'RE NOT SUPPOSED TO BE IN THERE..
3-11
SCHULZ

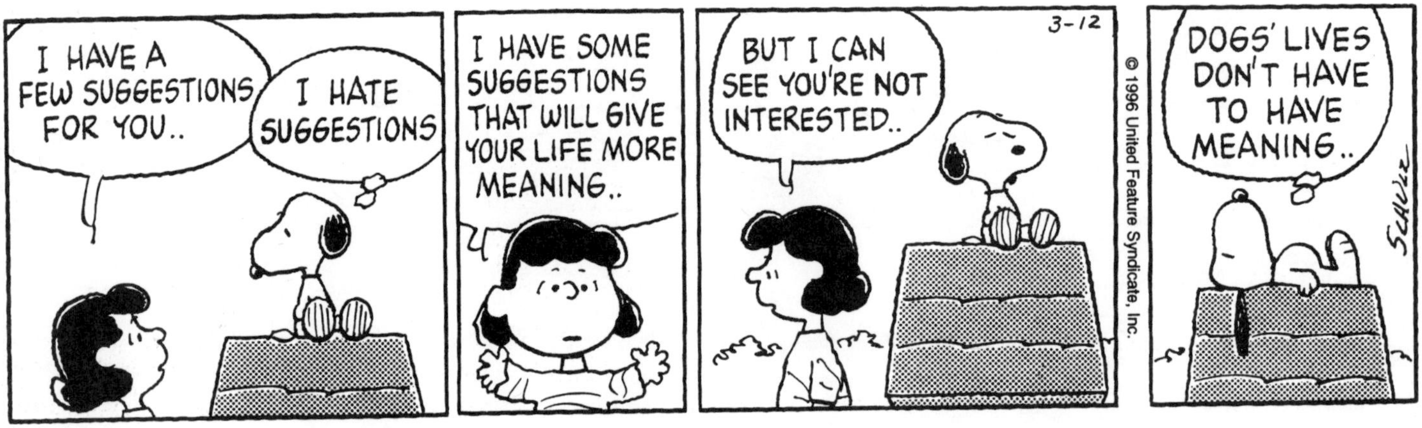
I HAVE A FEW SUGGESTIONS FOR YOU..
I HATE SUGGESTIONS
I HAVE SOME SUGGESTIONS THAT WILL GIVE YOUR LIFE MORE MEANING..
BUT I CAN SEE YOU'RE NOT INTERESTED..
3-12
© 1996 United Feature Syndicate, Inc.
DOGS' LIVES DON'T HAVE TO HAVE MEANING..
SCHULZ

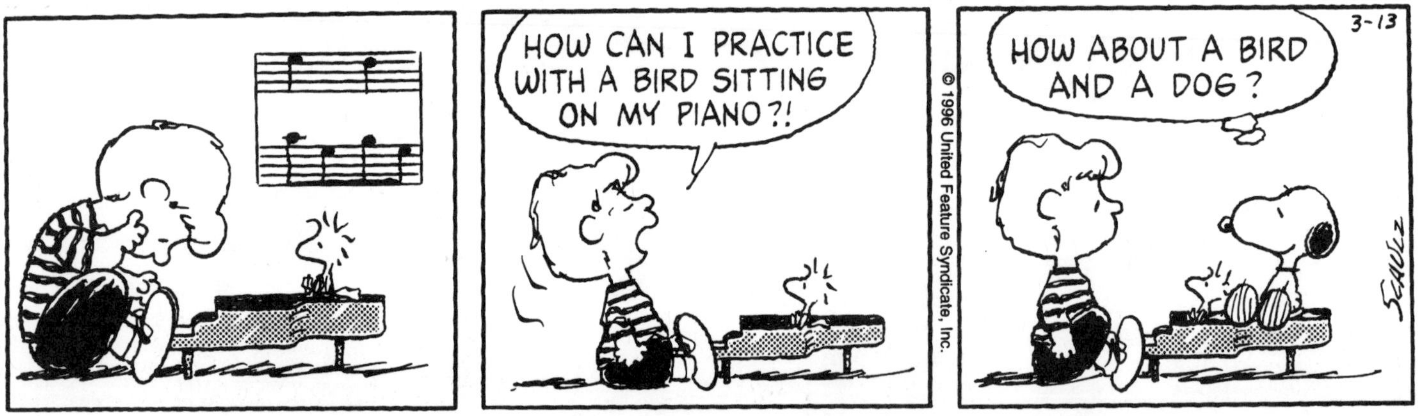
HOW CAN I PRACTICE WITH A BIRD SITTING ON MY PIANO?!
© 1996 United Feature Syndicate, Inc.
3-13
HOW ABOUT A BIRD AND A DOG?
SCHULZ

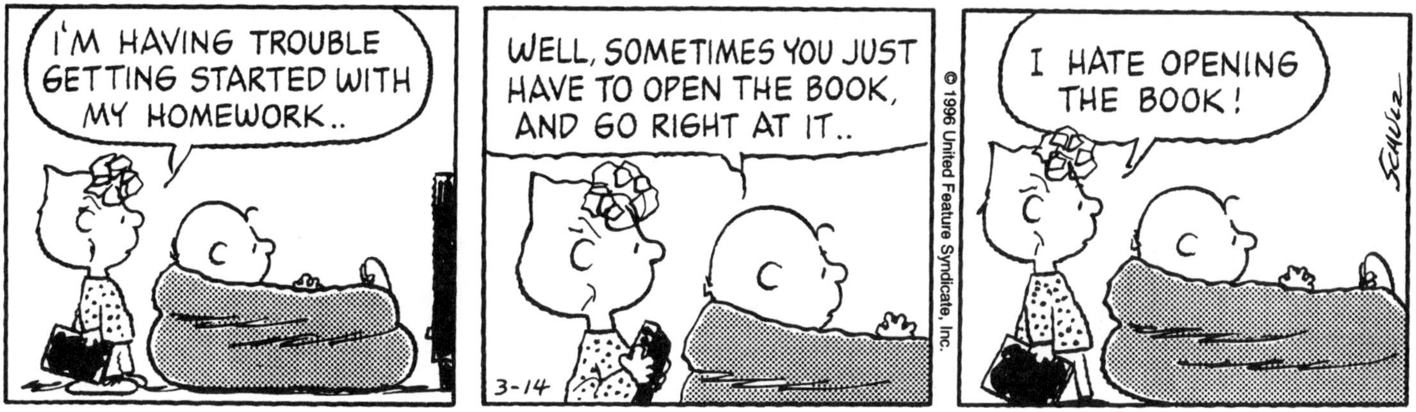
I'M HAVING TROUBLE GETTING STARTED WITH MY HOMEWORK..
WELL, SOMETIMES YOU JUST HAVE TO OPEN THE BOOK, AND GO RIGHT AT IT..
3-14
© 1996 United Feature Syndicate, Inc.
I HATE OPENING THE BOOK!
SCHULZ

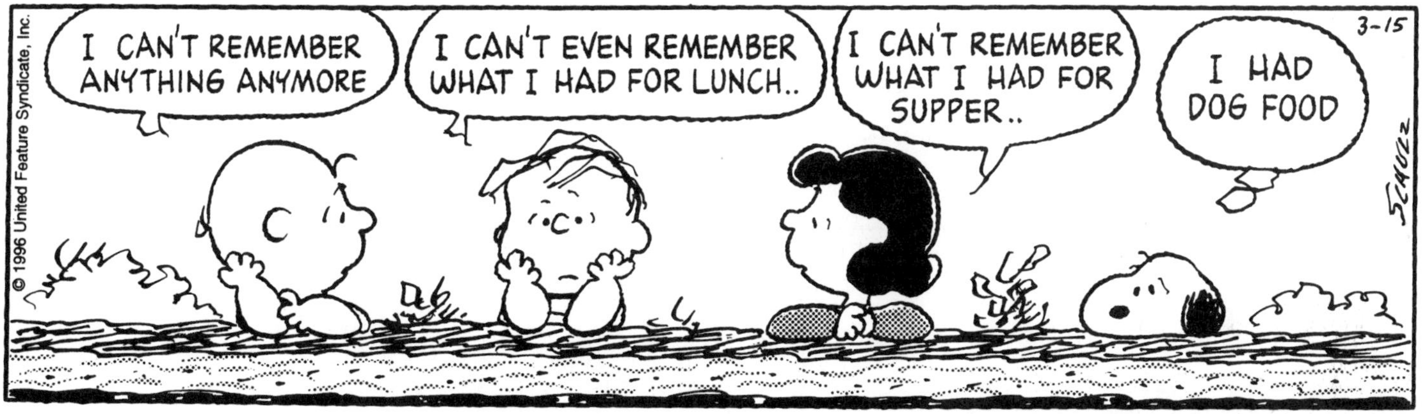
© 1996 United Feature Syndicate, Inc.
I CAN'T REMEMBER ANYTHING ANYMORE
I CAN'T EVEN REMEMBER WHAT I HAD FOR LUNCH..
I CAN'T REMEMBER WHAT I HAD FOR SUPPER..
3-15
I HAD DOG FOOD
SCHULZ

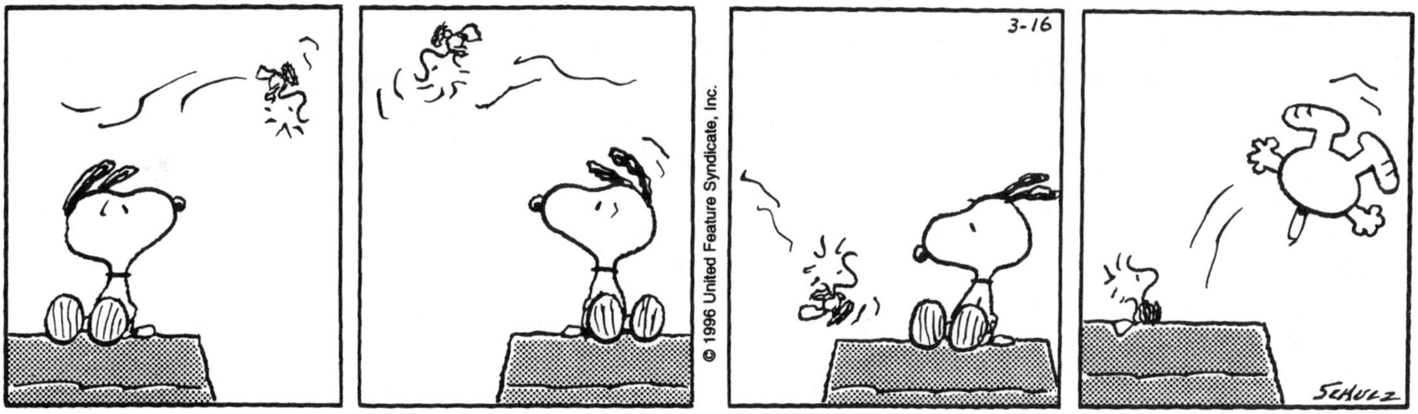
© 1996 United Feature Syndicate, Inc.
3-16
SCHULZ

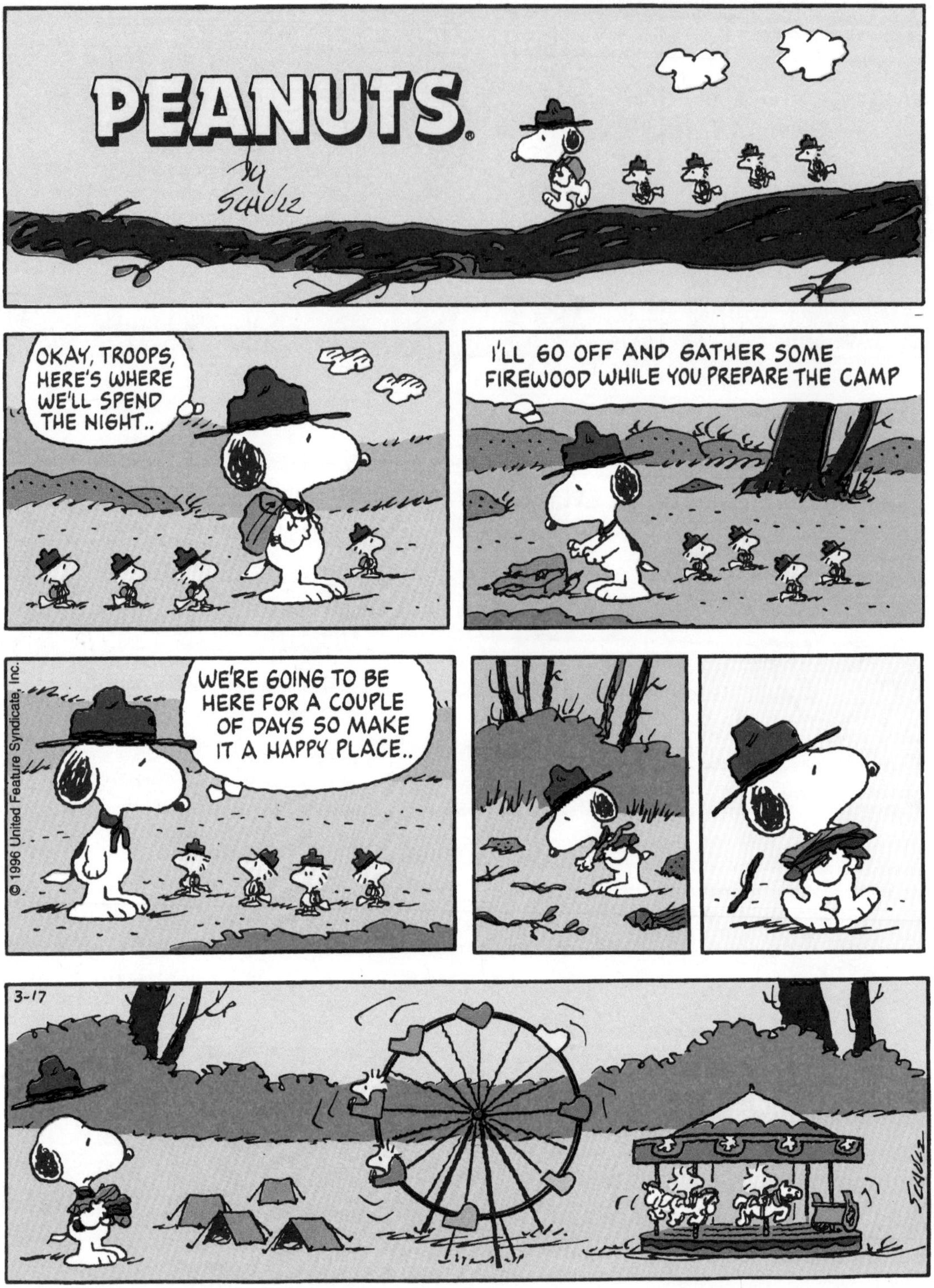
PEANUTS
by SCHULZ
OKAY, TROOPS, HERE'S WHERE WE'LL SPEND THE NIGHT..
I'LL GO OFF AND GATHER SOME FIREWOOD WHILE YOU PREPARE THE CAMP
© 1996 United Feature Syndicate, Inc.
WE'RE GOING TO BE HERE FOR A COUPLE OF DAYS SO MAKE IT A HAPPY PLACE..
3-17
SCHULZ

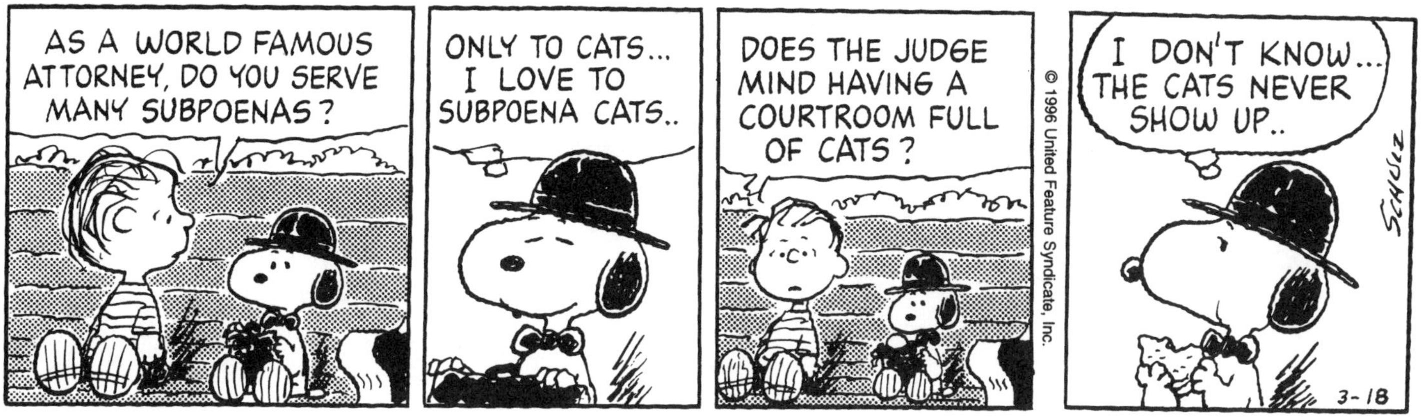
AS A WORLD FAMOUS ATTORNEY, DO YOU SERVE MANY SUBPOENAS?
ONLY TO CATS... I LOVE TO SUBPOENA CATS..
DOES THE JUDGE MIND HAVING A COURTROOM FULL OF CATS?
I DON'T KNOW... THE CATS NEVER SHOW UP..
SCHULZ
3-18

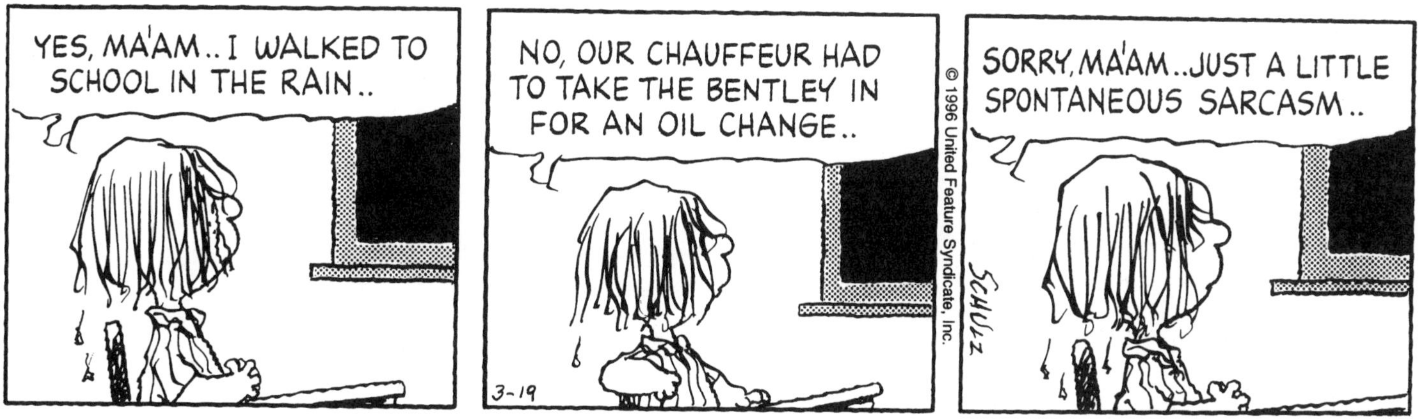
YES, MA'AM.. I WALKED TO SCHOOL IN THE RAIN..
NO, OUR CHAUFFEUR HAD TO TAKE THE BENTLEY IN FOR AN OIL CHANGE..
3-19
SORRY, MA'AM.. JUST A LITTLE SPONTANEOUS SARCASM..
SCHULZ

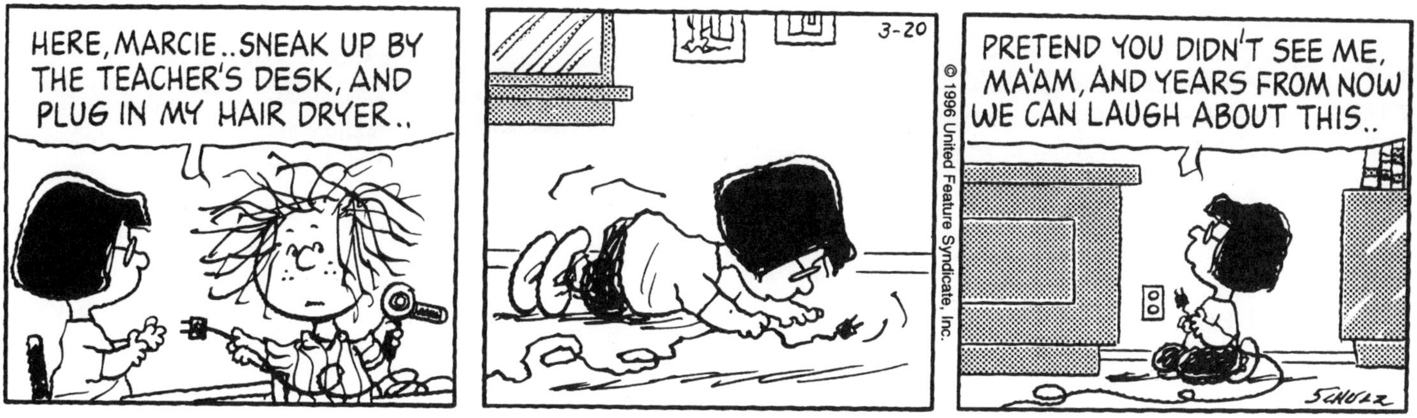
HERE, MARCIE.. SNEAK UP BY THE TEACHER'S DESK, AND PLUG IN MY HAIR DRYER..
3-20
PRETEND YOU DIDN'T SEE ME, MA'AM, AND YEARS FROM NOW WE CAN LAUGH ABOUT THIS..
SCHULZ

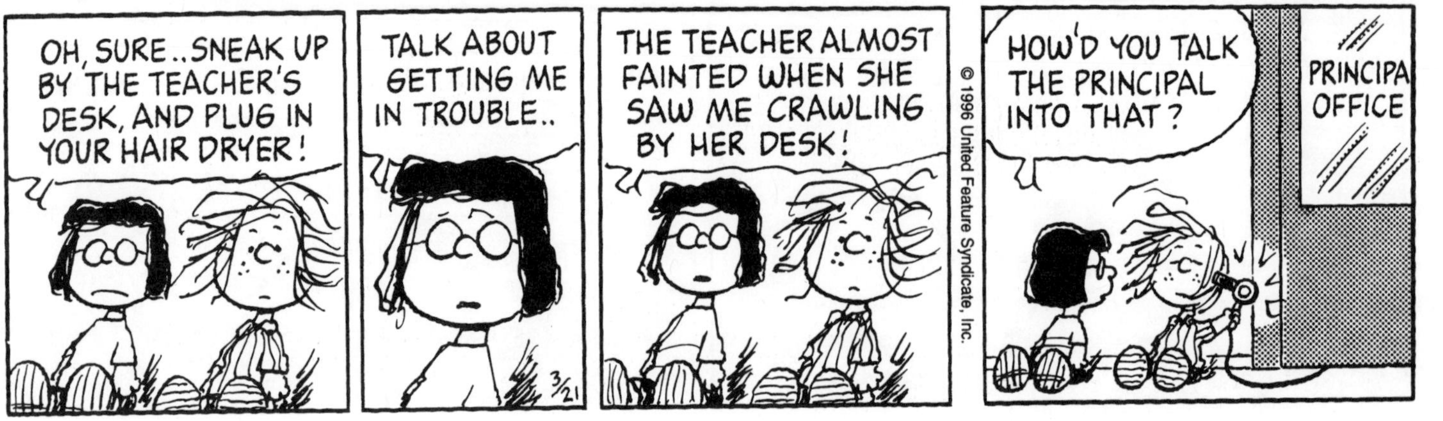
OH, SURE..SNEAK UP BY THE TEACHER'S DESK, AND PLUG IN YOUR HAIR DRYER!
TALK ABOUT GETTING ME IN TROUBLE..
3/21
THE TEACHER ALMOST FAINTED WHEN SHE SAW ME CRAWLING BY HER DESK!
© 1996 United Feature Syndicate, Inc.
HOW'D YOU TALK THE PRINCIPAL INTO THAT?
PRINCIPA OFFICE

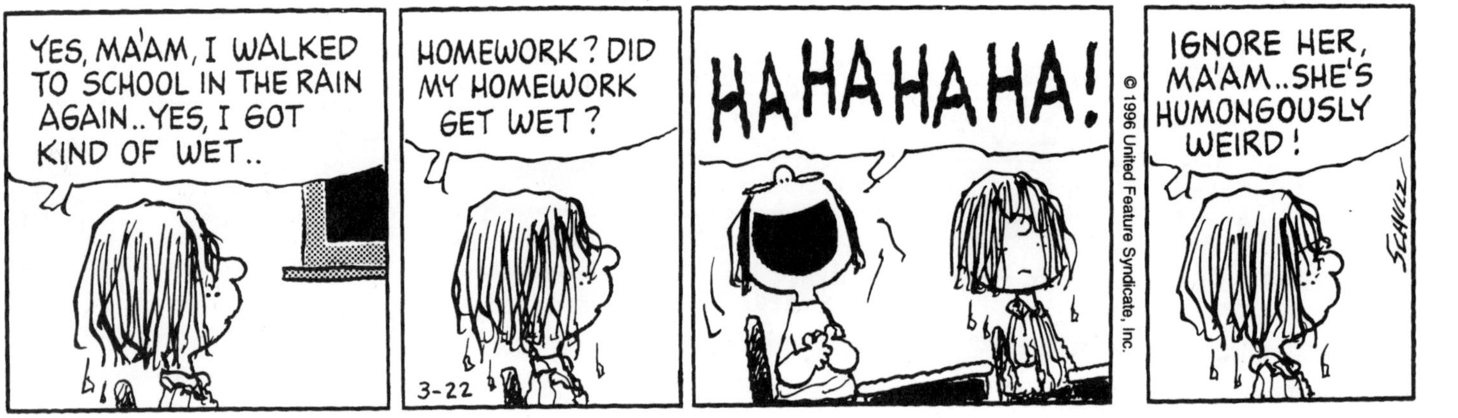
YES, MA'AM, I WALKED TO SCHOOL IN THE RAIN AGAIN..YES, I GOT KIND OF WET..
HOMEWORK? DID MY HOMEWORK GET WET?
3-22
HAHAHAHA!
© 1996 United Feature Syndicate, Inc.
IGNORE HER, MA'AM..SHE'S HUMONGOUSLY WEIRD!
SCHULZ

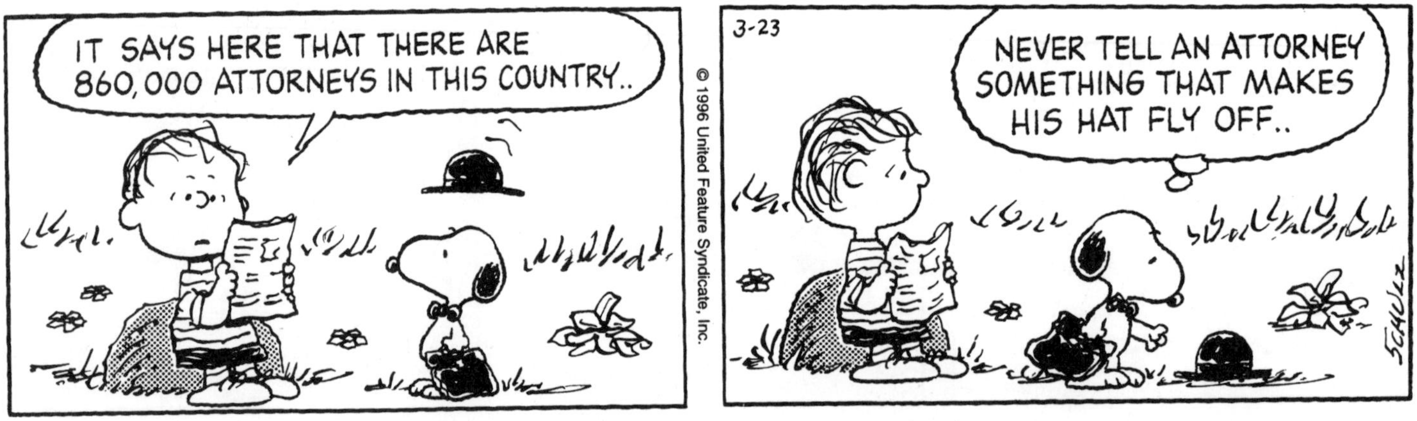
IT SAYS HERE THAT THERE ARE 860,000 ATTORNEYS IN THIS COUNTRY..
© 1996 United Feature Syndicate, Inc.
3-23
NEVER TELL AN ATTORNEY SOMETHING THAT MAKES HIS HAT FLY OFF..
SCHULZ

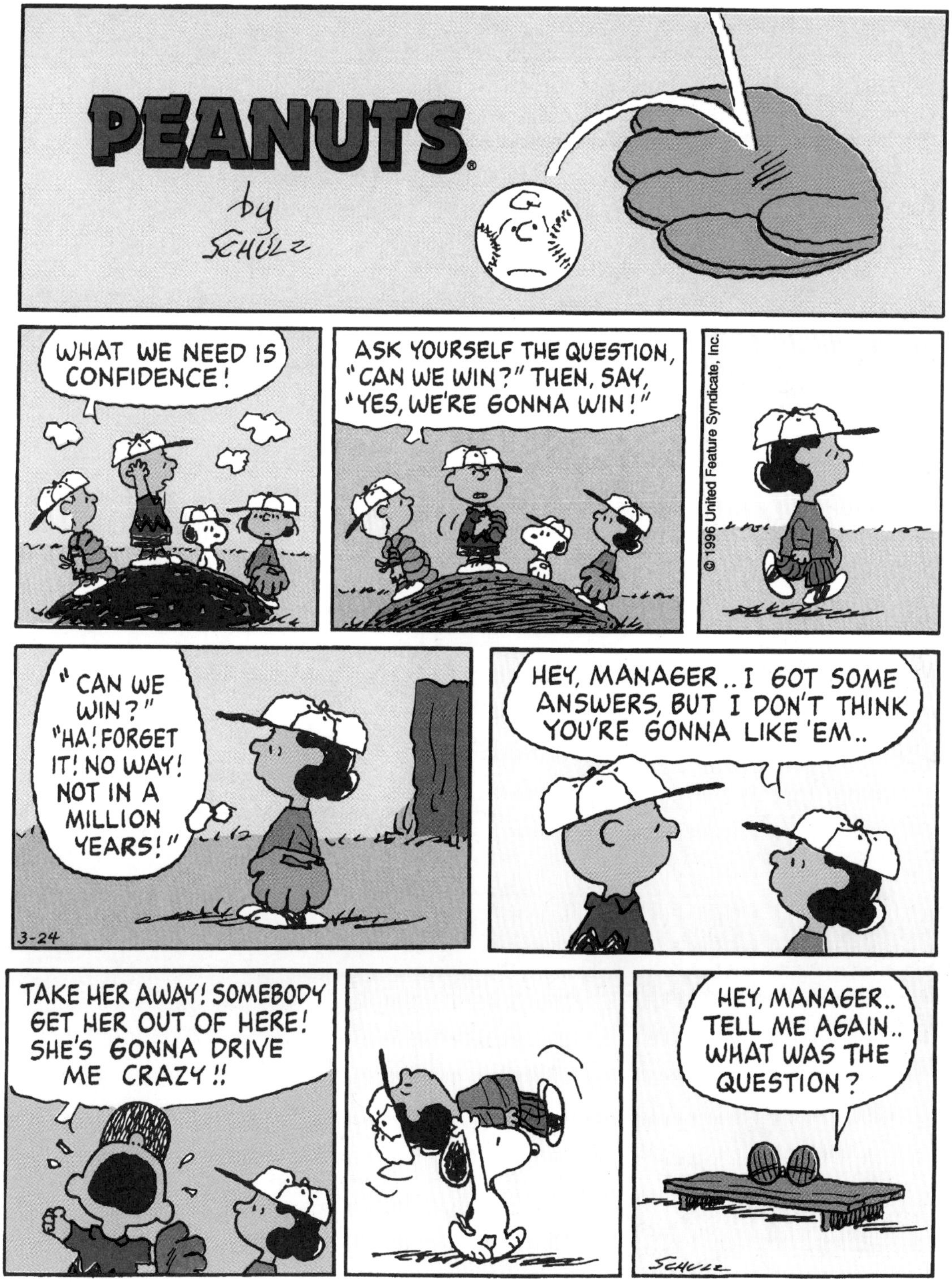
PEANUTS
by SCHULZ
WHAT WE NEED IS CONFIDENCE!
ASK YOURSELF THE QUESTION, "CAN WE WIN?" THEN, SAY, "YES, WE'RE GONNA WIN!"
© 1996 United Feature Syndicate, Inc.
"CAN WE WIN?" "HA! FORGET IT! NO WAY! NOT IN A MILLION YEARS!"
3-24
HEY, MANAGER.. I GOT SOME ANSWERS, BUT I DON'T THINK YOU'RE GONNA LIKE 'EM..
TAKE HER AWAY! SOMEBODY GET HER OUT OF HERE! SHE'S GONNA DRIVE ME CRAZY!!
HEY, MANAGER.. TELL ME AGAIN.. WHAT WAS THE QUESTION?
SCHULZ

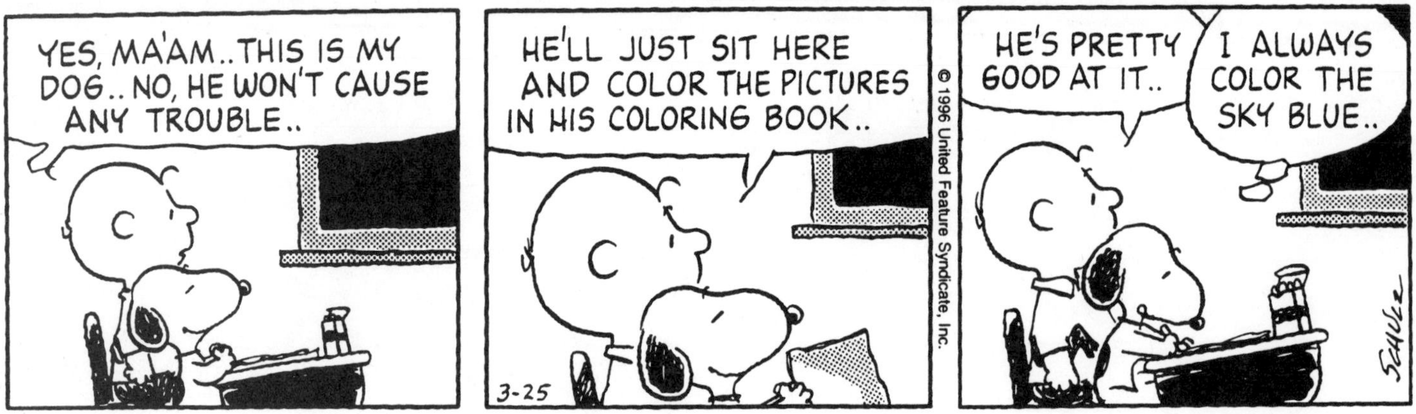

YES, MA'AM.. THIS IS MY DOG.. NO, HE WON'T CAUSE ANY TROUBLE..
HE'LL JUST SIT HERE AND COLOR THE PICTURES IN HIS COLORING BOOK..
3-25
© 1996 United Feature Syndicate, Inc.
HE'S PRETTY GOOD AT IT..
I ALWAYS COLOR THE SKY BLUE..
SCHULZ

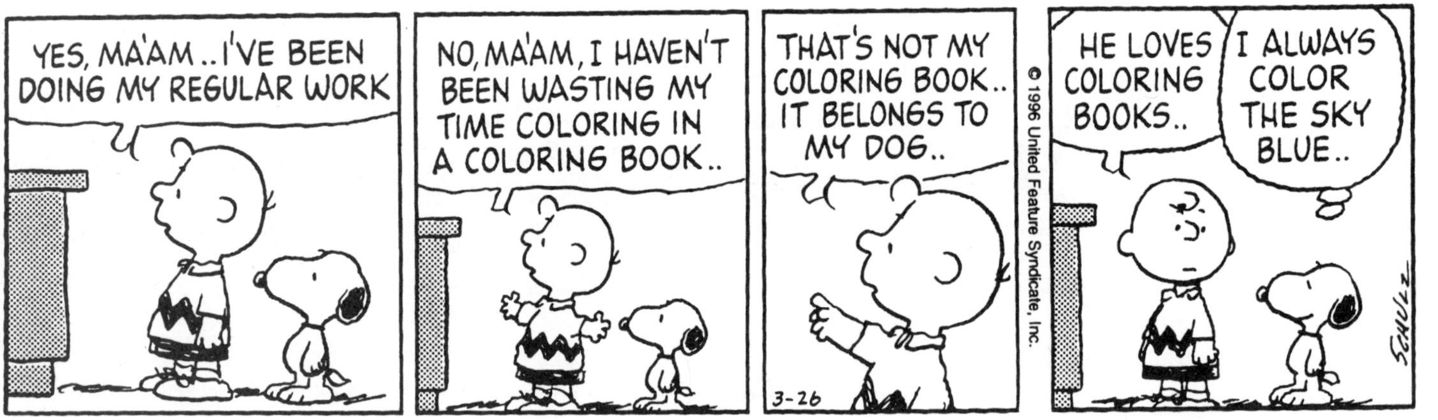

YES, MA'AM.. I'VE BEEN DOING MY REGULAR WORK
NO, MA'AM, I HAVEN'T BEEN WASTING MY TIME COLORING IN A COLORING BOOK..
THAT'S NOT MY COLORING BOOK.. IT BELONGS TO MY DOG..
3-26
© 1996 United Feature Syndicate, Inc.
HE LOVES COLORING BOOKS..
I ALWAYS COLOR THE SKY BLUE..
SCHULZ

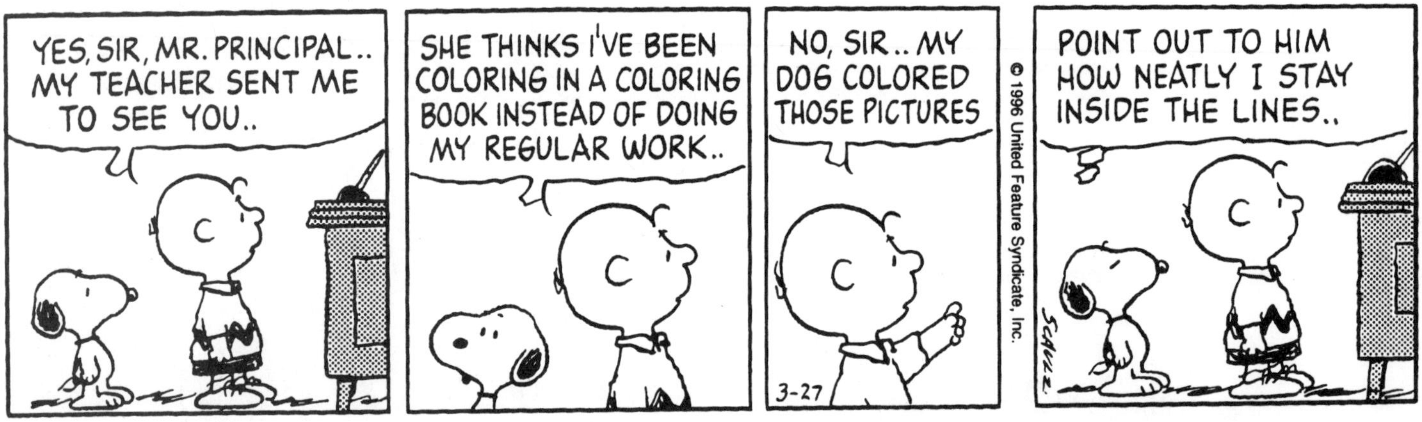

YES, SIR, MR. PRINCIPAL.. MY TEACHER SENT ME TO SEE YOU..
SHE THINKS I'VE BEEN COLORING IN A COLORING BOOK INSTEAD OF DOING MY REGULAR WORK..
NO, SIR.. MY DOG COLORED THOSE PICTURES
3-27
© 1996 United Feature Syndicate, Inc.
POINT OUT TO HIM HOW NEATLY I STAY INSIDE THE LINES..
SCHULZ

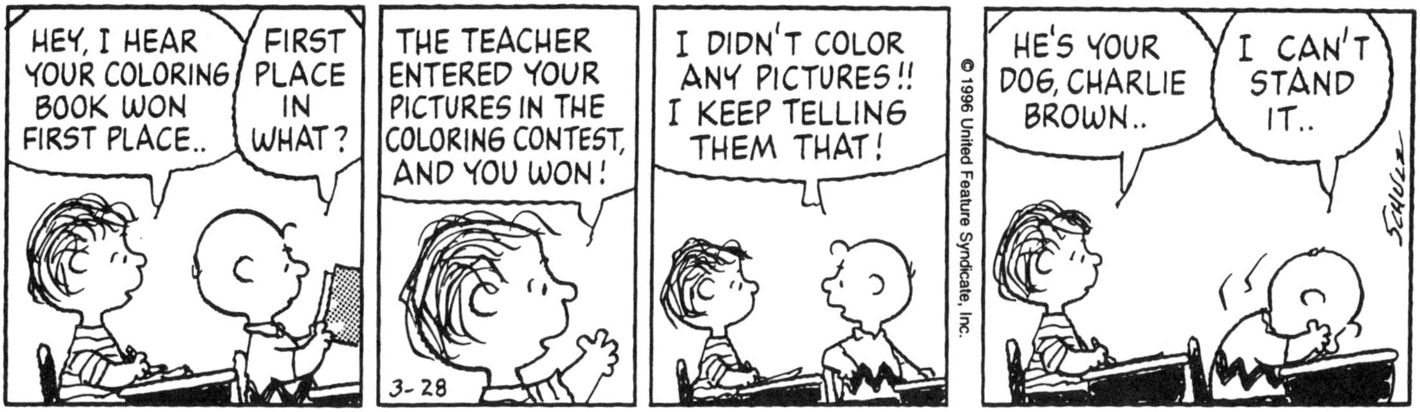
HEY, I HEAR YOUR COLORING BOOK WON FIRST PLACE..
FIRST PLACE IN WHAT?
THE TEACHER ENTERED YOUR PICTURES IN THE COLORING CONTEST, AND YOU WON!
3-28
I DIDN'T COLOR ANY PICTURES!! I KEEP TELLING THEM THAT!
© 1996 United Feature Syndicate, Inc.
HE'S YOUR DOG, CHARLIE BROWN..
I CAN'T STAND IT..
SCHULZ

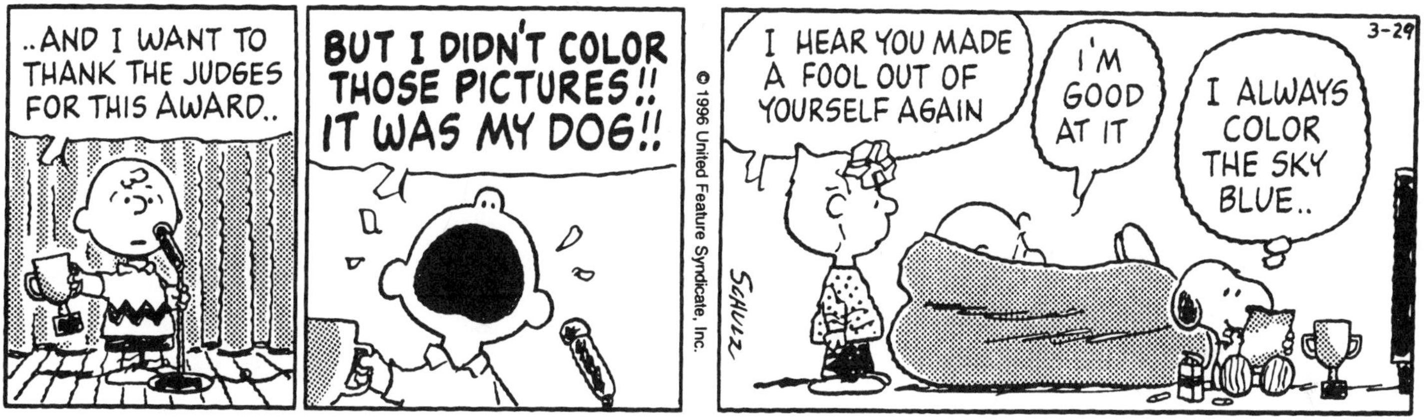
..AND I WANT TO THANK THE JUDGES FOR THIS AWARD..
BUT I DIDN'T COLOR THOSE PICTURES!! IT WAS MY DOG!!
© 1996 United Feature Syndicate, Inc.
3-29
I HEAR YOU MADE A FOOL OUT OF YOURSELF AGAIN
I'M GOOD AT IT
I ALWAYS COLOR THE SKY BLUE..
SCHULZ

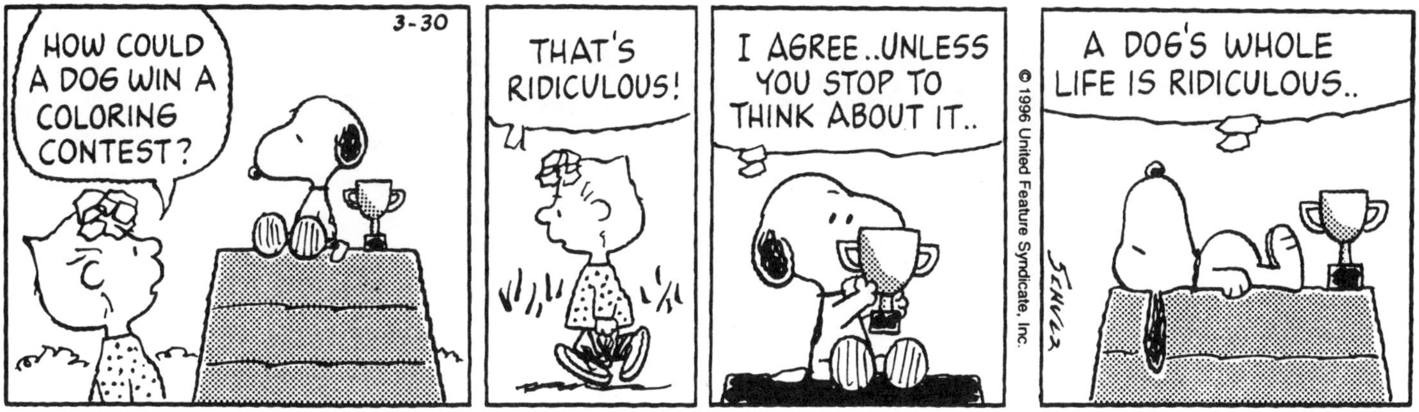
3-30
HOW COULD A DOG WIN A COLORING CONTEST?
THAT'S RIDICULOUS!
I AGREE..UNLESS YOU STOP TO THINK ABOUT IT..
© 1996 United Feature Syndicate, Inc.
A DOG'S WHOLE LIFE IS RIDICULOUS..
SCHULZ

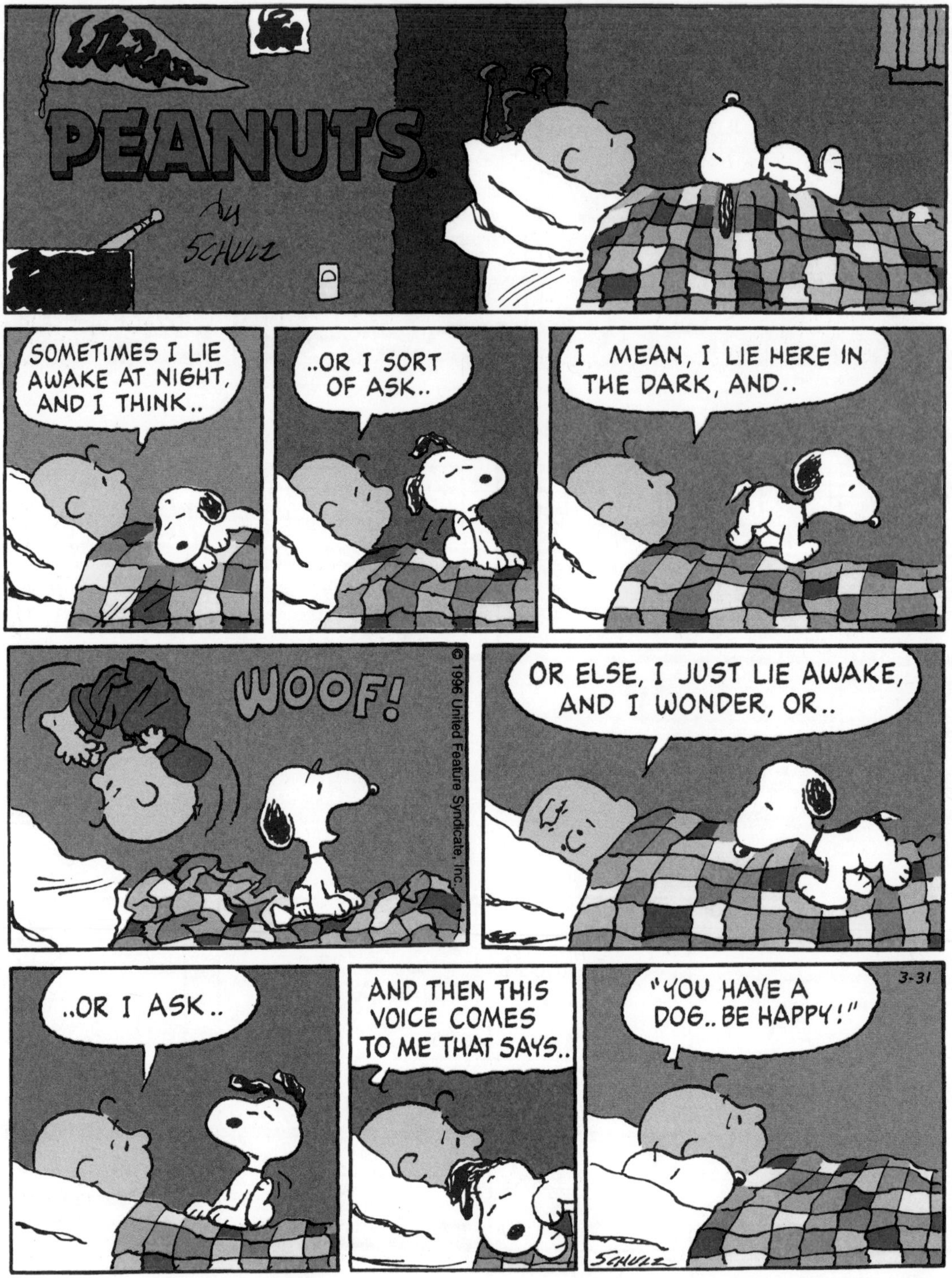
PEANUTS
by SCHULZ
SOMETIMES I LIE AWAKE AT NIGHT, AND I THINK..
..OR I SORT OF ASK..
I MEAN, I LIE HERE IN THE DARK, AND..
WOOF!
© 1996 United Feature Syndicate, Inc.
OR ELSE, I JUST LIE AWAKE, AND I WONDER, OR..
..OR I ASK..
AND THEN THIS VOICE COMES TO ME THAT SAYS..
3-31
"YOU HAVE A DOG.. BE HAPPY!"
SCHULZ

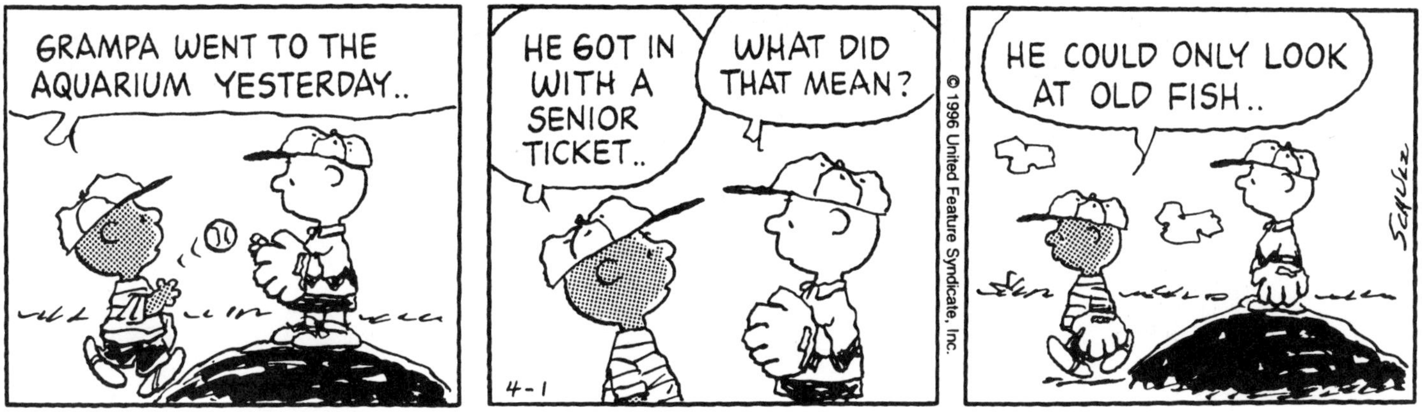
GRAMPA WENT TO THE AQUARIUM YESTERDAY..
HE GOT IN WITH A SENIOR TICKET..
WHAT DID THAT MEAN?
HE COULD ONLY LOOK AT OLD FISH..
4-1
© 1996 United Feature Syndicate, Inc.
SCHULZ

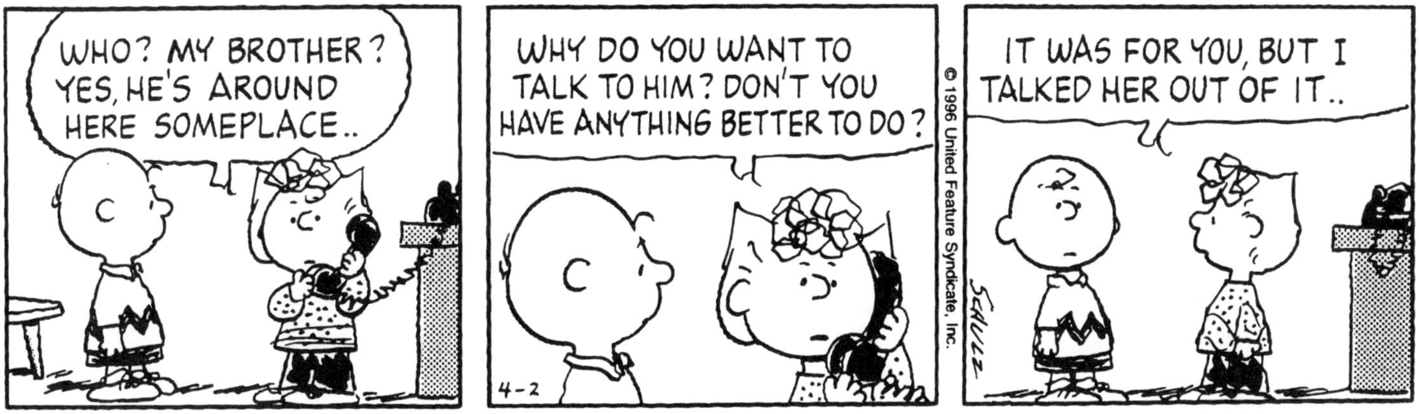
WHO? MY BROTHER? YES, HE'S AROUND HERE SOMEPLACE..
WHY DO YOU WANT TO TALK TO HIM? DON'T YOU HAVE ANYTHING BETTER TO DO?
IT WAS FOR YOU, BUT I TALKED HER OUT OF IT..
4-2
© 1996 United Feature Syndicate, Inc.
SCHULZ

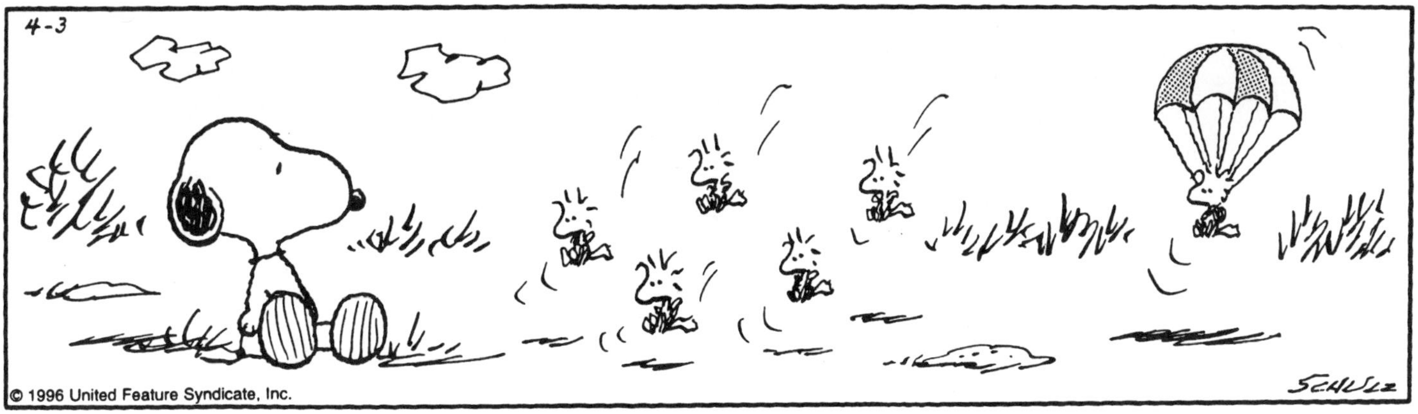
4-3
© 1996 United Feature Syndicate, Inc.
SCHULZ

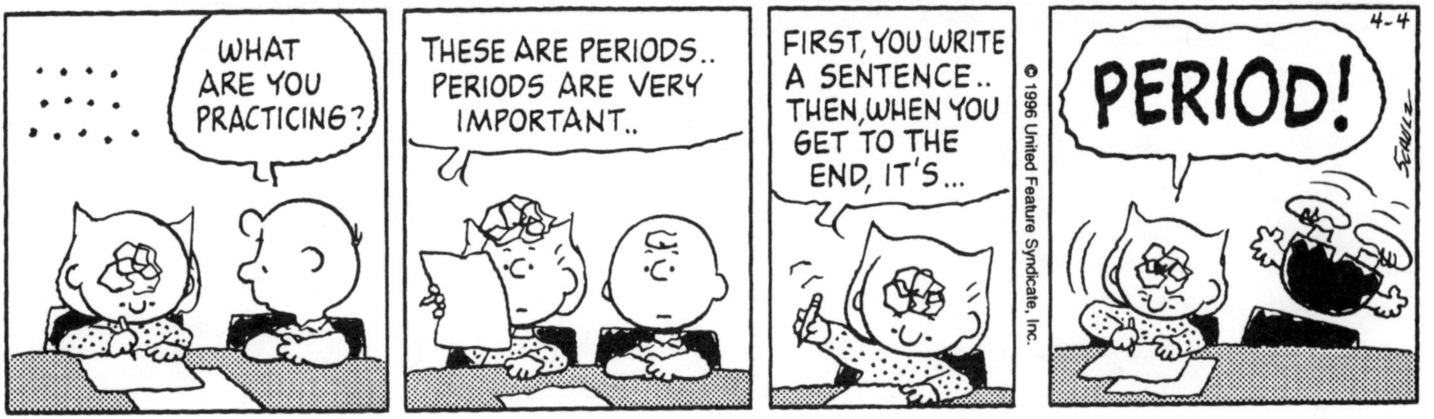
WHAT ARE YOU PRACTICING?
THESE ARE PERIODS.. PERIODS ARE VERY IMPORTANT..
FIRST, YOU WRITE A SENTENCE.. THEN, WHEN YOU GET TO THE END, IT'S...
PERIOD!
4-4
© 1996 United Feature Syndicate, Inc.
SCHULZ

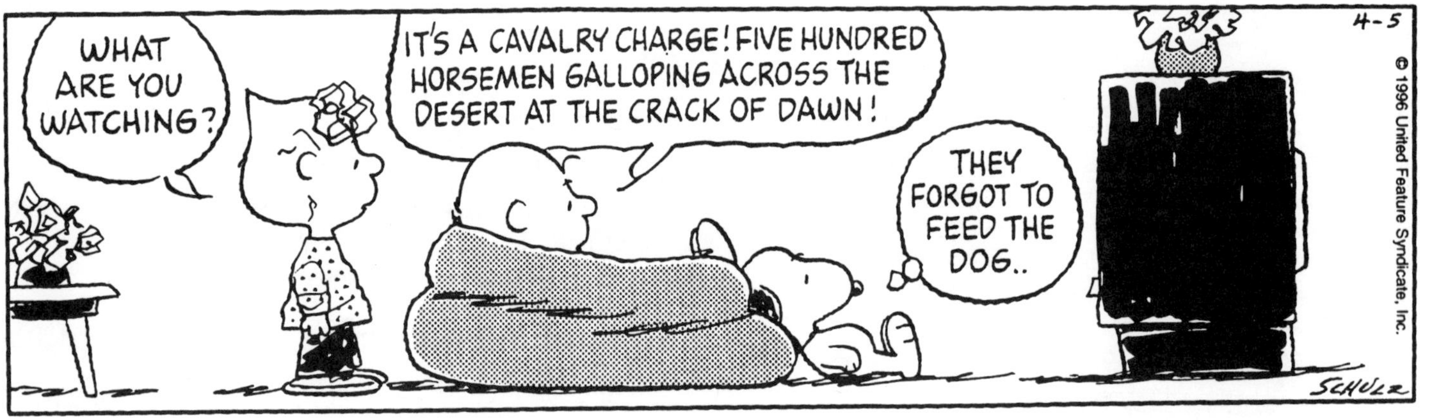
WHAT ARE YOU WATCHING?
IT'S A CAVALRY CHARGE! FIVE HUNDRED HORSEMEN GALLOPING ACROSS THE DESERT AT THE CRACK OF DAWN!
THEY FORGOT TO FEED THE DOG..
4-5
© 1996 United Feature Syndicate, Inc.
SCHULZ

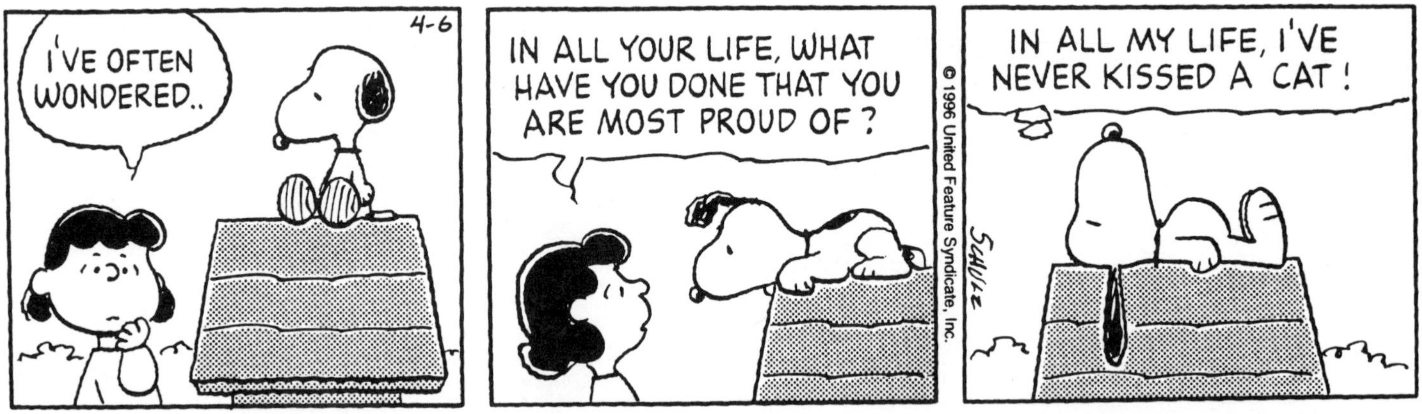
I'VE OFTEN WONDERED..
IN ALL YOUR LIFE, WHAT HAVE YOU DONE THAT YOU ARE MOST PROUD OF?
IN ALL MY LIFE, I'VE NEVER KISSED A CAT!
4-6
© 1996 United Feature Syndicate, Inc.
SCHULZ

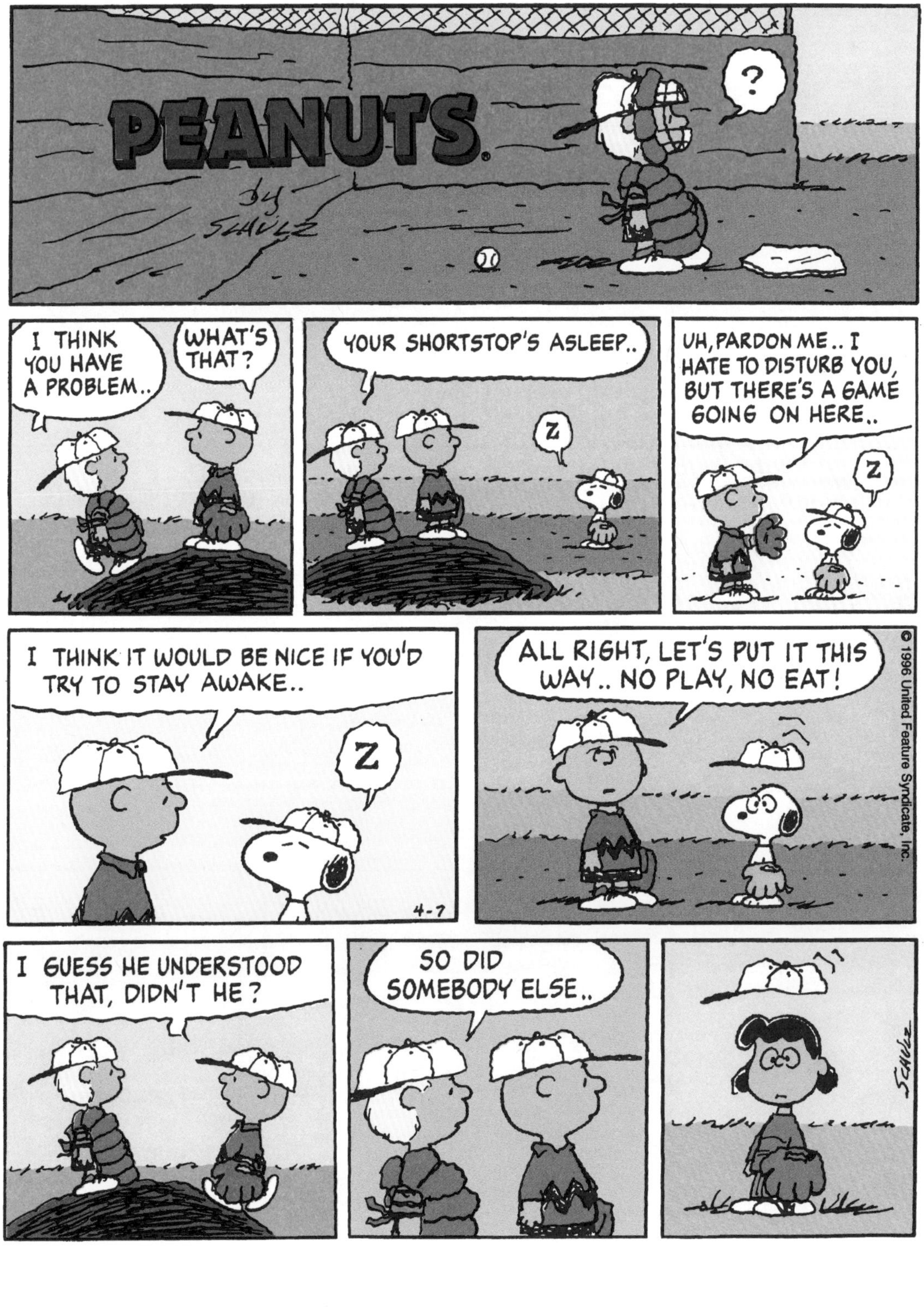
PEANUTS
by SCHULZ
?
I THINK YOU HAVE A PROBLEM..
WHAT'S THAT?
YOUR SHORTSTOP'S ASLEEP..
Z
UH, PARDON ME.. I HATE TO DISTURB YOU, BUT THERE'S A GAME GOING ON HERE..
Z
I THINK IT WOULD BE NICE IF YOU'D TRY TO STAY AWAKE..
Z
4-7
ALL RIGHT, LET'S PUT IT THIS WAY.. NO PLAY, NO EAT!
© 1996 United Feature Syndicate, Inc.
I GUESS HE UNDERSTOOD THAT, DIDN'T HE?
SO DID SOMEBODY ELSE..
SCHULZ

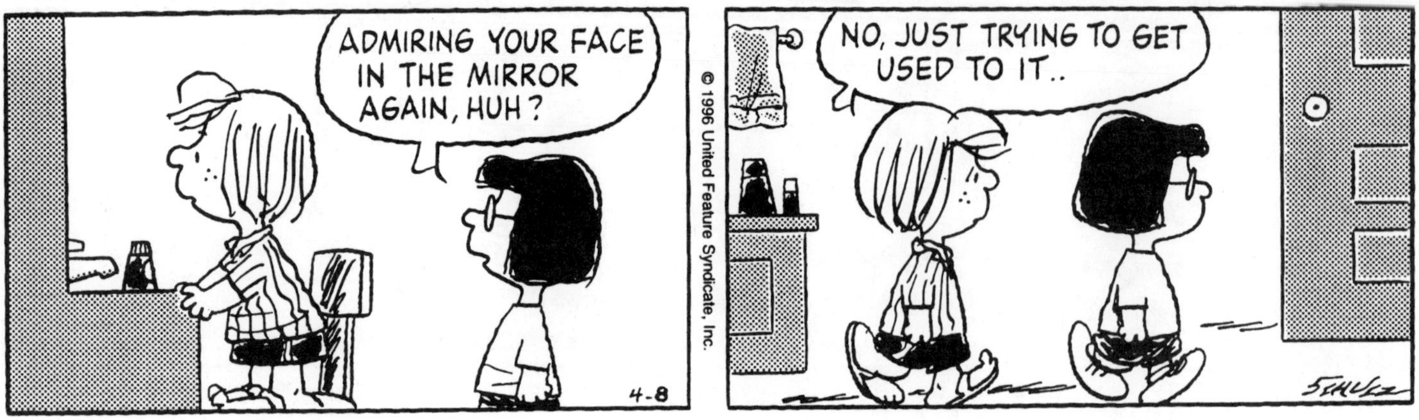
ADMIRING YOUR FACE IN THE MIRROR AGAIN, HUH?
© 1996 United Feature Syndicate, Inc.
4-8
NO, JUST TRYING TO GET USED TO IT..
SCHULZ

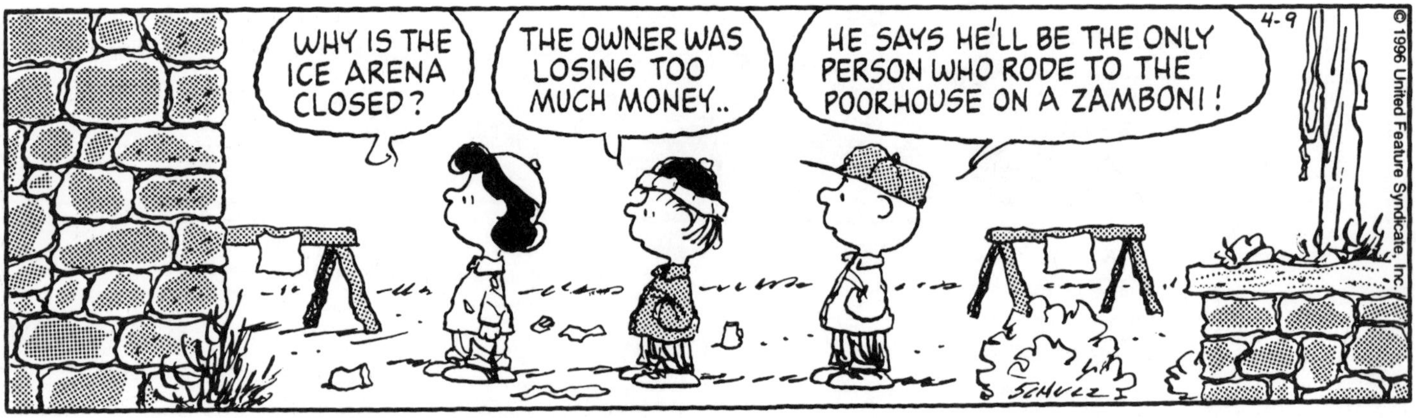
WHY IS THE ICE ARENA CLOSED?
THE OWNER WAS LOSING TOO MUCH MONEY..
HE SAYS HE'LL BE THE ONLY PERSON WHO RODE TO THE POORHOUSE ON A ZAMBONI!
4-9
© 1996 United Feature Syndicate, Inc.
SCHULZ

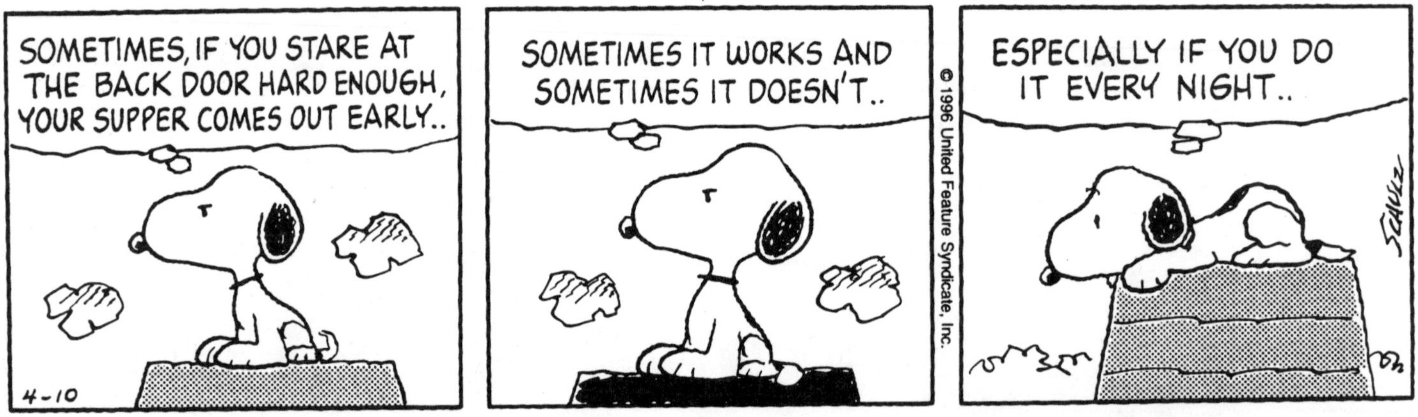
SOMETIMES, IF YOU STARE AT THE BACK DOOR HARD ENOUGH, YOUR SUPPER COMES OUT EARLY..
4-10
SOMETIMES IT WORKS AND SOMETIMES IT DOESN'T..
© 1996 United Feature Syndicate, Inc.
ESPECIALLY IF YOU DO IT EVERY NIGHT..
SCHULZ

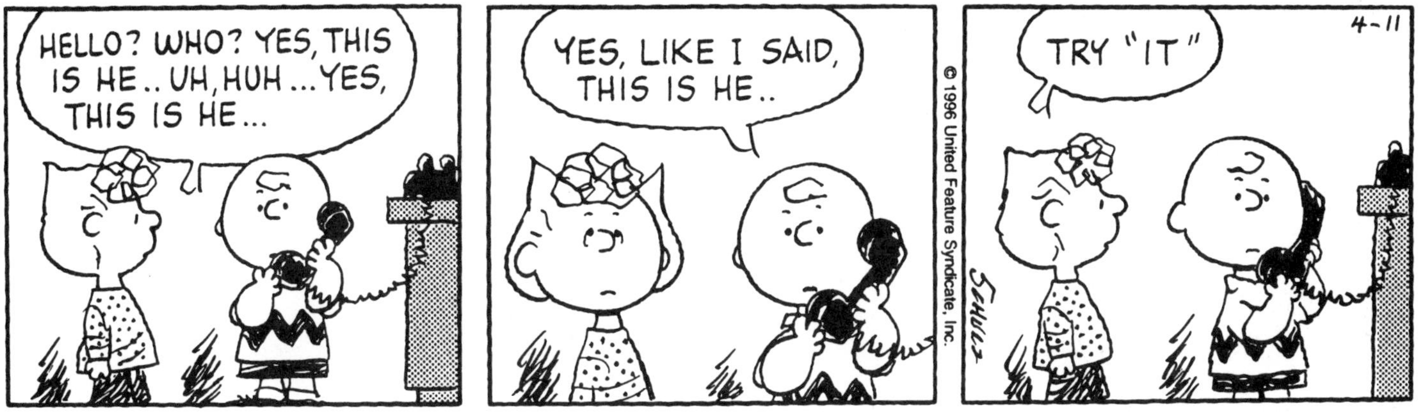
HELLO? WHO? YES, THIS IS HE.. UH, HUH ... YES, THIS IS HE...
YES, LIKE I SAID, THIS IS HE..
© 1996 United Feature Syndicate, Inc.
4-11
TRY "IT"
SCHULZ

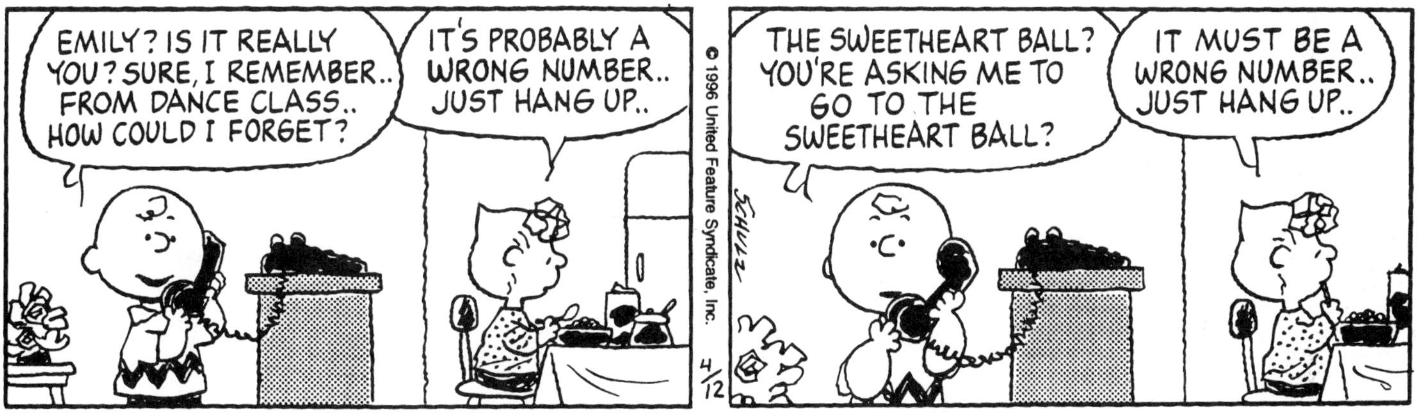
EMILY? IS IT REALLY YOU? SURE, I REMEMBER.. FROM DANCE CLASS.. HOW COULD I FORGET?
IT'S PROBABLY A WRONG NUMBER.. JUST HANG UP..
© 1996 United Feature Syndicate, Inc.
4/12
SCHULZ
THE SWEETHEART BALL? YOU'RE ASKING ME TO GO TO THE SWEETHEART BALL?
IT MUST BE A WRONG NUMBER.. JUST HANG UP..

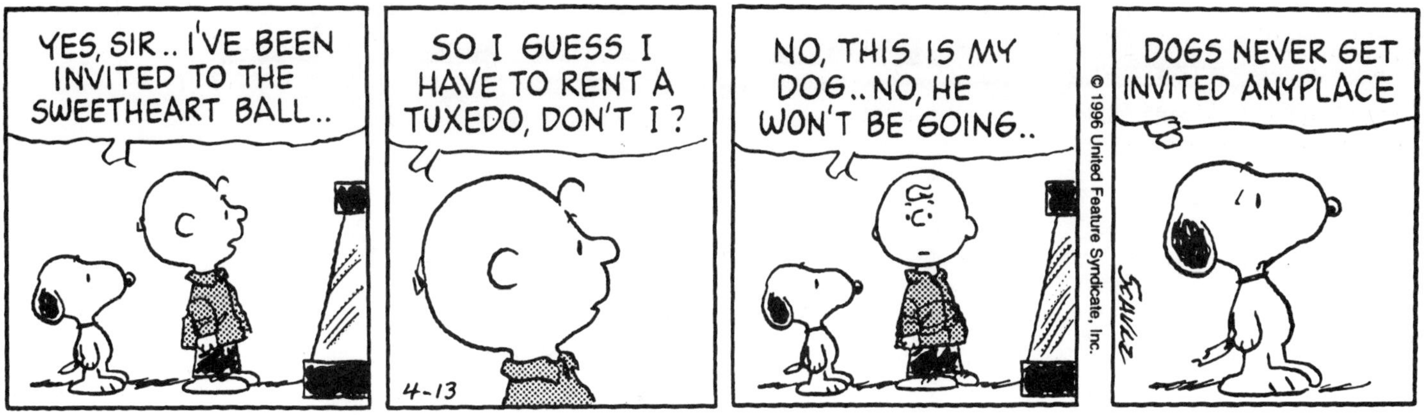
YES, SIR.. I'VE BEEN INVITED TO THE SWEETHEART BALL..
SO I GUESS I HAVE TO RENT A TUXEDO, DON'T I?
4-13
NO, THIS IS MY DOG.. NO, HE WON'T BE GOING..
© 1996 United Feature Syndicate, Inc.
DOGS NEVER GET INVITED ANYPLACE
SCHULZ

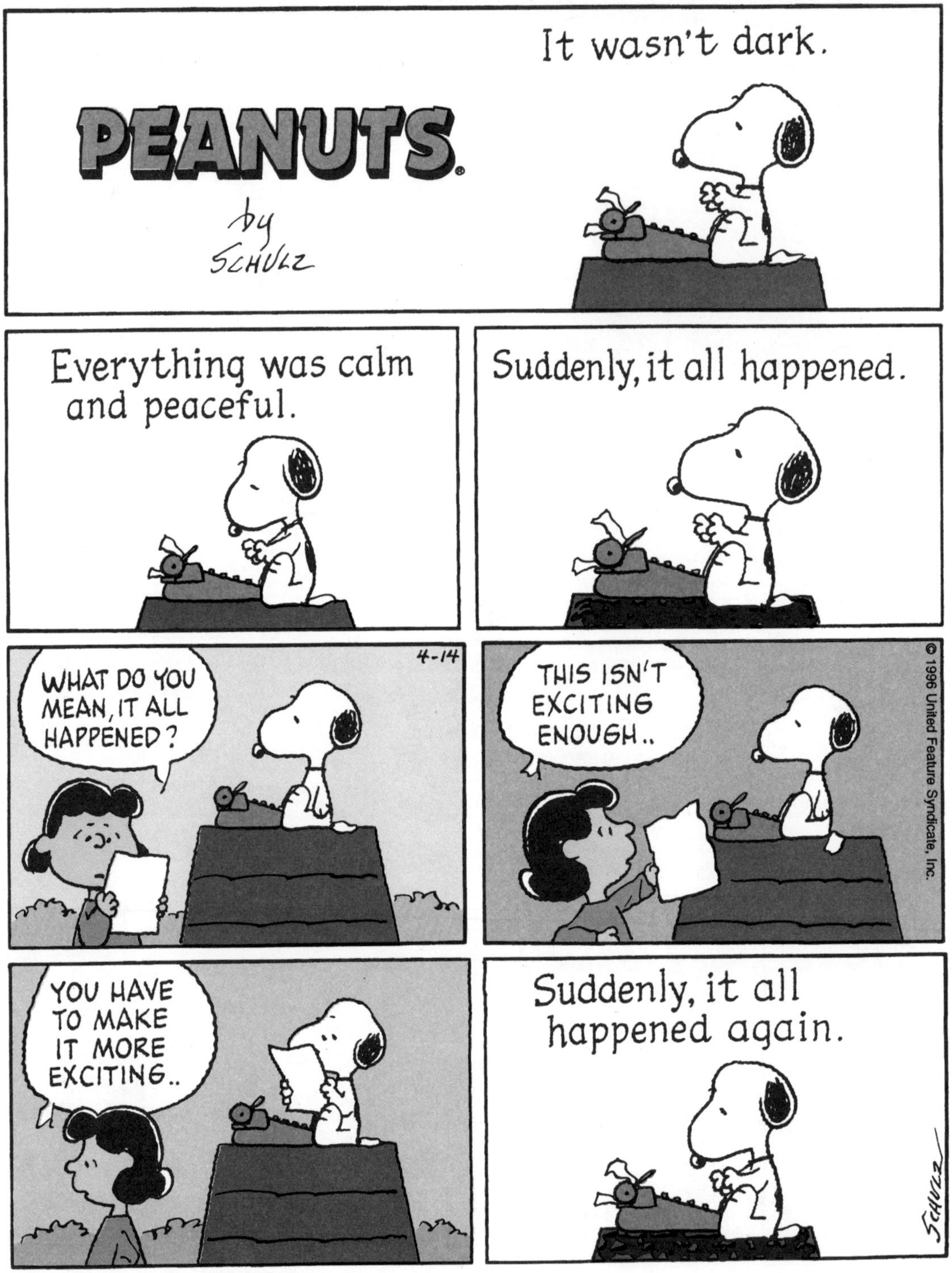
PEANUTS
by SCHULZ
It wasn't dark.
Everything was calm and peaceful.
Suddenly, it all happened.
4-14
WHAT DO YOU MEAN, IT ALL HAPPENED?
THIS ISN'T EXCITING ENOUGH..
© 1996 United Feature Syndicate, Inc.
YOU HAVE TO MAKE IT MORE EXCITING..
Suddenly, it all happened again.
SCHULZ

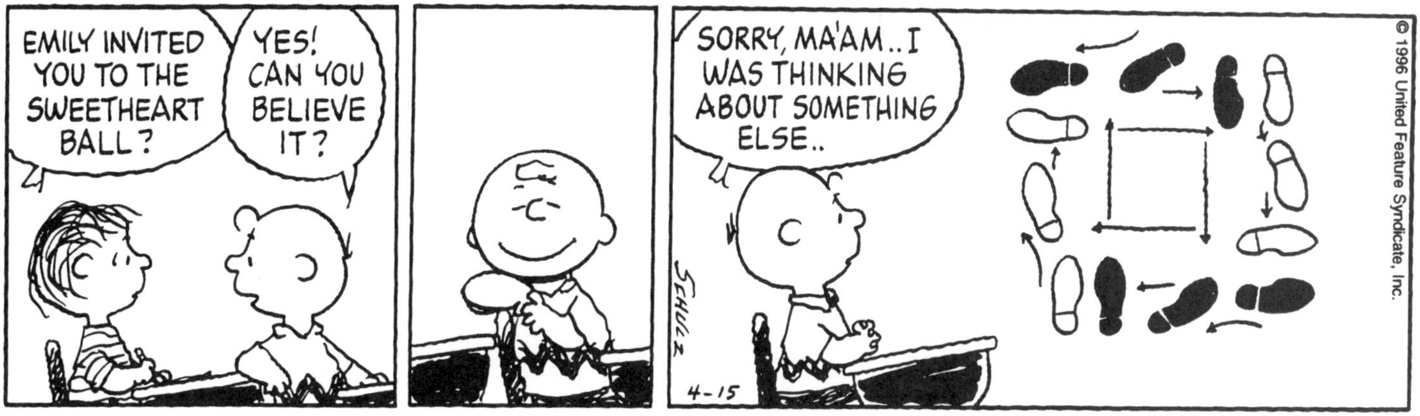
EMILY INVITED YOU TO THE SWEETHEART BALL?
YES! CAN YOU BELIEVE IT?
SORRY, MA'AM.. I WAS THINKING ABOUT SOMETHING ELSE..
4-15
SCHULZ
© 1996 United Feature Syndicate, Inc.

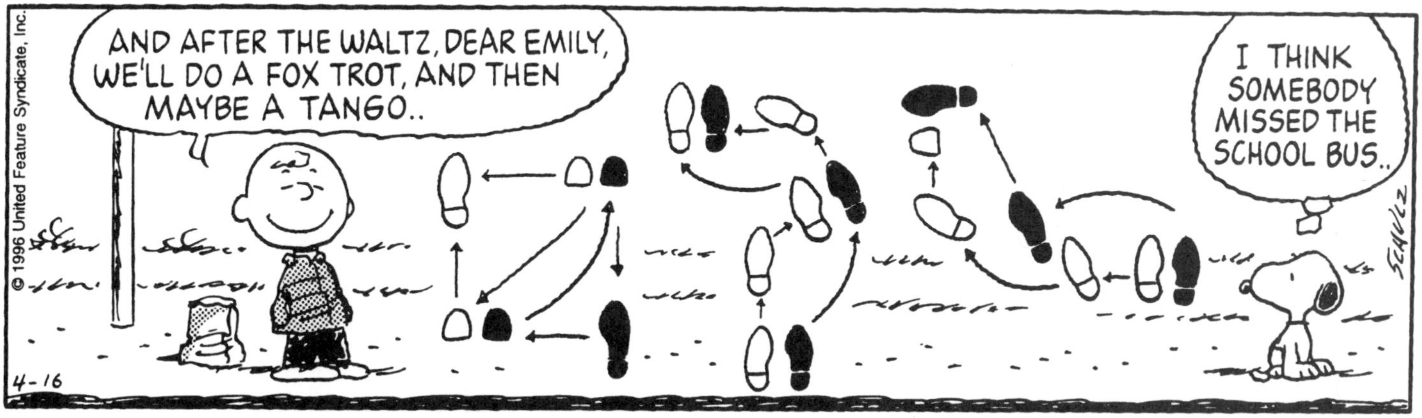
AND AFTER THE WALTZ, DEAR EMILY, WE'LL DO A FOX TROT, AND THEN MAYBE A TANGO..
I THINK SOMEBODY MISSED THE SCHOOL BUS..
4-16
SCHULZ
© 1996 United Feature Syndicate, Inc.

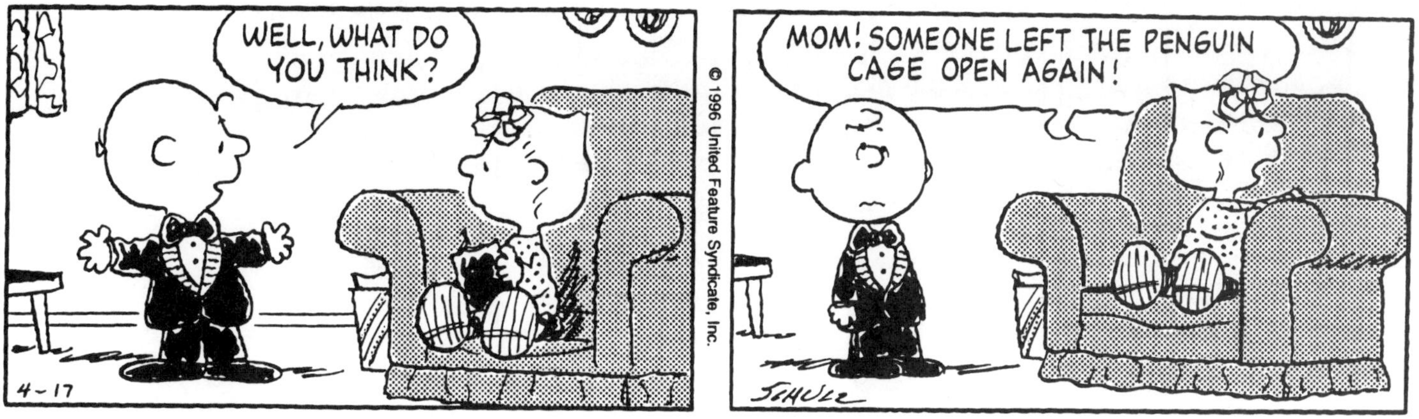
WELL, WHAT DO YOU THINK?
MOM! SOMEONE LEFT THE PENGUIN CAGE OPEN AGAIN!
4-17
SCHULZ
© 1996 United Feature Syndicate, Inc.

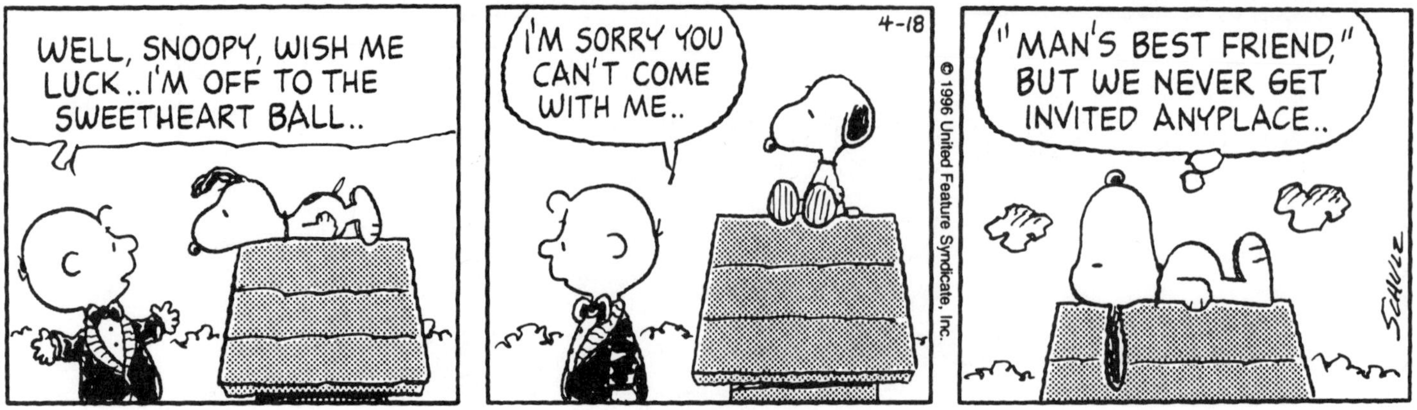
WELL, SNOOPY, WISH ME LUCK..I'M OFF TO THE SWEETHEART BALL..
I'M SORRY YOU CAN'T COME WITH ME..
4-18
© 1996 United Feature Syndicate, Inc.
"MAN'S BEST FRIEND," BUT WE NEVER GET INVITED ANYPLACE..
SCHULZ

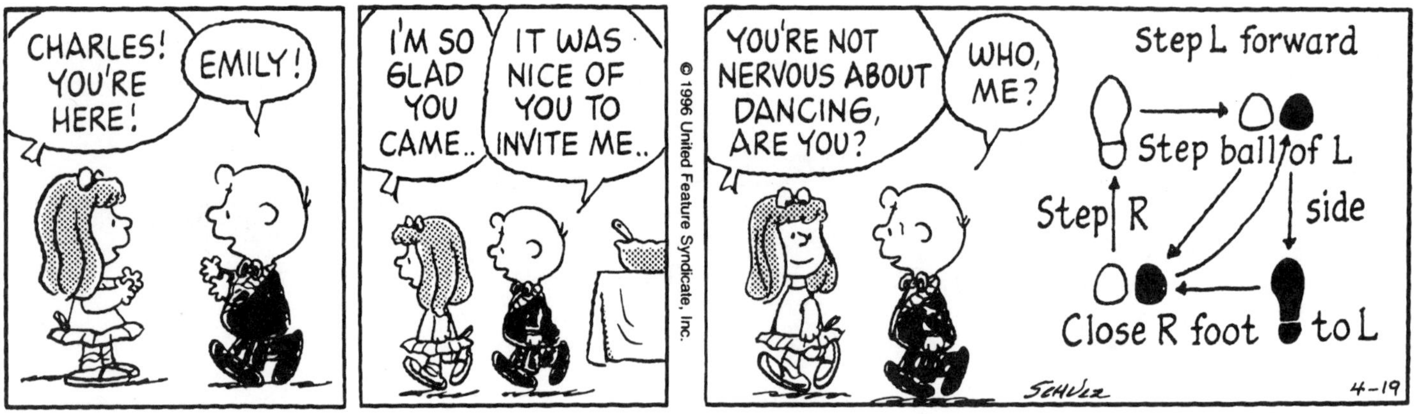
CHARLES! YOU'RE HERE!
EMILY!
I'M SO GLAD YOU CAME..
IT WAS NICE OF YOU TO INVITE ME..
© 1996 United Feature Syndicate, Inc.
YOU'RE NOT NERVOUS ABOUT DANCING, ARE YOU?
WHO, ME?
Step L forward
Step ball of L
Step R
side
Close R foot
to L
SCHULZ
4-19

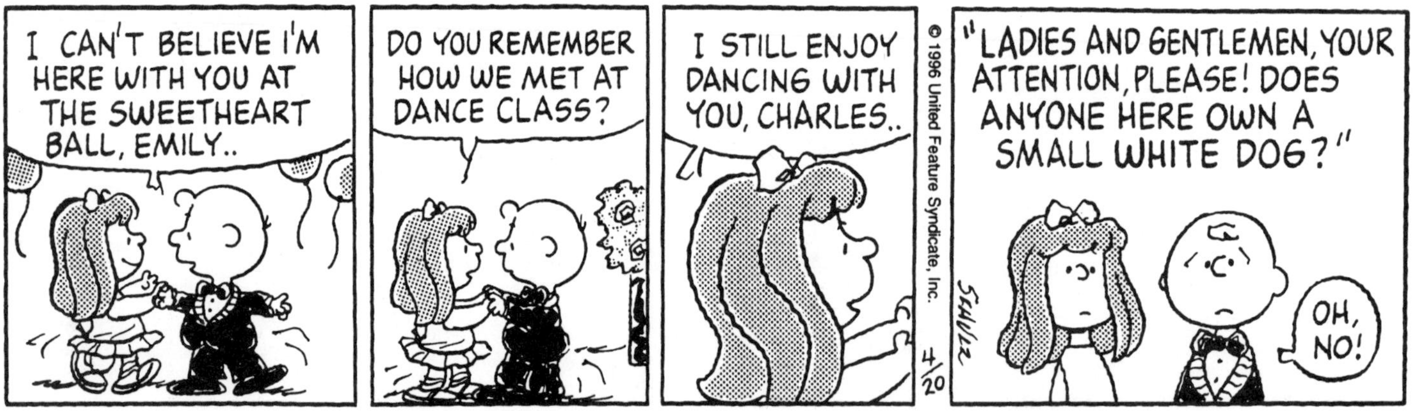
I CAN'T BELIEVE I'M HERE WITH YOU AT THE SWEETHEART BALL, EMILY..
DO YOU REMEMBER HOW WE MET AT DANCE CLASS?
I STILL ENJOY DANCING WITH YOU, CHARLES..
4/20
© 1996 United Feature Syndicate, Inc.
SCHULZ
"LADIES AND GENTLEMEN, YOUR ATTENTION, PLEASE! DOES ANYONE HERE OWN A SMALL WHITE DOG?"
OH, NO!

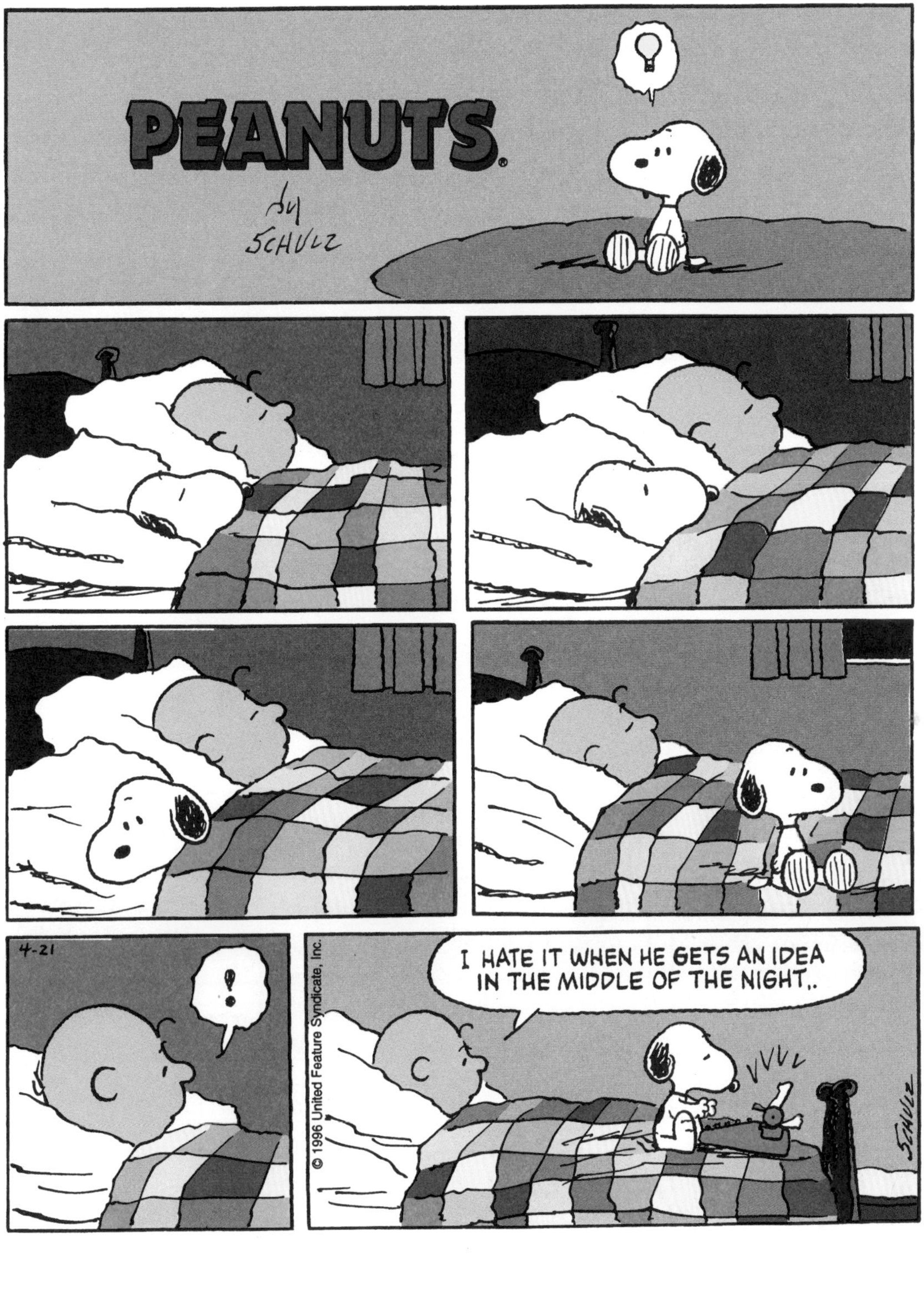
PEANUTS
SCHULZ
4-21
!
I HATE IT WHEN HE GETS AN IDEA IN THE MIDDLE OF THE NIGHT..
VVVV
© 1996 United Feature Syndicate, Inc.
SCHULZ

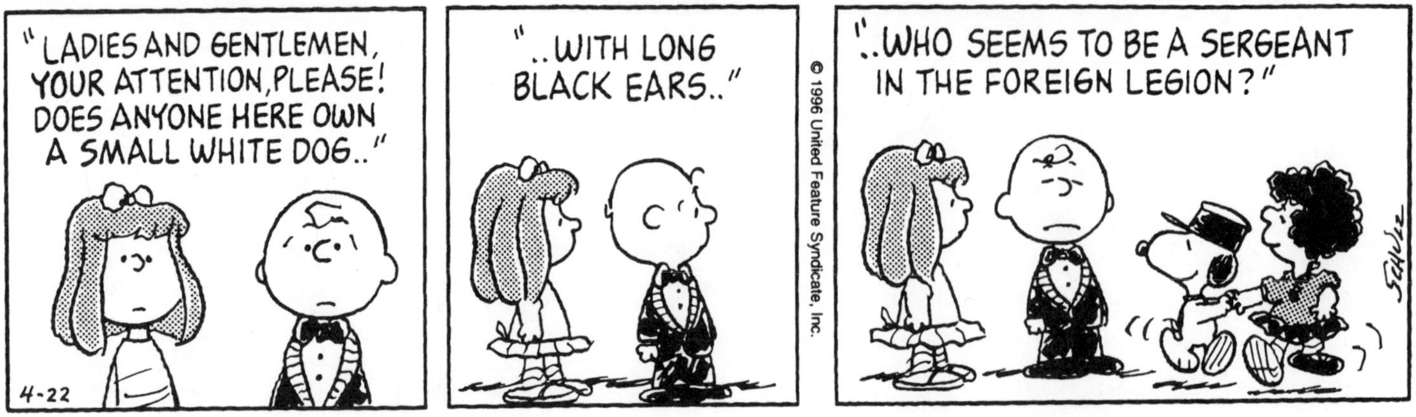
"LADIES AND GENTLEMEN, YOUR ATTENTION, PLEASE! DOES ANYONE HERE OWN A SMALL WHITE DOG.."
4-22
"..WITH LONG BLACK EARS.."
© 1996 United Feature Syndicate, Inc.
"..WHO SEEMS TO BE A SERGEANT IN THE FOREIGN LEGION?"
SCHULZ

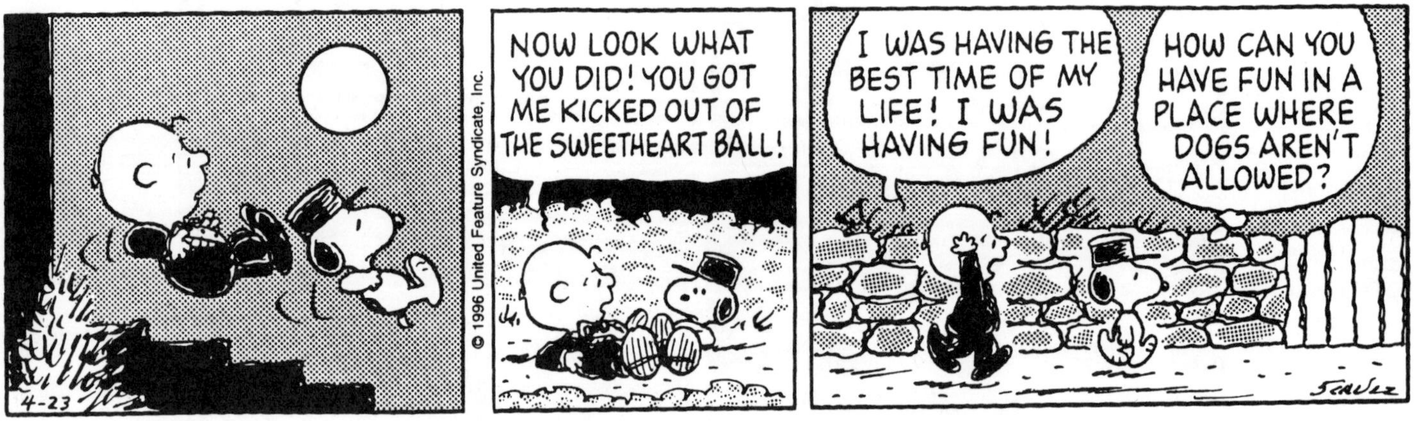
4-23
© 1996 United Feature Syndicate, Inc.
NOW LOOK WHAT YOU DID! YOU GOT ME KICKED OUT OF THE SWEETHEART BALL!
I WAS HAVING THE BEST TIME OF MY LIFE! I WAS HAVING FUN!
HOW CAN YOU HAVE FUN IN A PLACE WHERE DOGS AREN'T ALLOWED?
SCHULZ

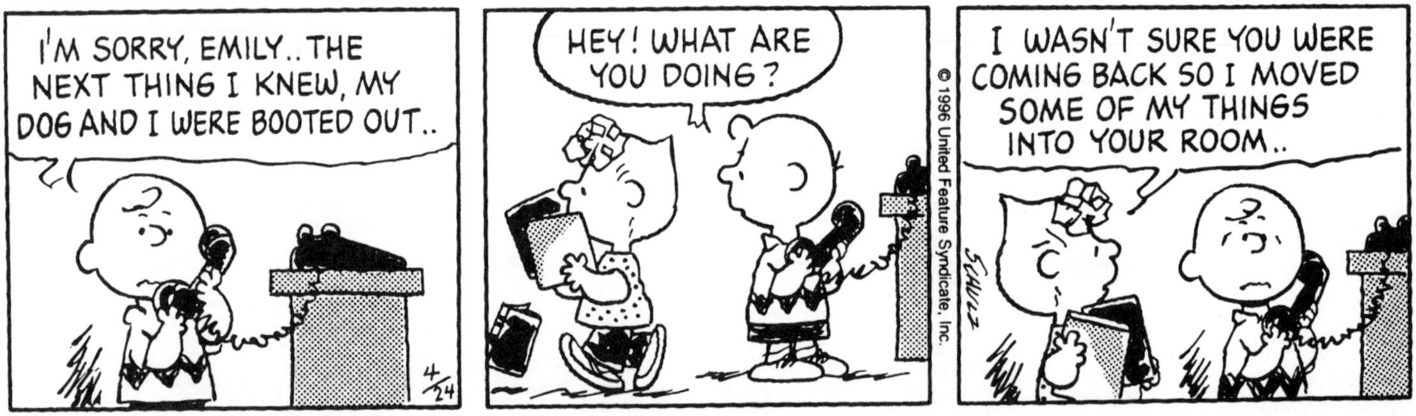
I'M SORRY, EMILY.. THE NEXT THING I KNEW, MY DOG AND I WERE BOOTED OUT..
4/24
HEY! WHAT ARE YOU DOING?
© 1996 United Feature Syndicate, Inc.
SCHULZ
I WASN'T SURE YOU WERE COMING BACK SO I MOVED SOME OF MY THINGS INTO YOUR ROOM..

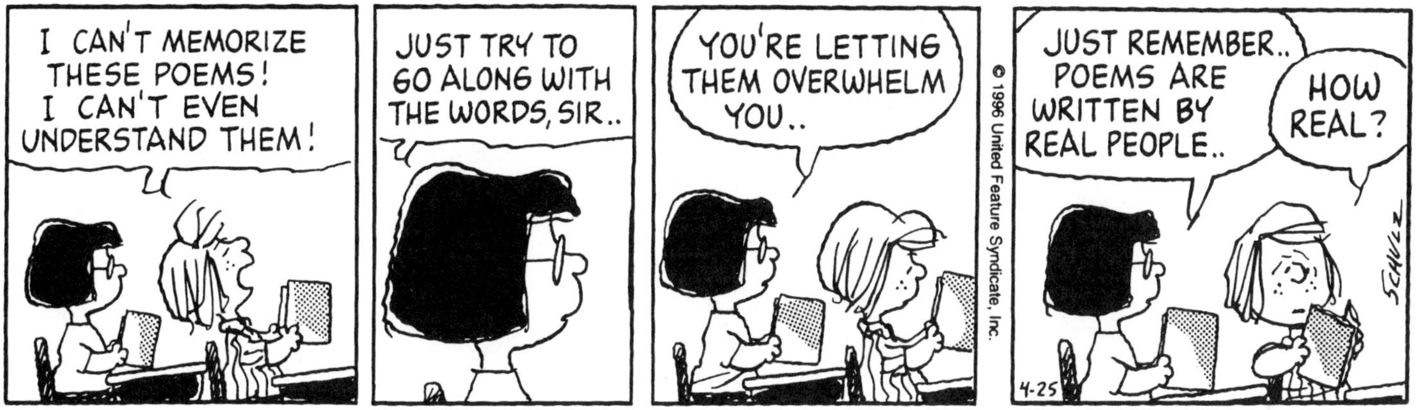
I CAN'T MEMORIZE THESE POEMS! I CAN'T EVEN UNDERSTAND THEM!
JUST TRY TO GO ALONG WITH THE WORDS, SIR..
YOU'RE LETTING THEM OVERWHELM YOU..
© 1996 United Feature Syndicate, Inc.
JUST REMEMBER.. POEMS ARE WRITTEN BY REAL PEOPLE..
HOW REAL?
SCHULZ
4-25

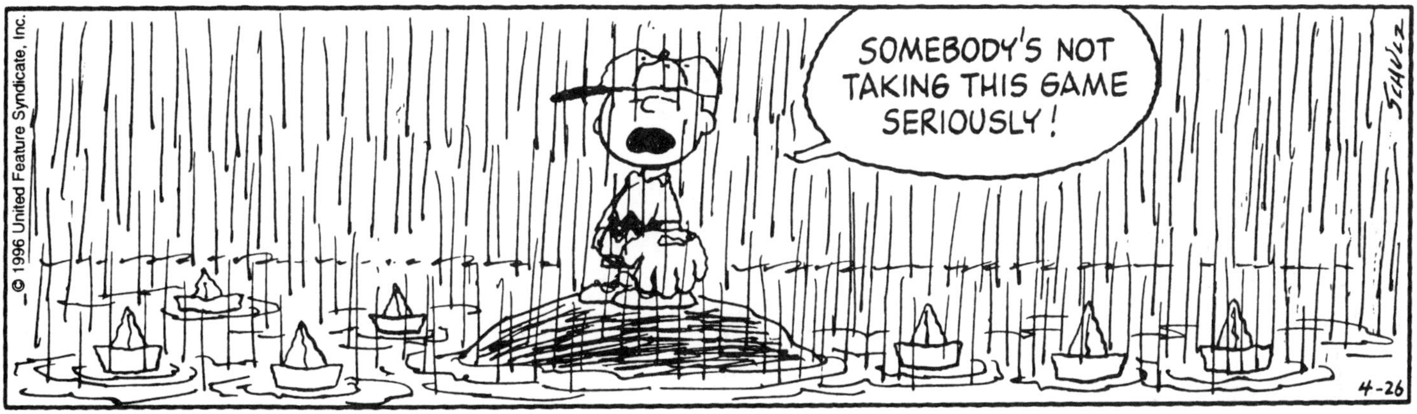
© 1996 United Feature Syndicate, Inc.
SOMEBODY'S NOT TAKING THIS GAME SERIOUSLY!
SCHULZ
4-26

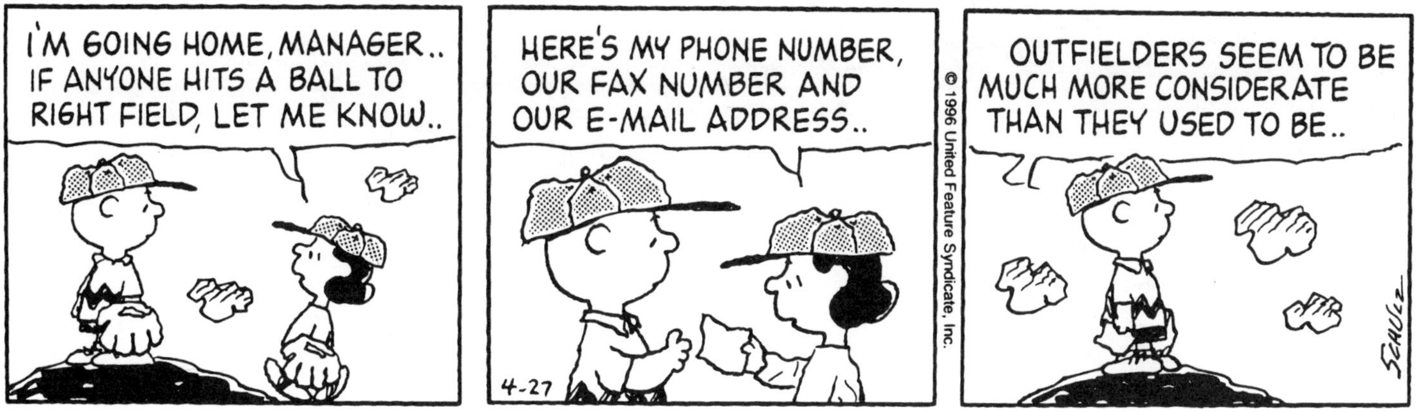
I'M GOING HOME, MANAGER.. IF ANYONE HITS A BALL TO RIGHT FIELD, LET ME KNOW..
HERE'S MY PHONE NUMBER, OUR FAX NUMBER AND OUR E-MAIL ADDRESS..
4-27
© 1996 United Feature Syndicate, Inc.
OUTFIELDERS SEEM TO BE MUCH MORE CONSIDERATE THAN THEY USED TO BE..
SCHULZ

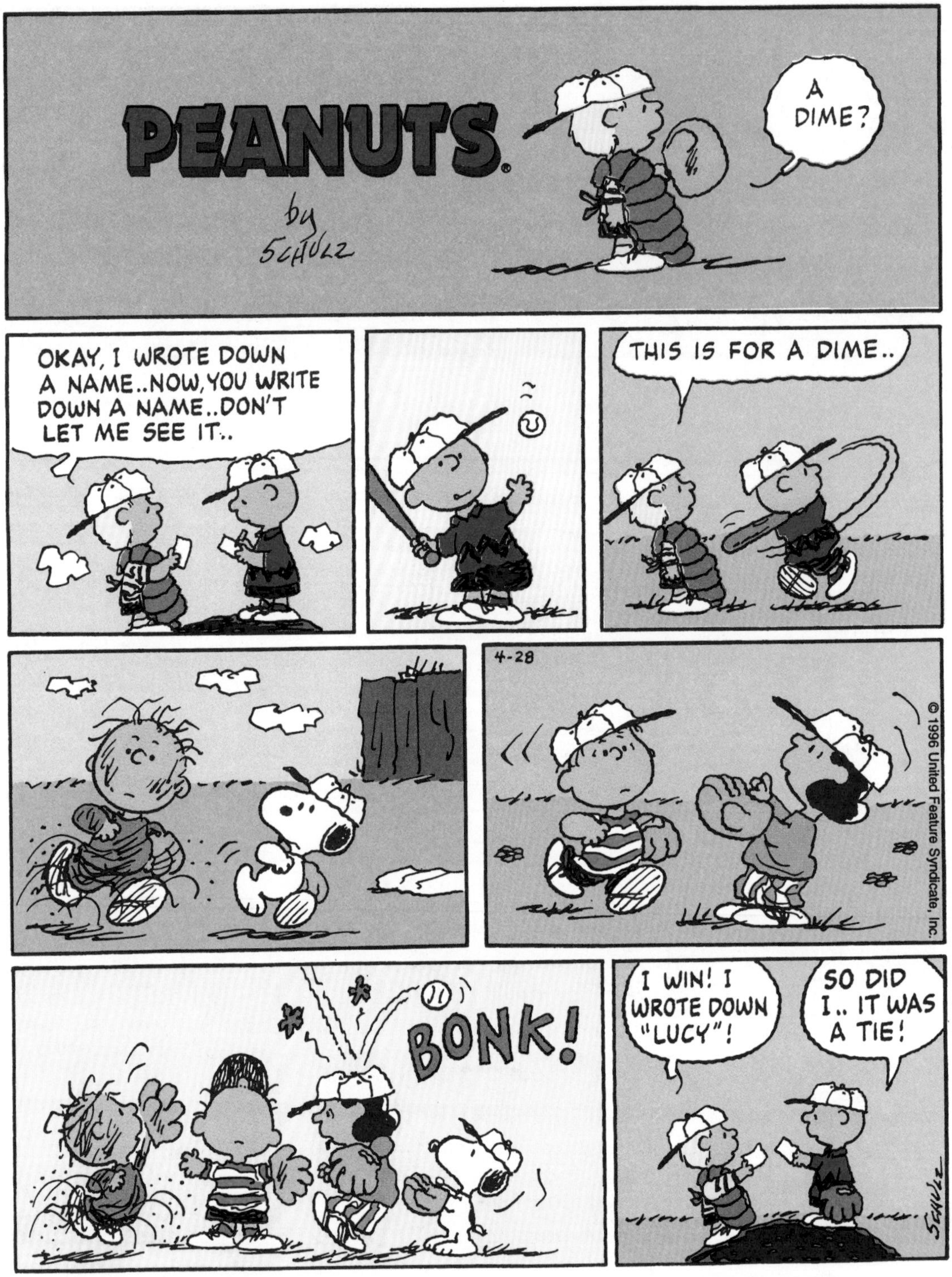
PEANUTS®
by SCHULZ
A DIME?
OKAY, I WROTE DOWN A NAME..NOW, YOU WRITE DOWN A NAME..DON'T LET ME SEE IT..
THIS IS FOR A DIME..
4-28
© 1996 United Feature Syndicate, Inc.
BONK!
I WIN! I WROTE DOWN "LUCY"!
SO DID I.. IT WAS A TIE!
SCHULZ

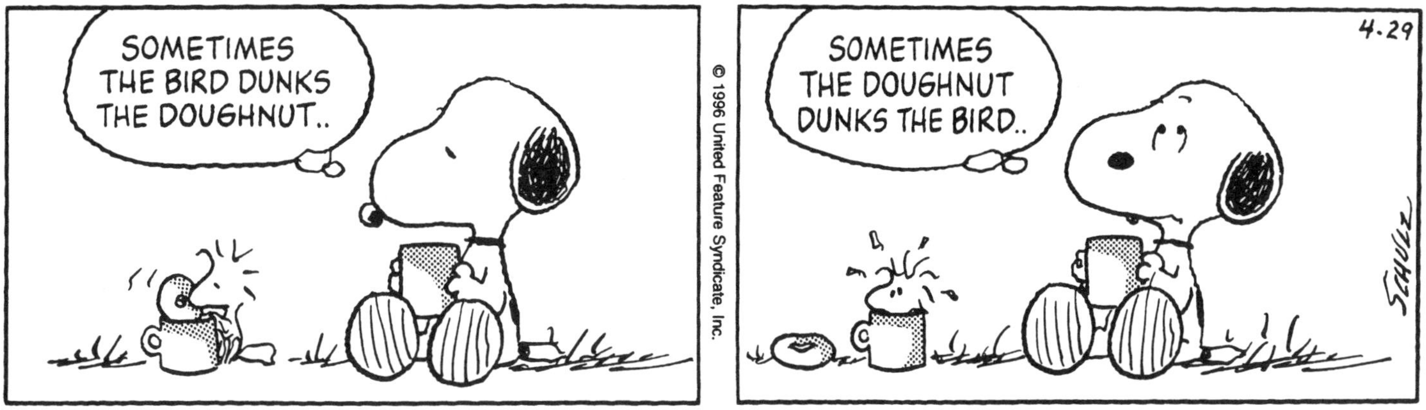
SOMETIMES THE BIRD DUNKS THE DOUGHNUT..
© 1996 United Feature Syndicate, Inc.
4-29
SOMETIMES THE DOUGHNUT DUNKS THE BIRD..
SCHULZ

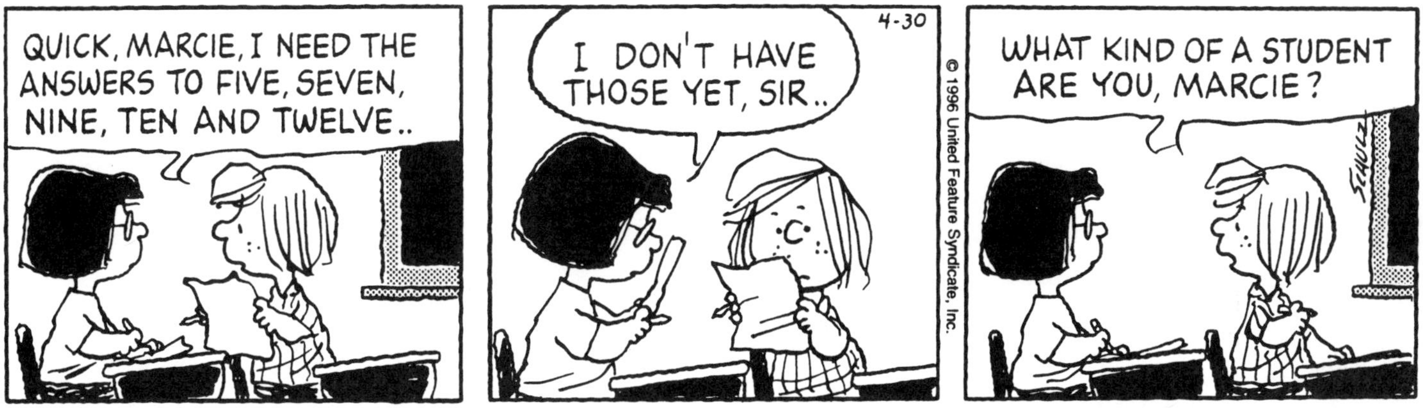
QUICK, MARCIE, I NEED THE ANSWERS TO FIVE, SEVEN, NINE, TEN AND TWELVE..
4-30
I DON'T HAVE THOSE YET, SIR..
© 1996 United Feature Syndicate, Inc.
WHAT KIND OF A STUDENT ARE YOU, MARCIE?
SCHULZ

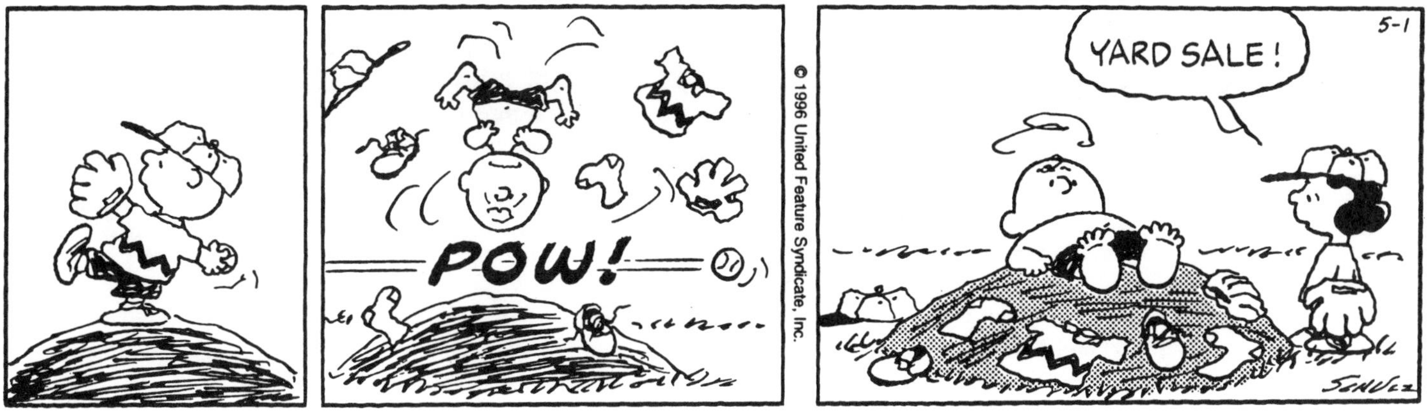
POW!
© 1996 United Feature Syndicate, Inc.
5-1
YARD SALE!
SCHULZ

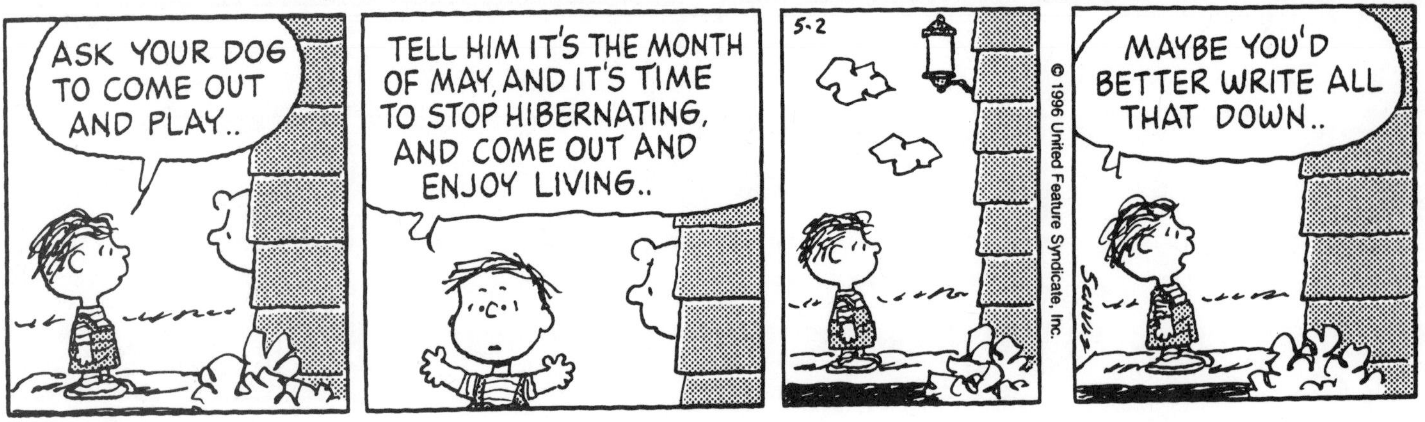
ASK YOUR DOG TO COME OUT AND PLAY..
TELL HIM IT'S THE MONTH OF MAY, AND IT'S TIME TO STOP HIBERNATING, AND COME OUT AND ENJOY LIVING..
5-2
© 1996 United Feature Syndicate, Inc.
MAYBE YOU'D BETTER WRITE ALL THAT DOWN..

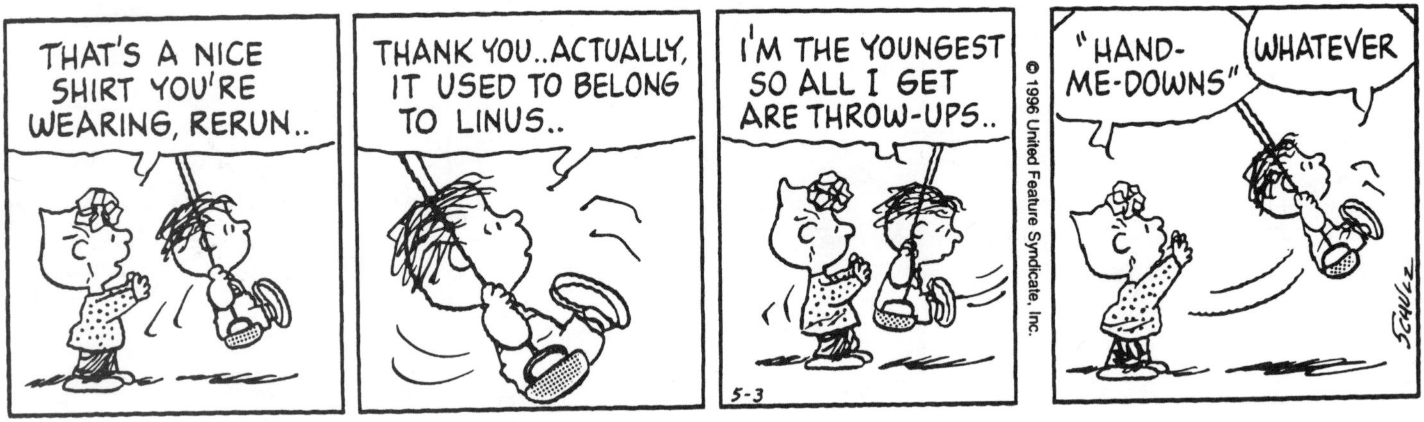
THAT'S A NICE SHIRT YOU'RE WEARING, RERUN..
THANK YOU..ACTUALLY, IT USED TO BELONG TO LINUS..
I'M THE YOUNGEST SO ALL I GET ARE THROW-UPS..
5-3
© 1996 United Feature Syndicate, Inc.
"HAND-ME-DOWNS"
WHATEVER

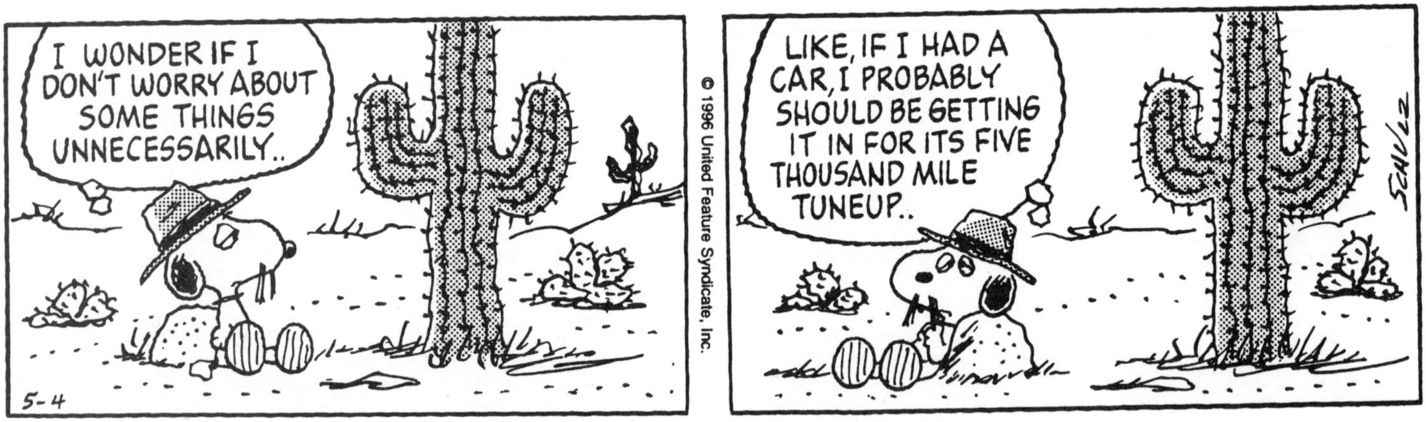
I WONDER IF I DON'T WORRY ABOUT SOME THINGS UNNECESSARILY..
5-4
© 1996 United Feature Syndicate, Inc.
LIKE, IF I HAD A CAR, I PROBABLY SHOULD BE GETTING IT IN FOR ITS FIVE THOUSAND MILE TUNEUP..

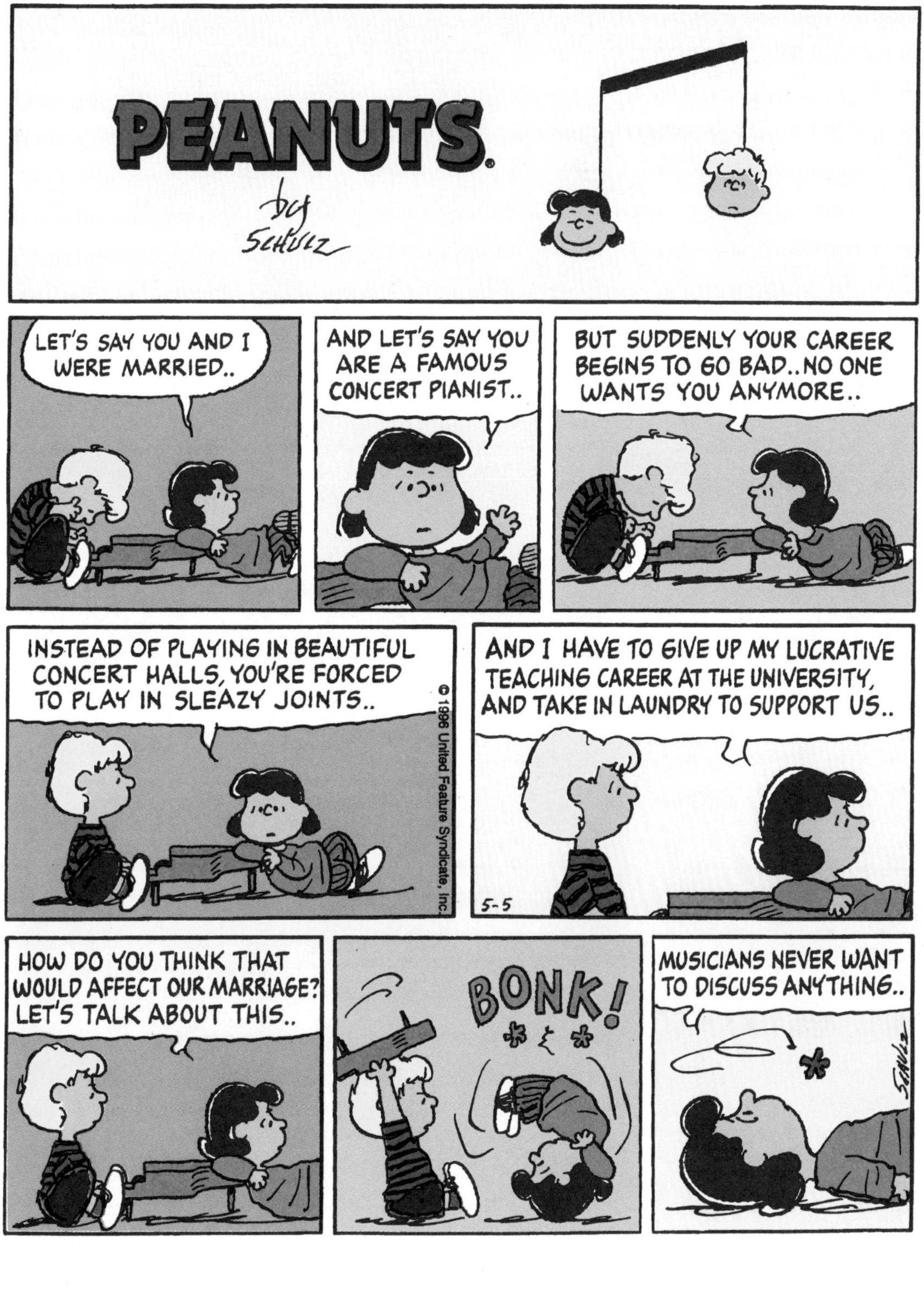
PEANUTS
SCHULZ
LET'S SAY YOU AND I WERE MARRIED..
AND LET'S SAY YOU ARE A FAMOUS CONCERT PIANIST..
BUT SUDDENLY YOUR CAREER BEGINS TO GO BAD..NO ONE WANTS YOU ANYMORE..
INSTEAD OF PLAYING IN BEAUTIFUL CONCERT HALLS, YOU'RE FORCED TO PLAY IN SLEAZY JOINTS..
© 1996 United Feature Syndicate, Inc.
AND I HAVE TO GIVE UP MY LUCRATIVE TEACHING CAREER AT THE UNIVERSITY, AND TAKE IN LAUNDRY TO SUPPORT US..
5-5
HOW DO YOU THINK THAT WOULD AFFECT OUR MARRIAGE? LET'S TALK ABOUT THIS..
BONK!
MUSICIANS NEVER WANT TO DISCUSS ANYTHING..
SCHULZ

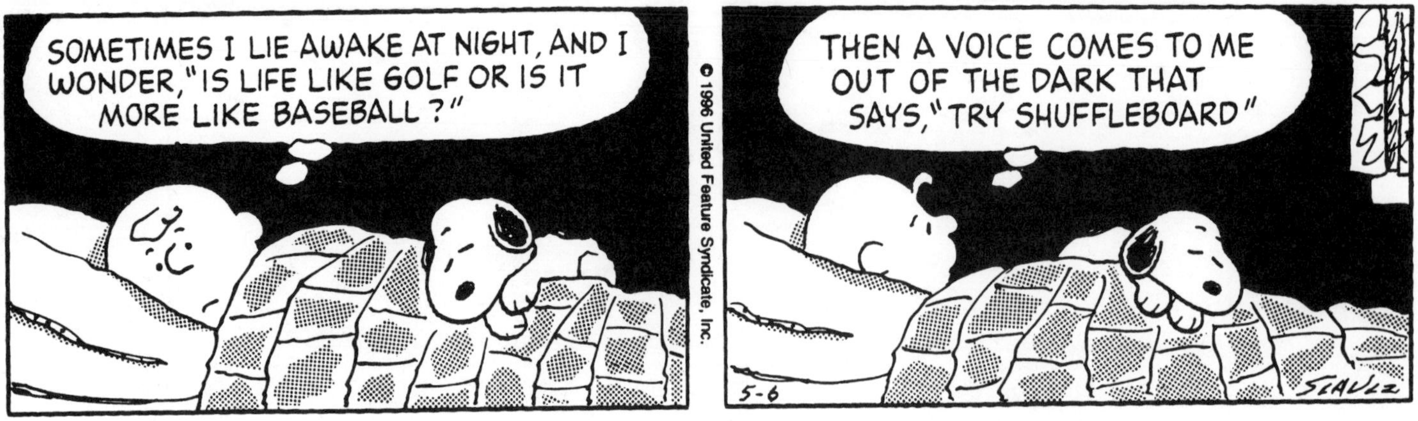
SOMETIMES I LIE AWAKE AT NIGHT, AND I WONDER, "IS LIFE LIKE GOLF OR IS IT MORE LIKE BASEBALL?"
THEN A VOICE COMES TO ME OUT OF THE DARK THAT SAYS, "TRY SHUFFLEBOARD"
© 1996 United Feature Syndicate, Inc.

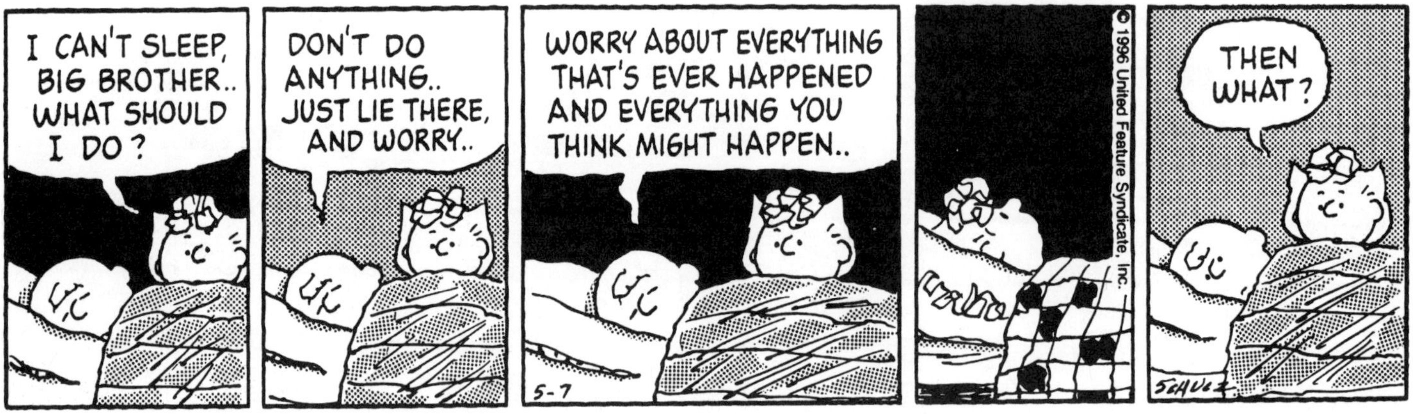
I CAN'T SLEEP, BIG BROTHER.. WHAT SHOULD I DO?
DON'T DO ANYTHING.. JUST LIE THERE, AND WORRY..
WORRY ABOUT EVERYTHING THAT'S EVER HAPPENED AND EVERYTHING YOU THINK MIGHT HAPPEN..
THEN WHAT?
© 1996 United Feature Syndicate, Inc.

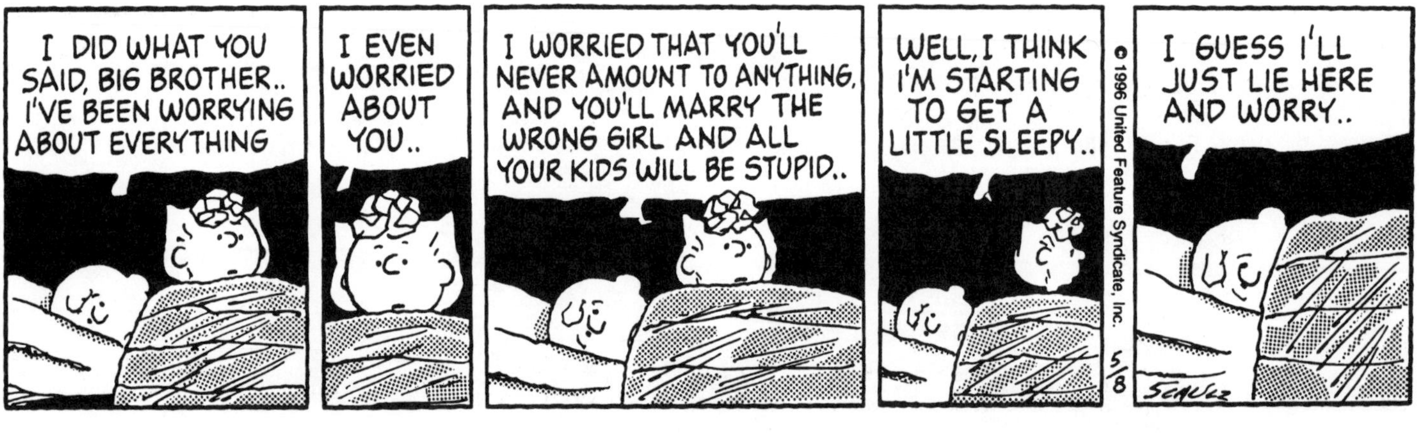
I DID WHAT YOU SAID, BIG BROTHER.. I'VE BEEN WORRYING ABOUT EVERYTHING
I EVEN WORRIED ABOUT YOU..
I WORRIED THAT YOU'LL NEVER AMOUNT TO ANYTHING, AND YOU'LL MARRY THE WRONG GIRL AND ALL YOUR KIDS WILL BE STUPID..
WELL, I THINK I'M STARTING TO GET A LITTLE SLEEPY..
I GUESS I'LL JUST LIE HERE AND WORRY..
© 1996 United Feature Syndicate, Inc.

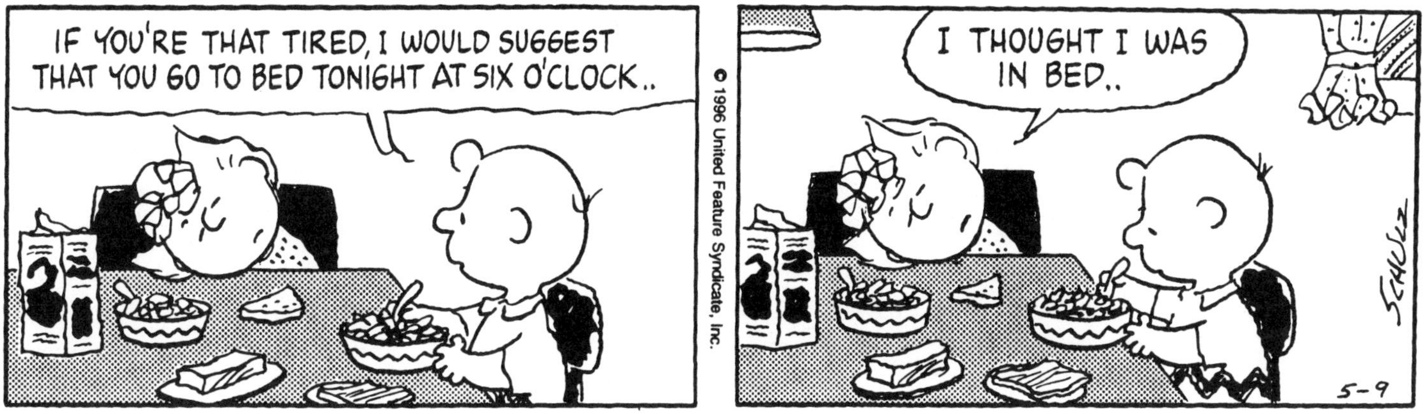
IF YOU'RE THAT TIRED, I WOULD SUGGEST THAT YOU GO TO BED TONIGHT AT SIX O'CLOCK..
© 1996 United Feature Syndicate, Inc.
I THOUGHT I WAS IN BED..
SCHULZ
5-9

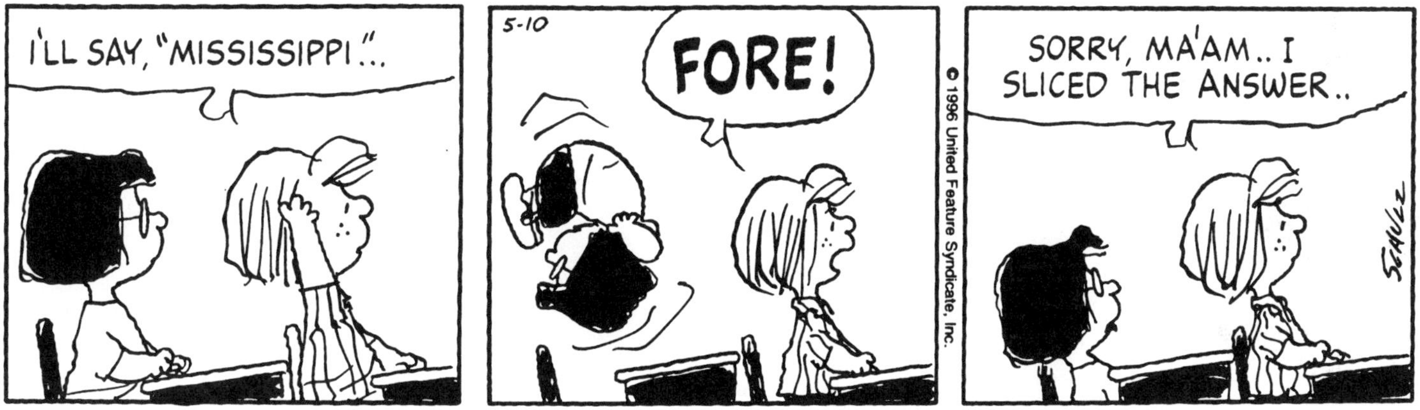
I'LL SAY, "MISSISSIPPI."..
5-10
FORE!
© 1996 United Feature Syndicate, Inc.
SORRY, MA'AM.. I SLICED THE ANSWER..
SCHULZ

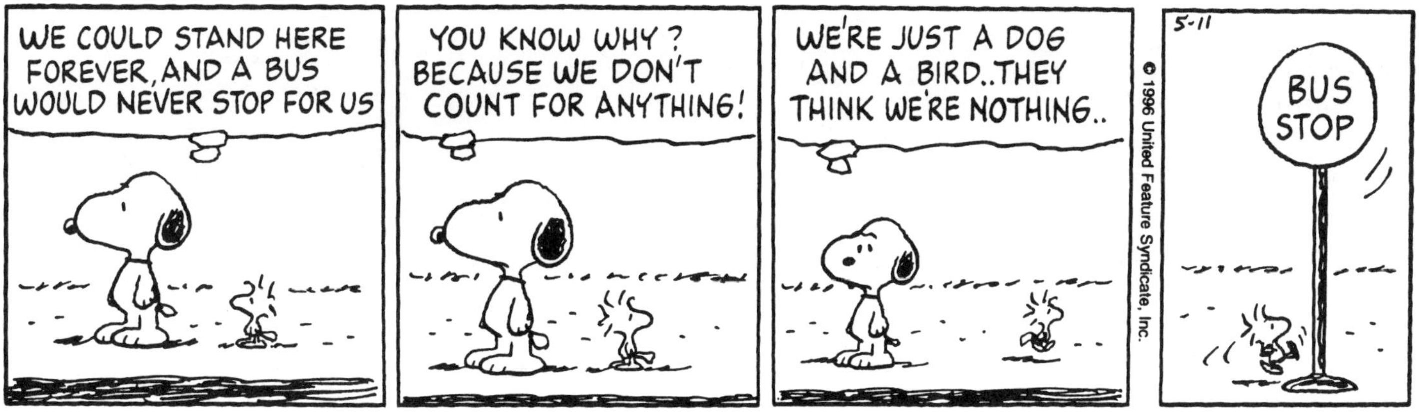
WE COULD STAND HERE FOREVER, AND A BUS WOULD NEVER STOP FOR US
YOU KNOW WHY? BECAUSE WE DON'T COUNT FOR ANYTHING!
WE'RE JUST A DOG AND A BIRD..THEY THINK WE'RE NOTHING..
© 1996 United Feature Syndicate, Inc.
5-11
BUS STOP

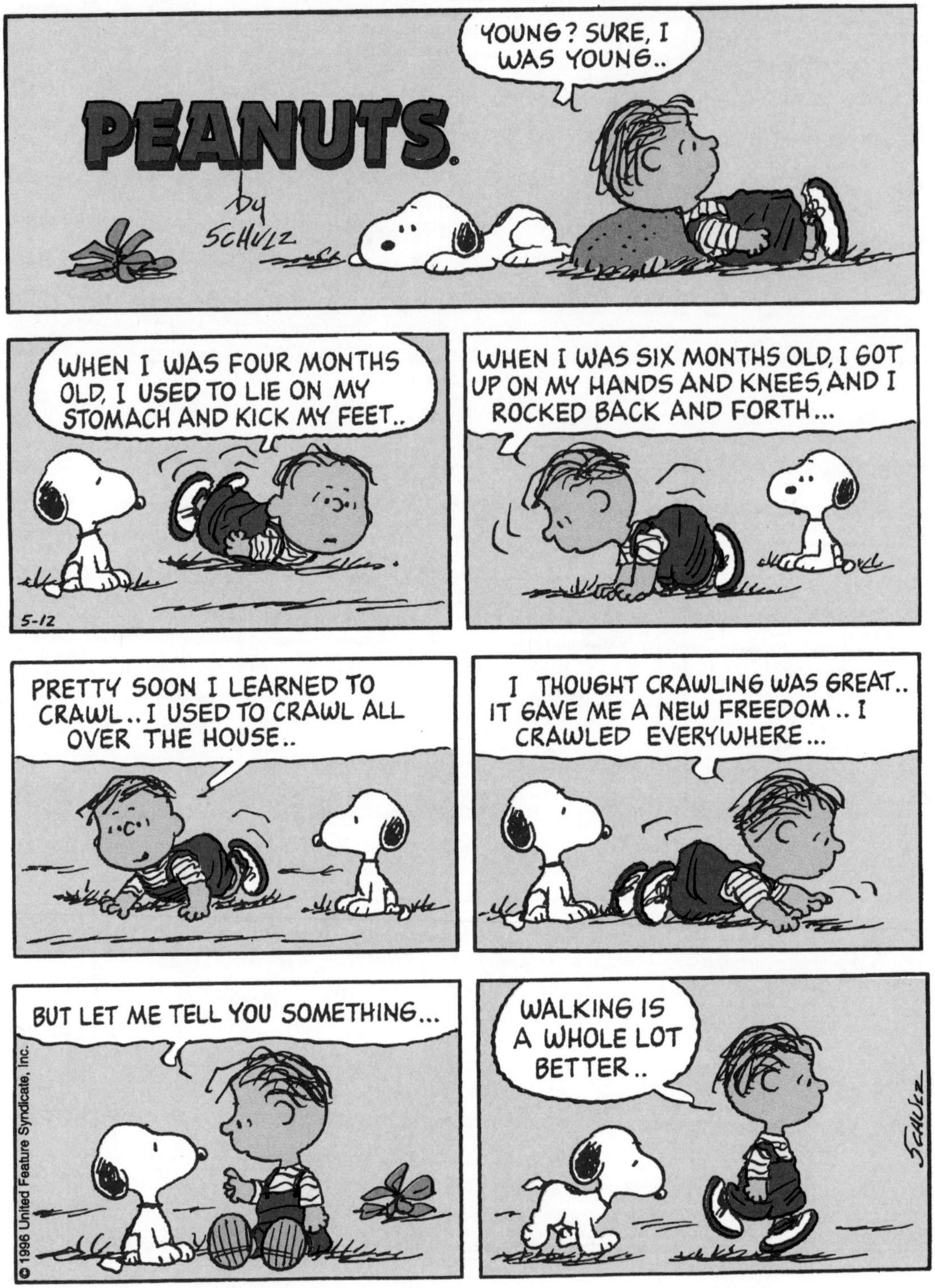
PEANUTS
by SCHULZ
YOUNG? SURE, I WAS YOUNG..
5-12
WHEN I WAS FOUR MONTHS OLD, I USED TO LIE ON MY STOMACH AND KICK MY FEET..
WHEN I WAS SIX MONTHS OLD, I GOT UP ON MY HANDS AND KNEES, AND I ROCKED BACK AND FORTH...
PRETTY SOON I LEARNED TO CRAWL.. I USED TO CRAWL ALL OVER THE HOUSE..
I THOUGHT CRAWLING WAS GREAT.. IT GAVE ME A NEW FREEDOM.. I CRAWLED EVERYWHERE...
BUT LET ME TELL YOU SOMETHING...
© 1996 United Feature Syndicate, Inc.
WALKING IS A WHOLE LOT BETTER..
SCHULZ

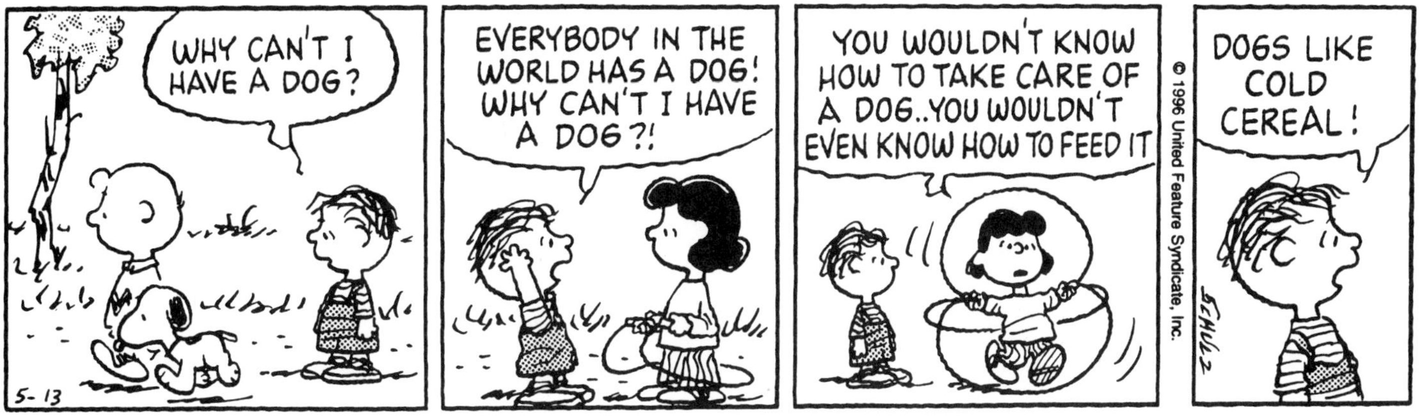
WHY CAN'T I HAVE A DOG?
EVERYBODY IN THE WORLD HAS A DOG! WHY CAN'T I HAVE A DOG?!
YOU WOULDN'T KNOW HOW TO TAKE CARE OF A DOG..YOU WOULDN'T EVEN KNOW HOW TO FEED IT
© 1996 United Feature Syndicate, Inc.
DOGS LIKE COLD CEREAL!
SCHULZ
5-13

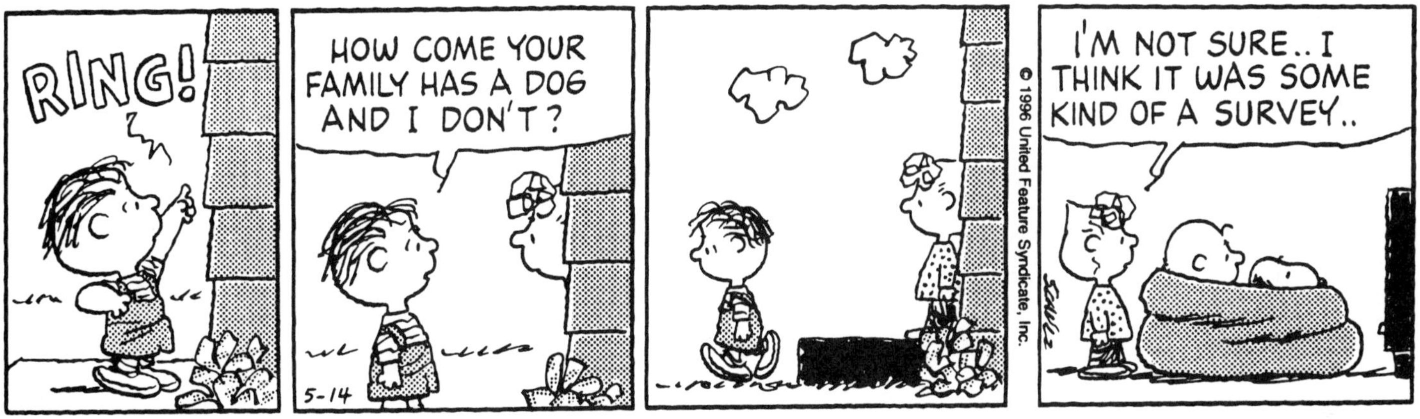
RING!
HOW COME YOUR FAMILY HAS A DOG AND I DON'T?
5-14
© 1996 United Feature Syndicate, Inc.
I'M NOT SURE.. I THINK IT WAS SOME KIND OF A SURVEY..
SCHULZ

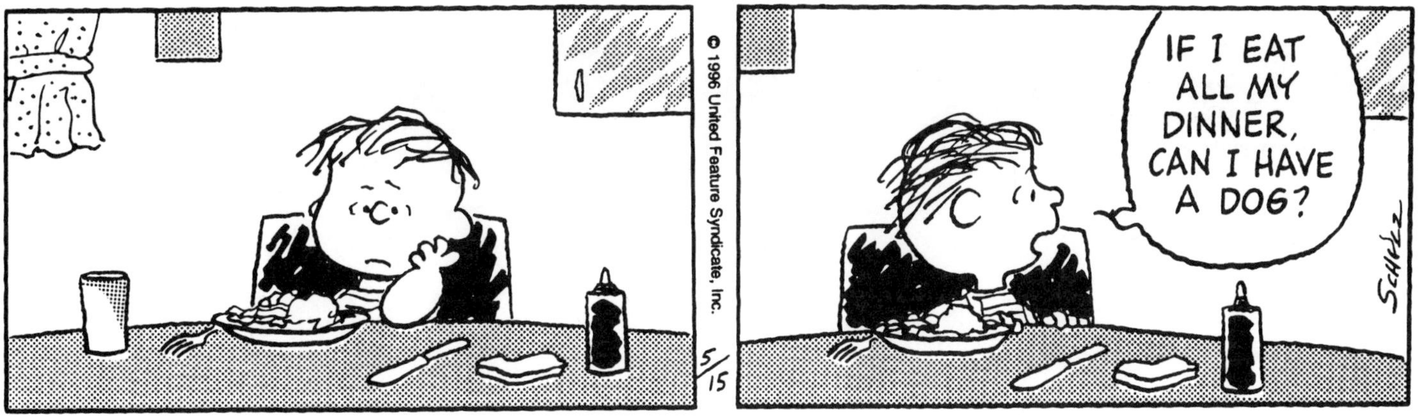
© 1996 United Feature Syndicate, Inc.
5/15
IF I EAT ALL MY DINNER, CAN I HAVE A DOG?
SCHULZ

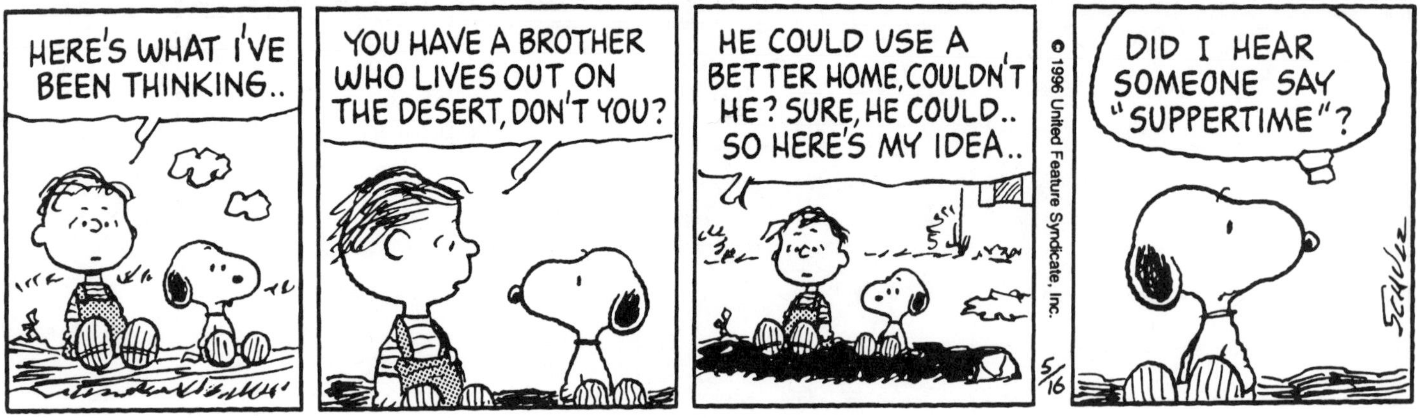
HERE'S WHAT I'VE BEEN THINKING..
YOU HAVE A BROTHER WHO LIVES OUT ON THE DESERT, DON'T YOU?
HE COULD USE A BETTER HOME, COULDN'T HE? SURE, HE COULD.. SO HERE'S MY IDEA..
© 1996 United Feature Syndicate, Inc.
5/16
DID I HEAR SOMEONE SAY "SUPPERTIME"?
SCHULZ

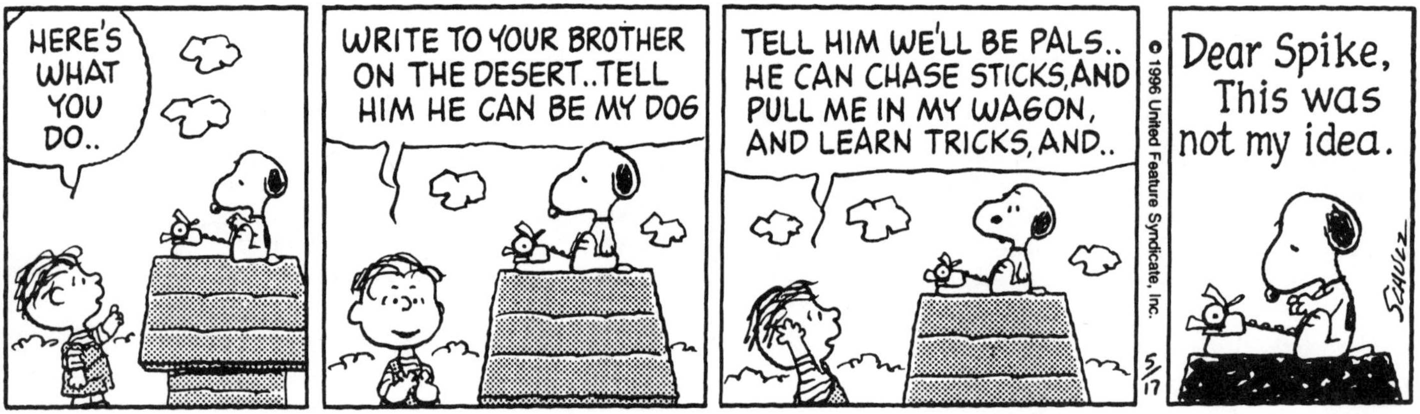
HERE'S WHAT YOU DO..
WRITE TO YOUR BROTHER ON THE DESERT..TELL HIM HE CAN BE MY DOG
TELL HIM WE'LL BE PALS.. HE CAN CHASE STICKS, AND PULL ME IN MY WAGON, AND LEARN TRICKS, AND..
© 1996 United Feature Syndicate, Inc.
5/17
Dear Spike, This was not my idea.
SCHULZ

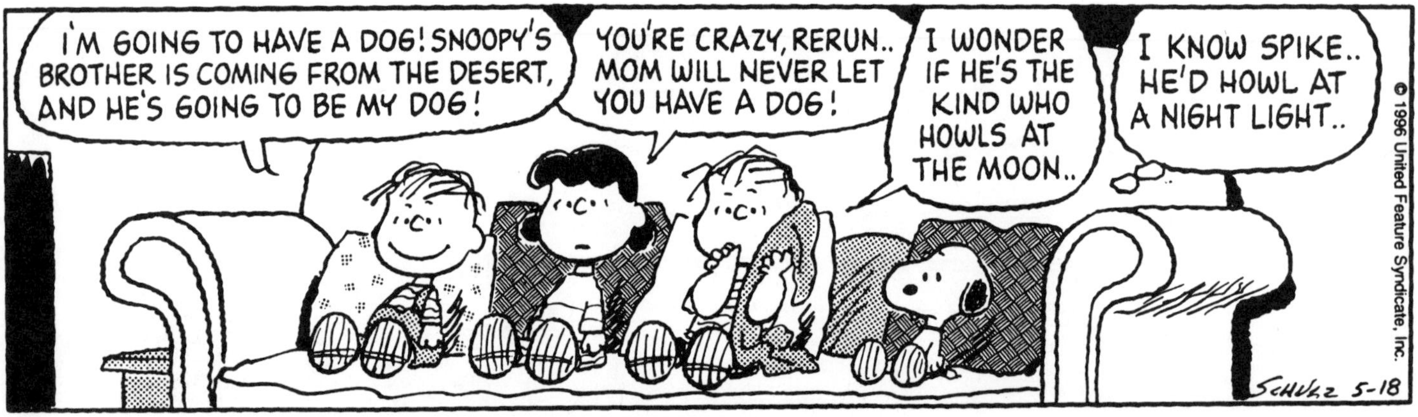
I'M GOING TO HAVE A DOG! SNOOPY'S BROTHER IS COMING FROM THE DESERT, AND HE'S GOING TO BE MY DOG!
YOU'RE CRAZY, RERUN.. MOM WILL NEVER LET YOU HAVE A DOG!
I WONDER IF HE'S THE KIND WHO HOWLS AT THE MOON..
I KNOW SPIKE.. HE'D HOWL AT A NIGHT LIGHT..
© 1996 United Feature Syndicate, Inc.
SCHULZ 5-18

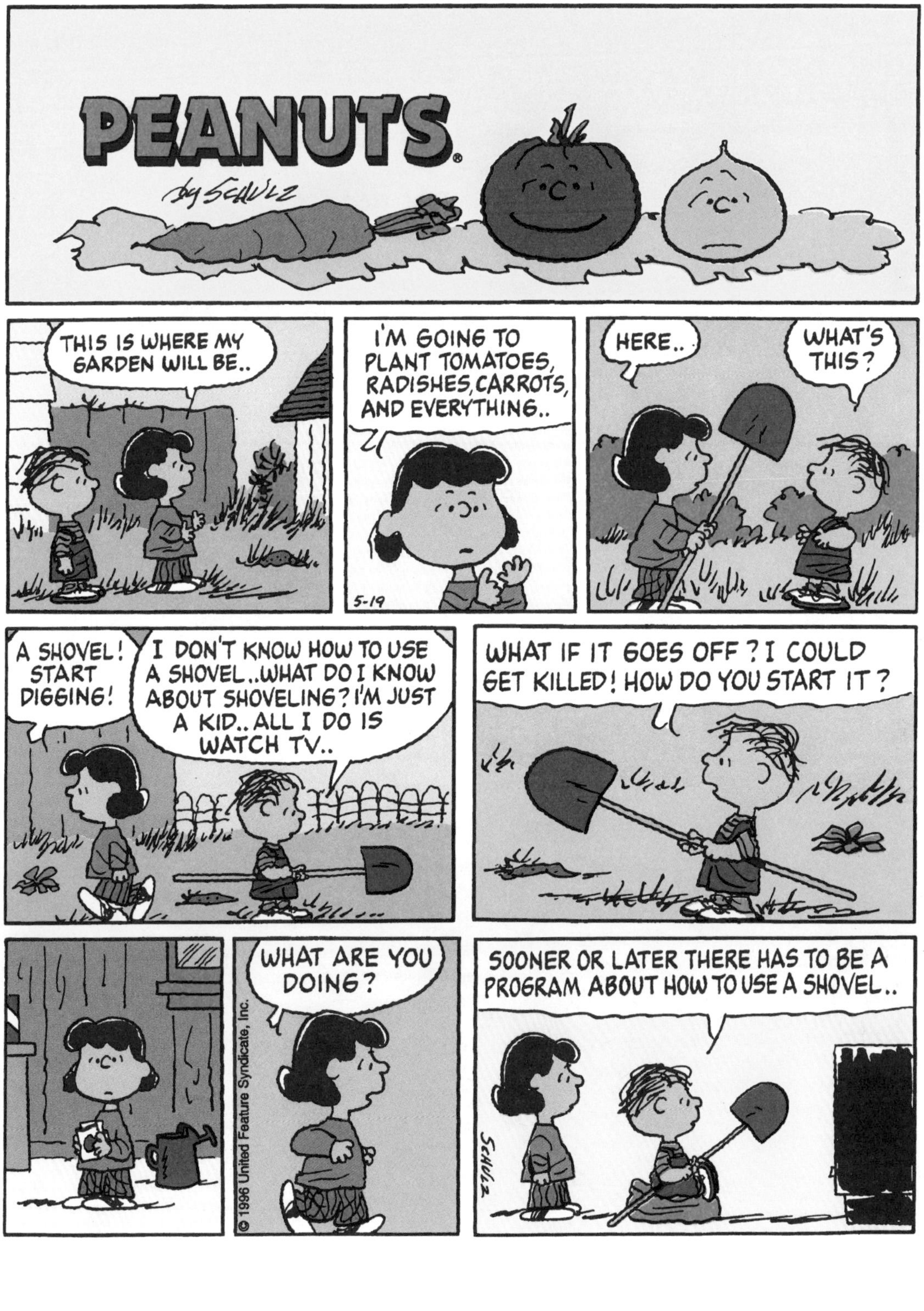
PEANUTS
by SCHULZ
THIS IS WHERE MY GARDEN WILL BE..
I'M GOING TO PLANT TOMATOES, RADISHES, CARROTS, AND EVERYTHING..
5-19
HERE..
WHAT'S THIS?
A SHOVEL! START DIGGING!
I DON'T KNOW HOW TO USE A SHOVEL..WHAT DO I KNOW ABOUT SHOVELING? I'M JUST A KID..ALL I DO IS WATCH TV..
WHAT IF IT GOES OFF? I COULD GET KILLED! HOW DO YOU START IT?
WHAT ARE YOU DOING?
© 1996 United Feature Syndicate, Inc.
SOONER OR LATER THERE HAS TO BE A PROGRAM ABOUT HOW TO USE A SHOVEL..
SCHULZ

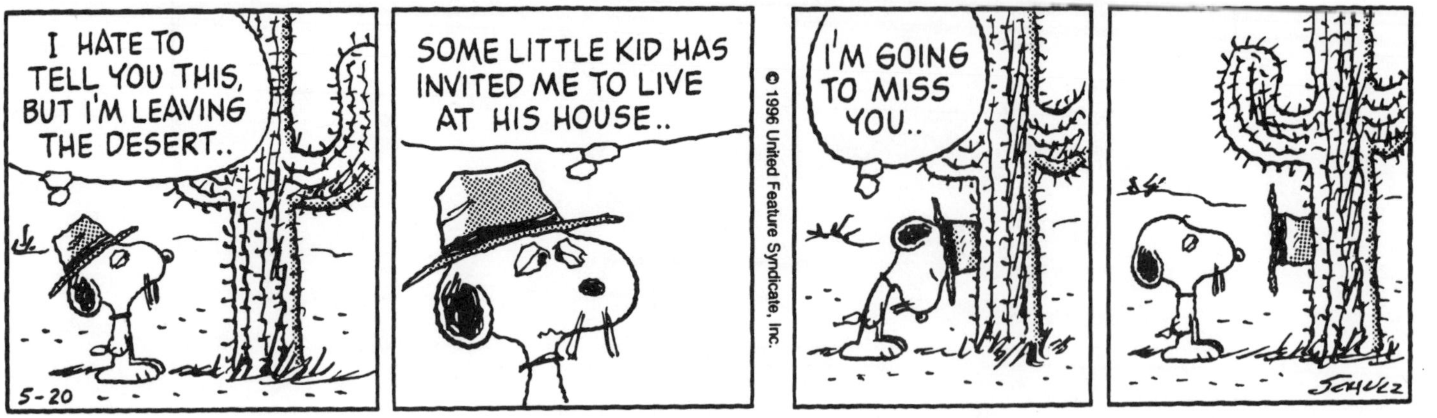
5-20
I HATE TO TELL YOU THIS, BUT I'M LEAVING THE DESERT..
SOME LITTLE KID HAS INVITED ME TO LIVE AT HIS HOUSE..
© 1996 United Feature Syndicate, Inc.
I'M GOING TO MISS YOU..
SCHULZ

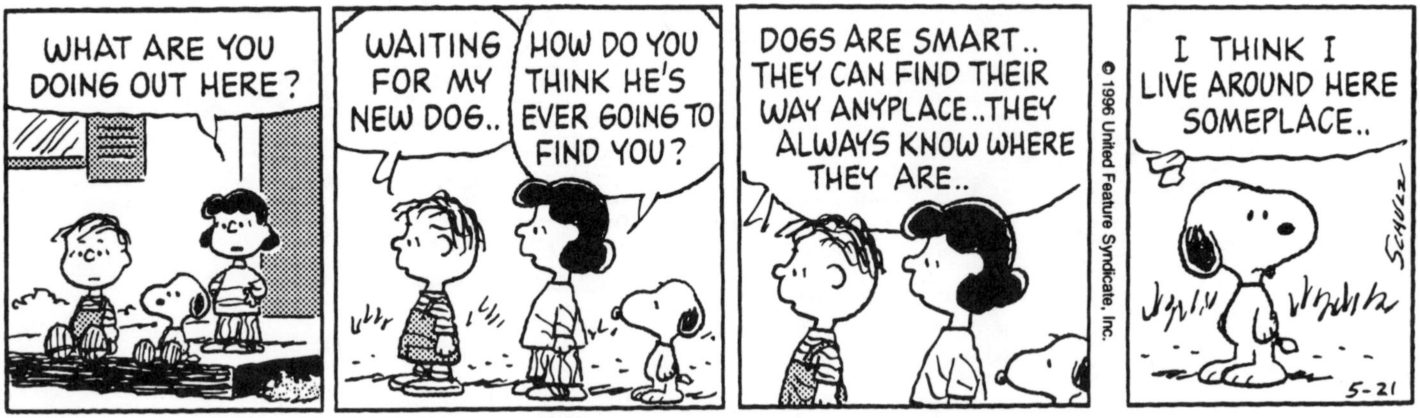
WHAT ARE YOU DOING OUT HERE?
WAITING FOR MY NEW DOG..
HOW DO YOU THINK HE'S EVER GOING TO FIND YOU?
DOGS ARE SMART.. THEY CAN FIND THEIR WAY ANYPLACE..THEY ALWAYS KNOW WHERE THEY ARE..
© 1996 United Feature Syndicate, Inc.
I THINK I LIVE AROUND HERE SOMEPLACE..
SCHULZ
5-21

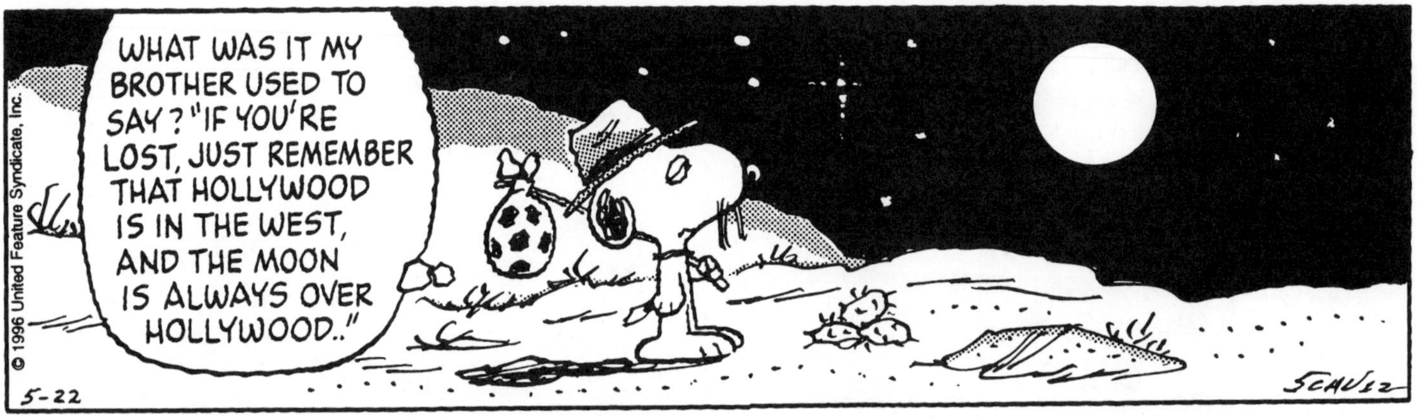
© 1996 United Feature Syndicate, Inc.
WHAT WAS IT MY BROTHER USED TO SAY? "IF YOU'RE LOST, JUST REMEMBER THAT HOLLYWOOD IS IN THE WEST, AND THE MOON IS ALWAYS OVER HOLLYWOOD.."
5-22
SCHULZ

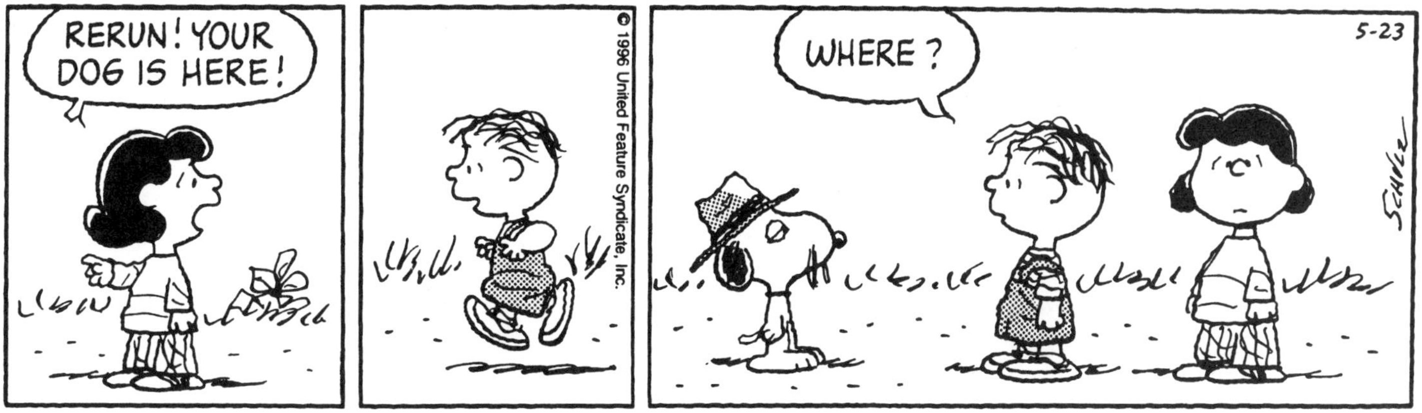
RERUN! YOUR DOG IS HERE!
© 1996 United Feature Syndicate, Inc.
5-23
WHERE?
SCHULZ

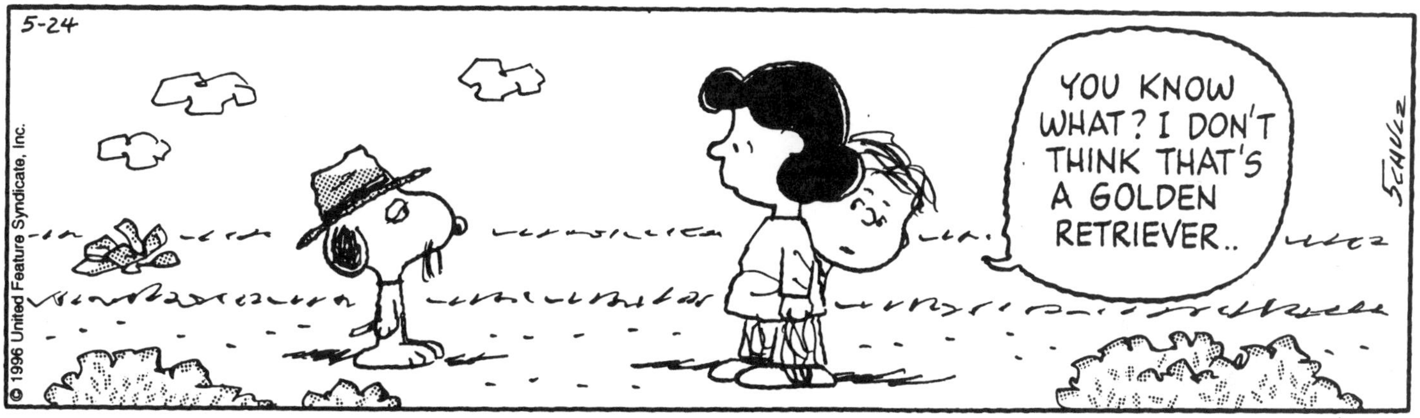
5-24
© 1996 United Feature Syndicate, Inc.
YOU KNOW WHAT? I DON'T THINK THAT'S A GOLDEN RETRIEVER..
SCHULZ

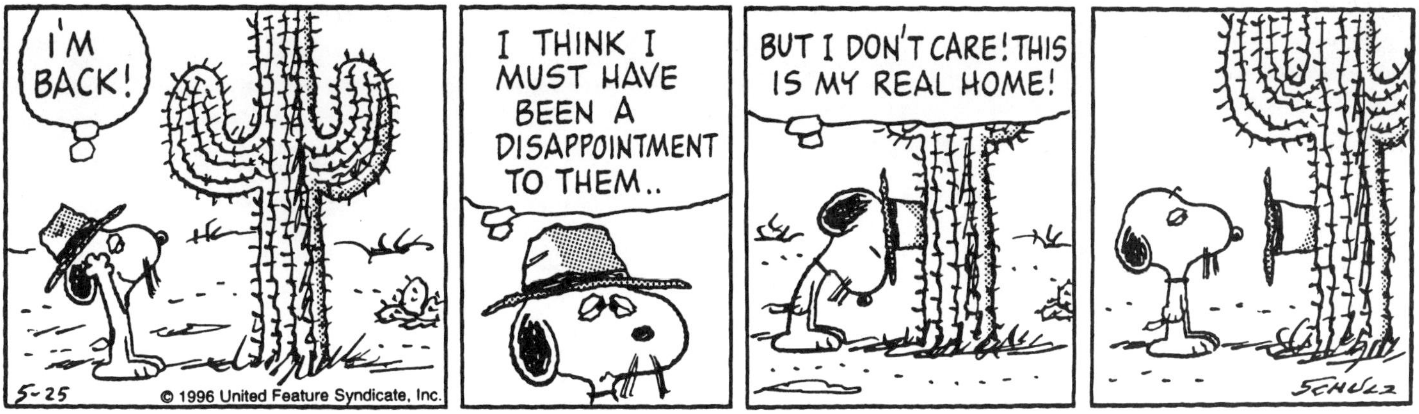
I'M BACK!
5-25
© 1996 United Feature Syndicate, Inc.
I THINK I MUST HAVE BEEN A DISAPPOINTMENT TO THEM..
BUT I DON'T CARE! THIS IS MY REAL HOME!
SCHULZ

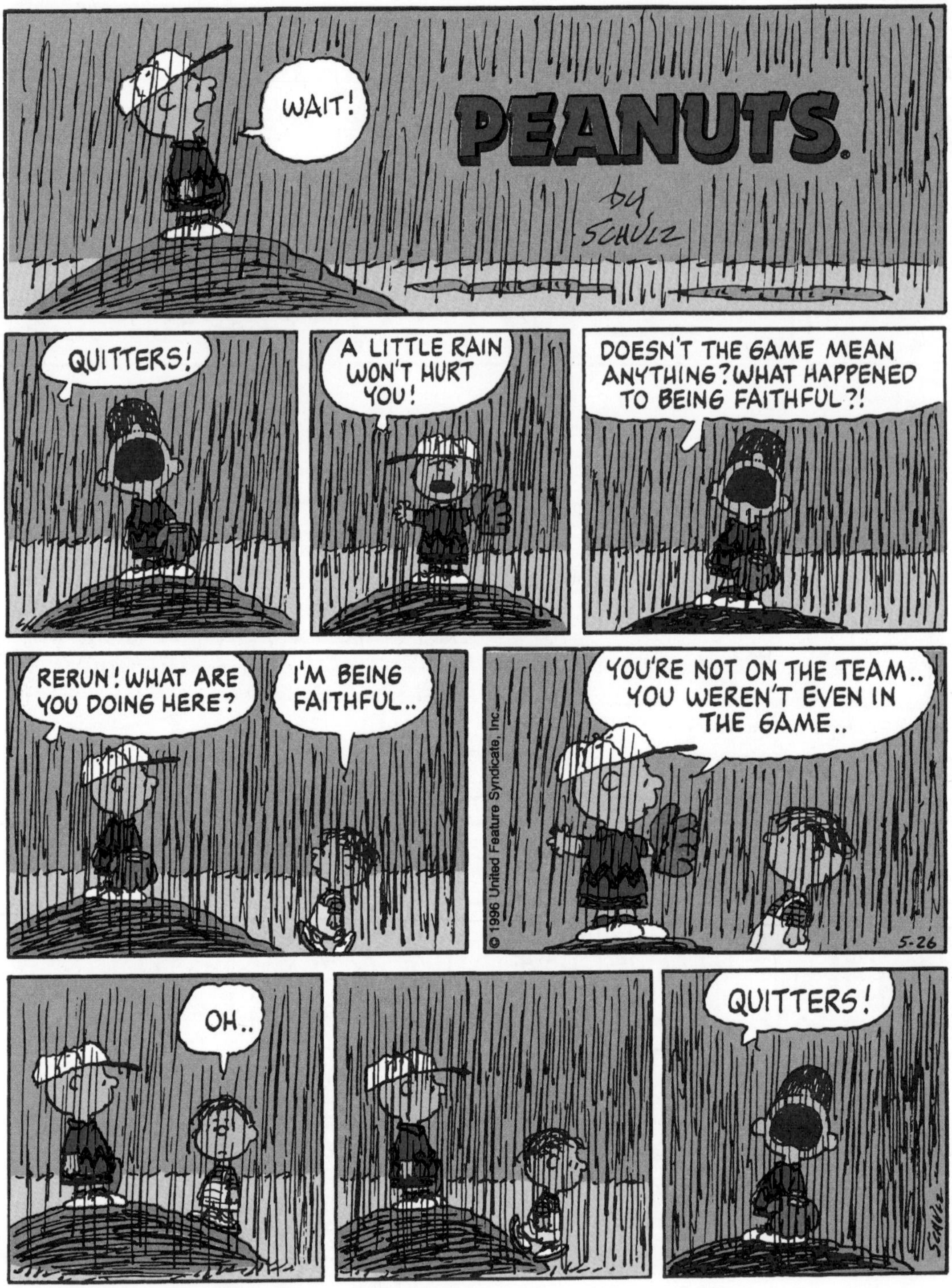
WAIT!
PEANUTS
by SCHULZ
QUITTERS!
A LITTLE RAIN WON'T HURT YOU!
DOESN'T THE GAME MEAN ANYTHING? WHAT HAPPENED TO BEING FAITHFUL?!
RERUN! WHAT ARE YOU DOING HERE?
I'M BEING FAITHFUL..
© 1996 United Feature Syndicate, Inc.
YOU'RE NOT ON THE TEAM.. YOU WEREN'T EVEN IN THE GAME..
5-26
OH..
QUITTERS!
SCHULZ

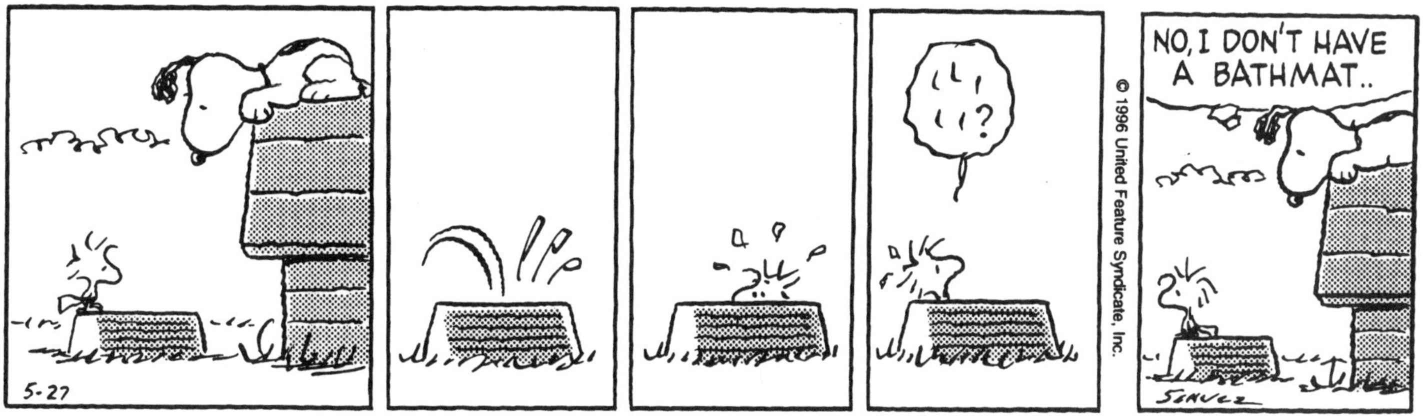
5-27
?
© 1996 United Feature Syndicate, Inc.
NO, I DON'T HAVE A BATHMAT..

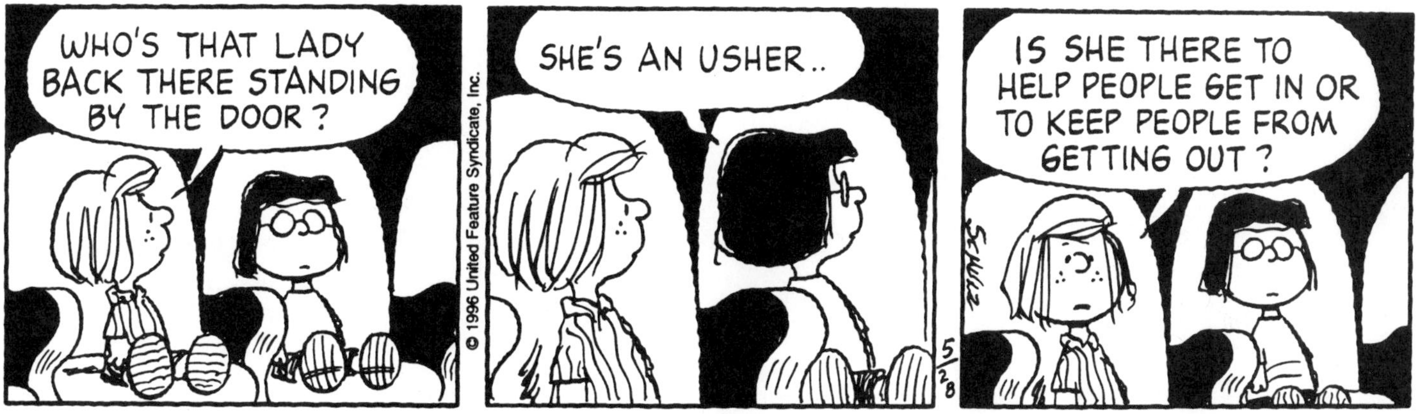
WHO'S THAT LADY BACK THERE STANDING BY THE DOOR ?
© 1996 United Feature Syndicate, Inc.
SHE'S AN USHER..
5/28
IS SHE THERE TO HELP PEOPLE GET IN OR TO KEEP PEOPLE FROM GETTING OUT ?

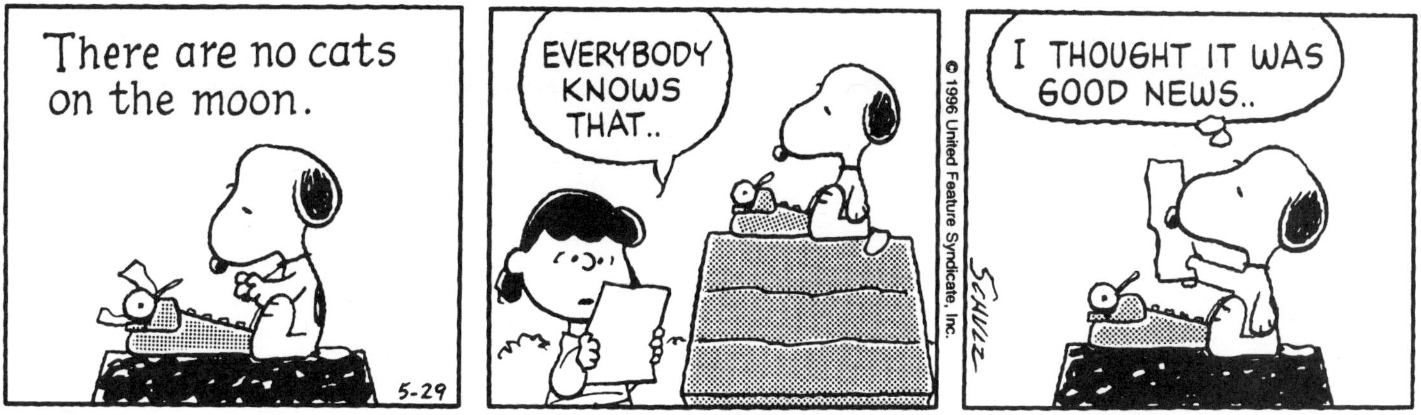
There are no cats on the moon.
5-29
EVERYBODY KNOWS THAT..
© 1996 United Feature Syndicate, Inc.
I THOUGHT IT WAS GOOD NEWS..

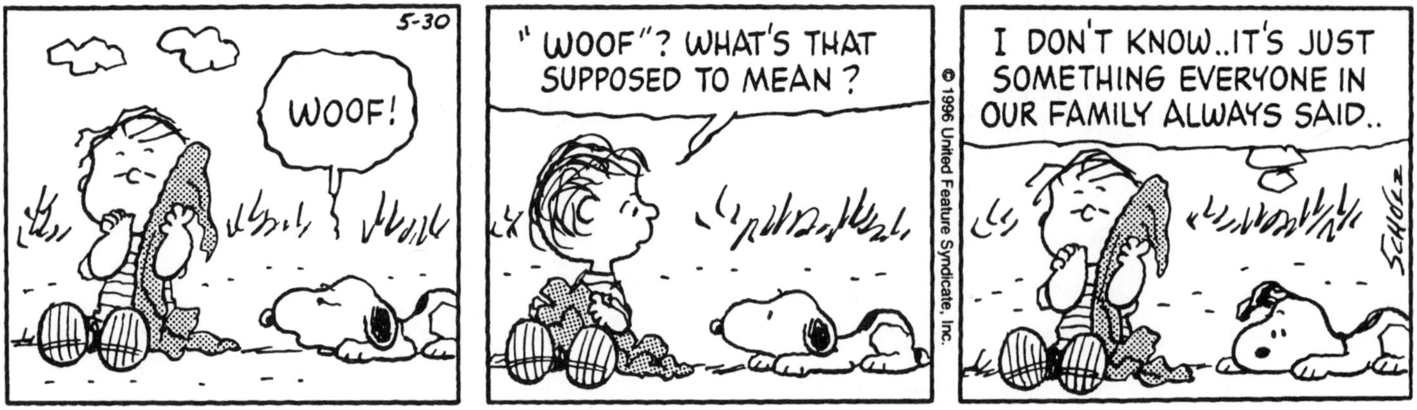
5-30
WOOF!
"WOOF"? WHAT'S THAT SUPPOSED TO MEAN?
I DON'T KNOW..IT'S JUST SOMETHING EVERYONE IN OUR FAMILY ALWAYS SAID..
© 1996 United Feature Syndicate, Inc.
SCHULZ

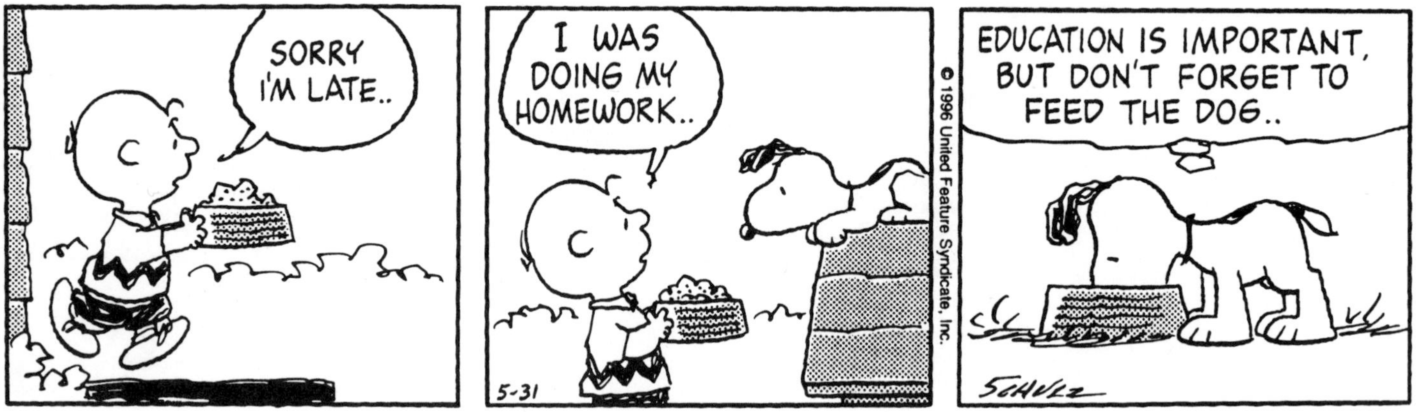
SORRY I'M LATE..
I WAS DOING MY HOMEWORK..
5-31
EDUCATION IS IMPORTANT, BUT DON'T FORGET TO FEED THE DOG..
© 1996 United Feature Syndicate, Inc.
SCHULZ

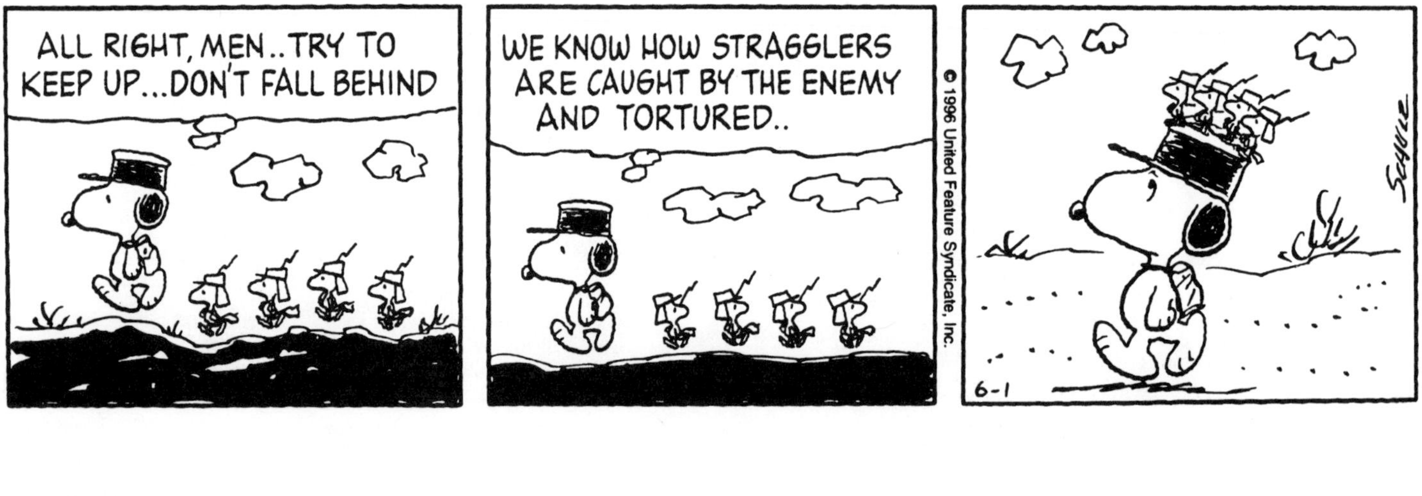
ALL RIGHT, MEN..TRY TO KEEP UP...DON'T FALL BEHIND
WE KNOW HOW STRAGGLERS ARE CAUGHT BY THE ENEMY AND TORTURED..
© 1996 United Feature Syndicate, Inc.
SCHULZ
6-1

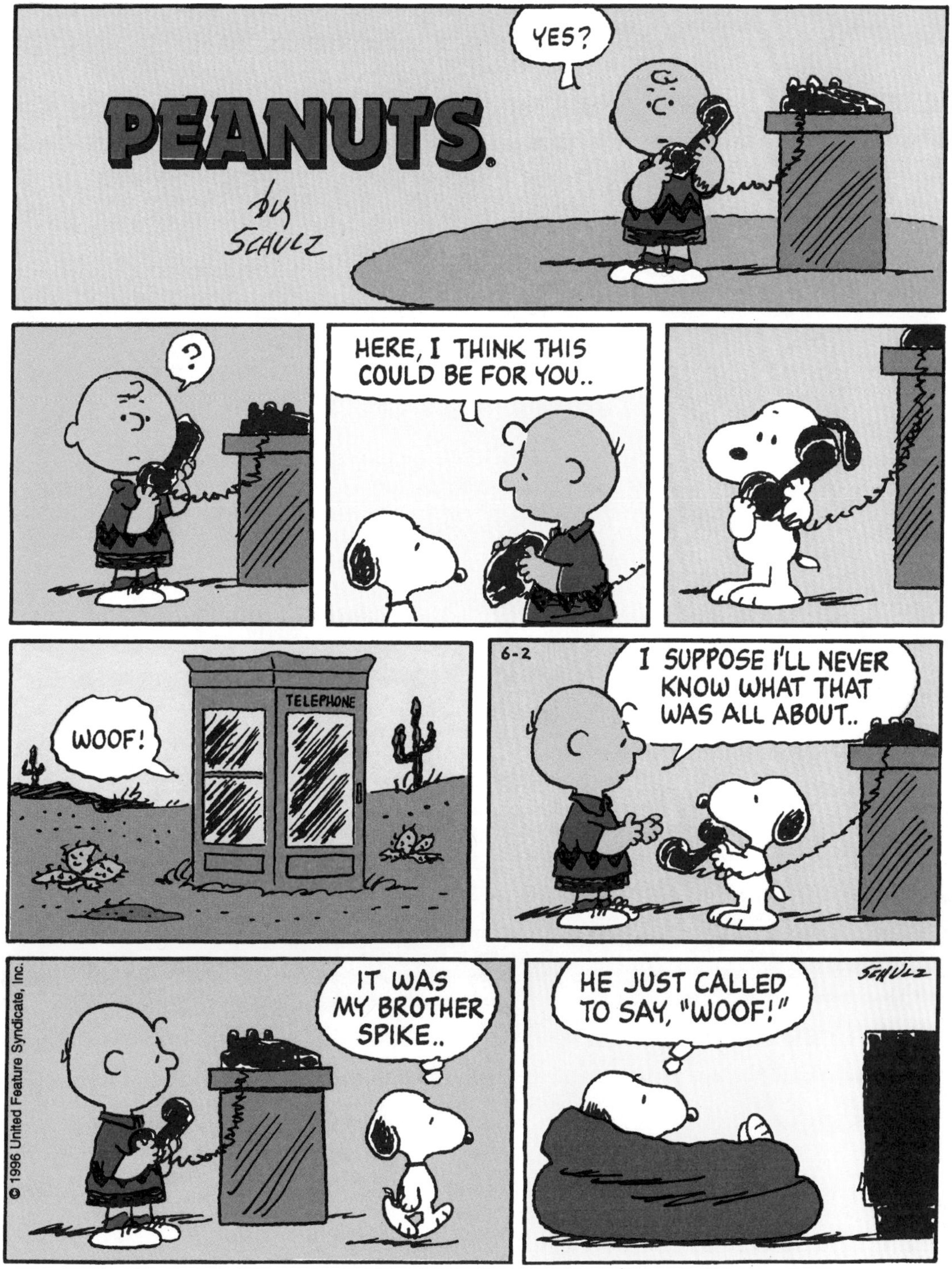
YES?
PEANUTS
by SCHULZ
?
HERE, I THINK THIS COULD BE FOR YOU..
WOOF!
TELEPHONE
6-2
I SUPPOSE I'LL NEVER KNOW WHAT THAT WAS ALL ABOUT..
© 1996 United Feature Syndicate, Inc.
IT WAS MY BROTHER SPIKE..
SCHULZ
HE JUST CALLED TO SAY, "WOOF!"

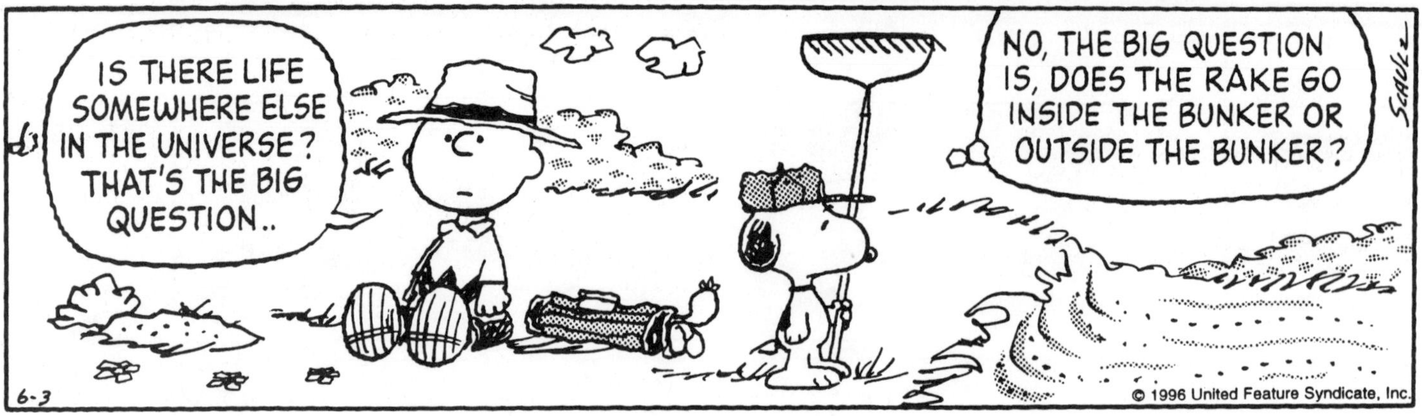
IS THERE LIFE SOMEWHERE ELSE IN THE UNIVERSE? THAT'S THE BIG QUESTION..
NO, THE BIG QUESTION IS, DOES THE RAKE GO INSIDE THE BUNKER OR OUTSIDE THE BUNKER?
SCHULZ
6-3
© 1996 United Feature Syndicate, Inc.

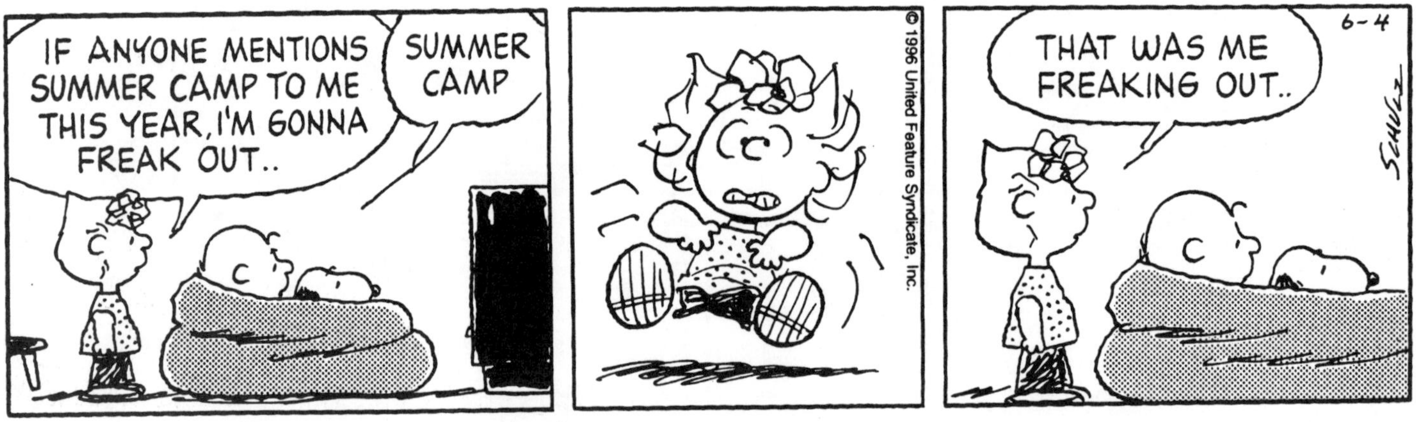
IF ANYONE MENTIONS SUMMER CAMP TO ME THIS YEAR, I'M GONNA FREAK OUT..
SUMMER CAMP
© 1996 United Feature Syndicate, Inc.
THAT WAS ME FREAKING OUT..
SCHULZ
6-4

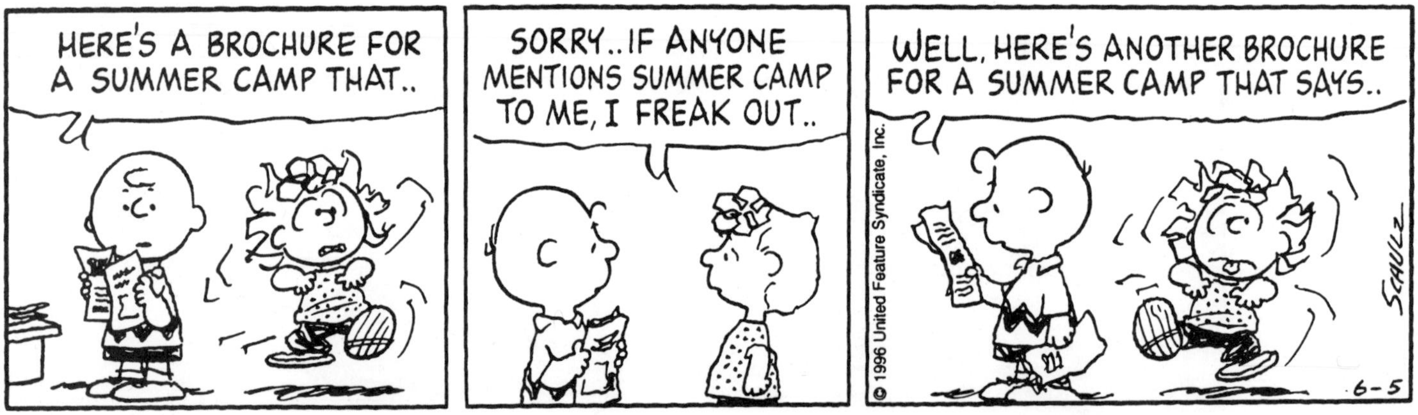
HERE'S A BROCHURE FOR A SUMMER CAMP THAT..
SORRY..IF ANYONE MENTIONS SUMMER CAMP TO ME, I FREAK OUT..
WELL, HERE'S ANOTHER BROCHURE FOR A SUMMER CAMP THAT SAYS..
© 1996 United Feature Syndicate, Inc.
SCHULZ
6-5

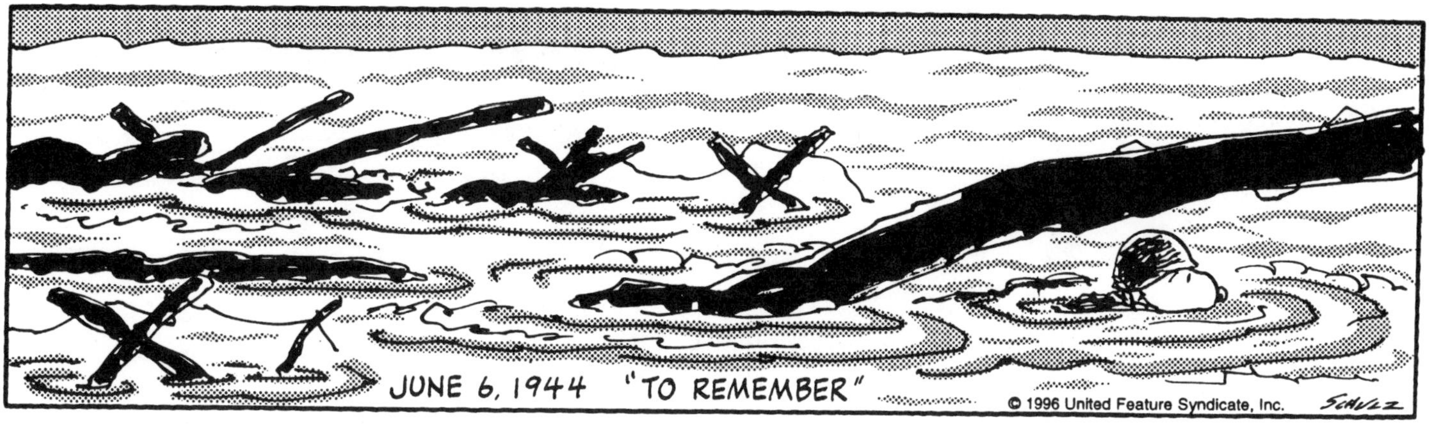
JUNE 6, 1944 "TO REMEMBER"
© 1996 United Feature Syndicate, Inc.
SCHULZ

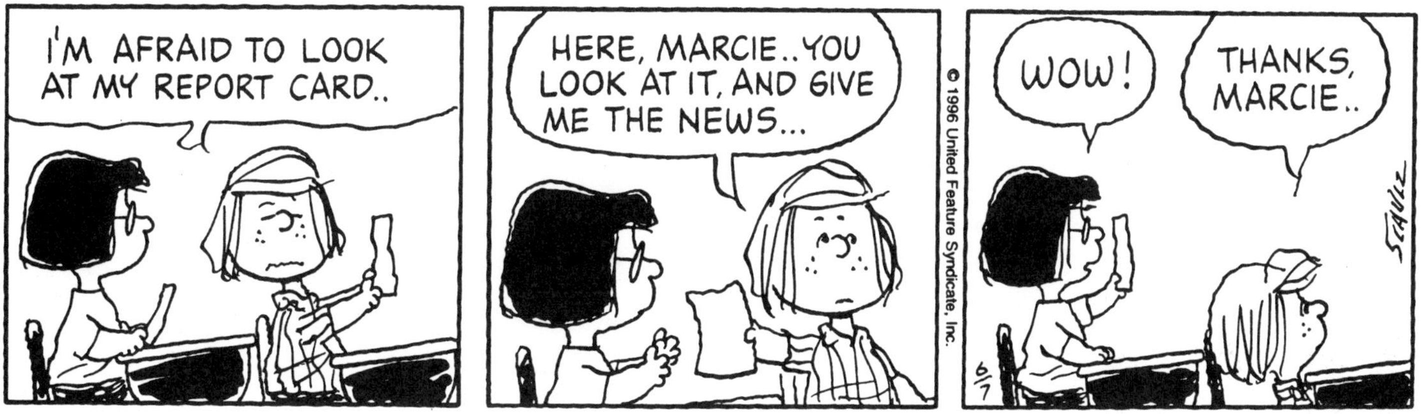
I'M AFRAID TO LOOK AT MY REPORT CARD..
HERE, MARCIE..YOU LOOK AT IT, AND GIVE ME THE NEWS...
© 1996 United Feature Syndicate, Inc.
WOW!
THANKS, MARCIE..
SCHULZ
6/7

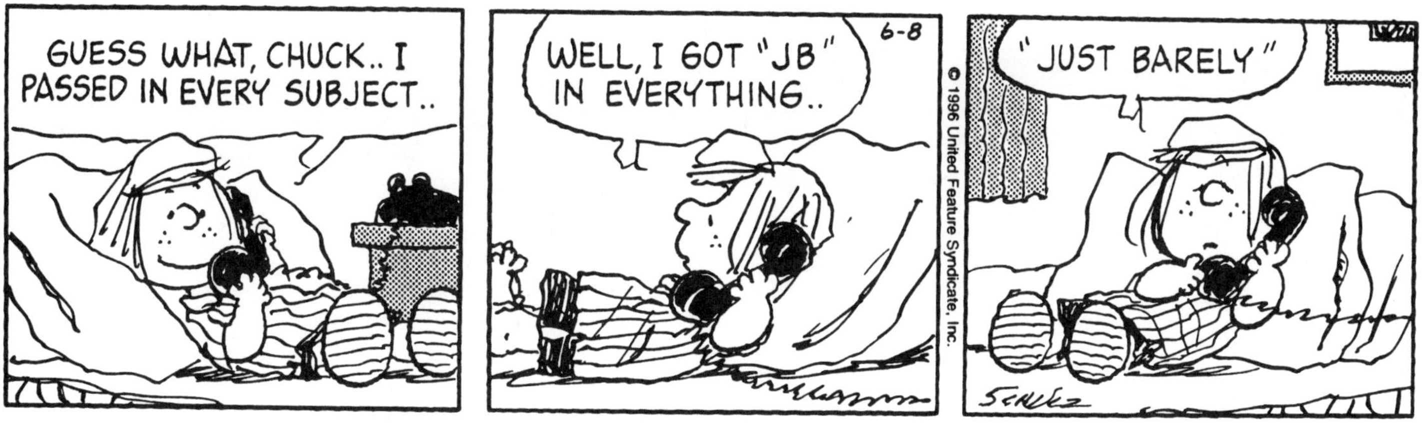
GUESS WHAT, CHUCK.. I PASSED IN EVERY SUBJECT..
6-8
WELL, I GOT "JB" IN EVERYTHING..
© 1996 United Feature Syndicate, Inc.
"JUST BARELY"
SCHULZ

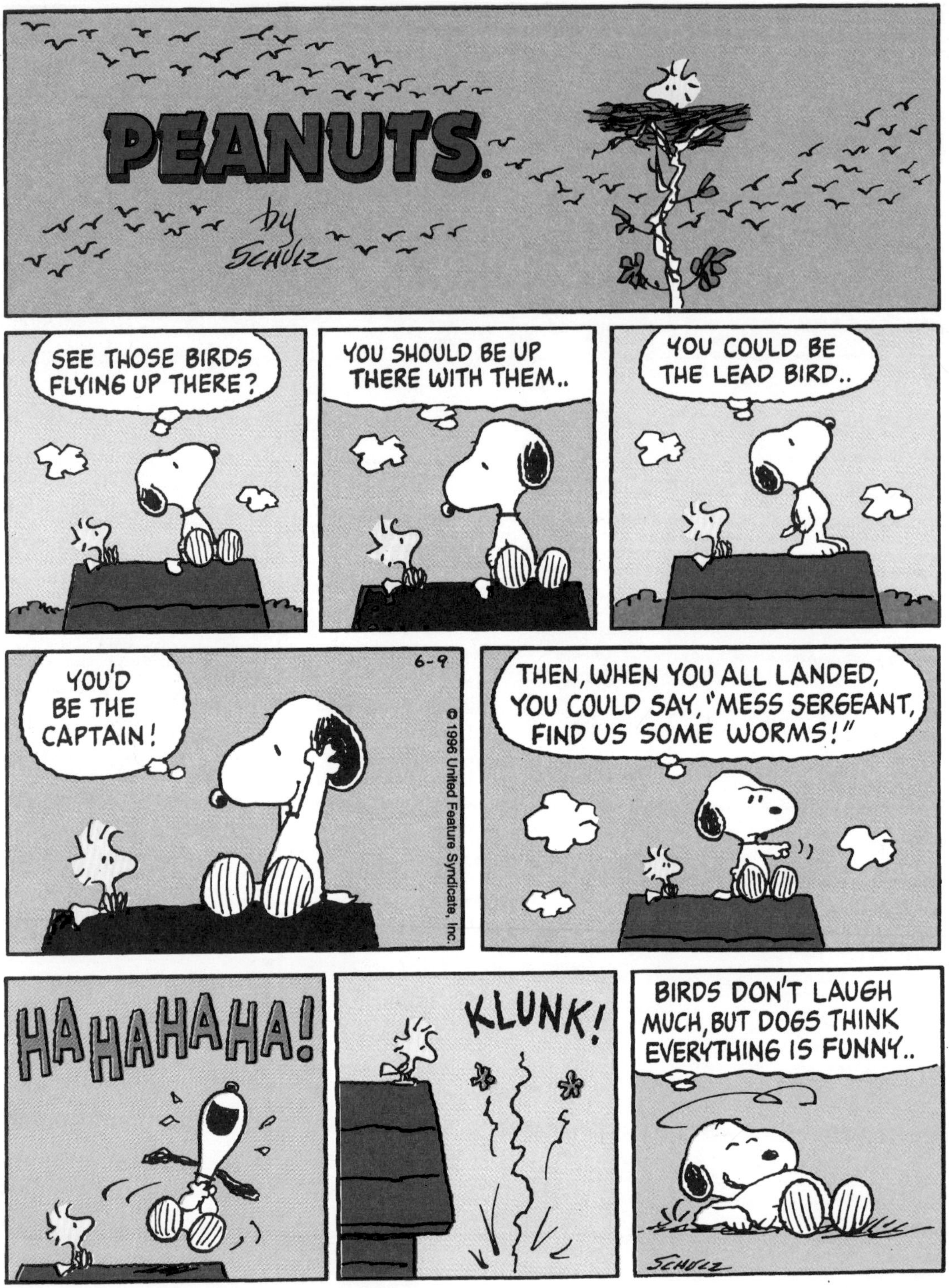
PEANUTS
by SCHULZ
SEE THOSE BIRDS FLYING UP THERE?
YOU SHOULD BE UP THERE WITH THEM..
YOU COULD BE THE LEAD BIRD..
YOU'D BE THE CAPTAIN!
6-9
© 1996 United Feature Syndicate, Inc.
THEN, WHEN YOU ALL LANDED, YOU COULD SAY, "MESS SERGEANT, FIND US SOME WORMS!"
HAHAHAHA!
KLUNK!
BIRDS DON'T LAUGH MUCH, BUT DOGS THINK EVERYTHING IS FUNNY..
SCHULZ

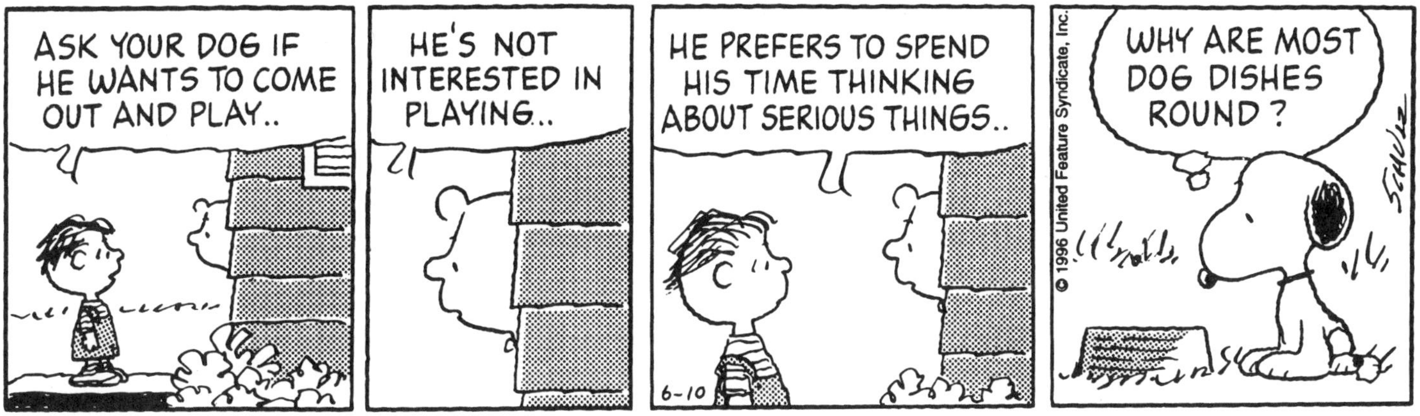
ASK YOUR DOG IF HE WANTS TO COME OUT AND PLAY..
HE'S NOT INTERESTED IN PLAYING..
HE PREFERS TO SPEND HIS TIME THINKING ABOUT SERIOUS THINGS..
WHY ARE MOST DOG DISHES ROUND?
6-10
© 1996 United Feature Syndicate, Inc.
SCHULZ

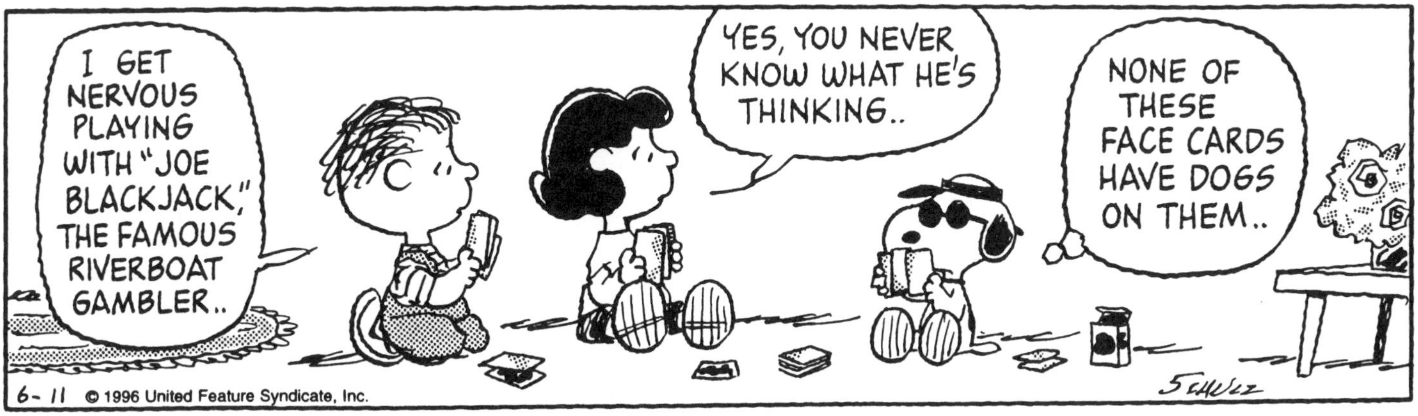
I GET NERVOUS PLAYING WITH "JOE BLACKJACK," THE FAMOUS RIVERBOAT GAMBLER..
YES, YOU NEVER KNOW WHAT HE'S THINKING..
NONE OF THESE FACE CARDS HAVE DOGS ON THEM..
6-11
© 1996 United Feature Syndicate, Inc.
SCHULZ

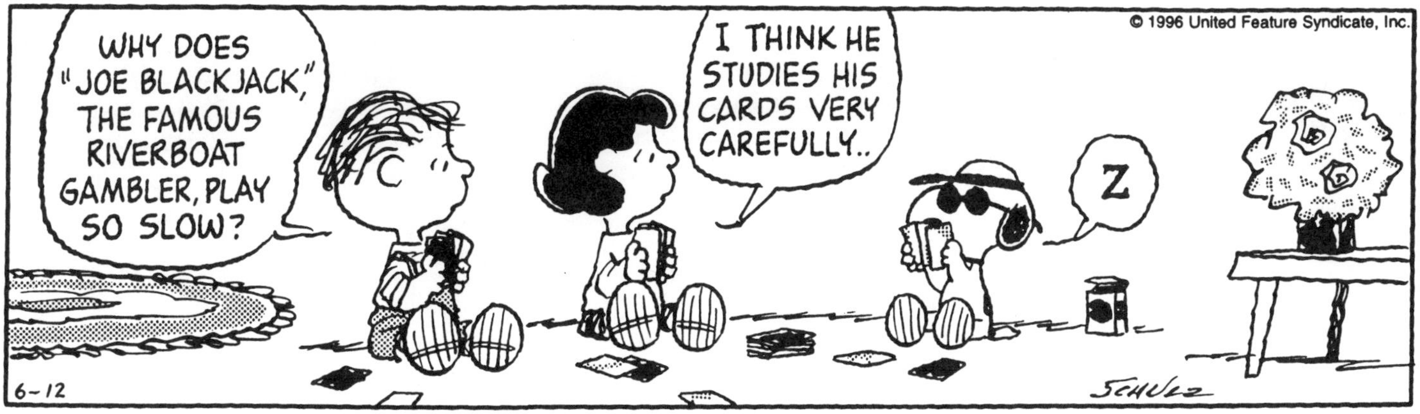
WHY DOES "JOE BLACKJACK," THE FAMOUS RIVERBOAT GAMBLER, PLAY SO SLOW?
I THINK HE STUDIES HIS CARDS VERY CAREFULLY..
Z
© 1996 United Feature Syndicate, Inc.
6-12
SCHULZ

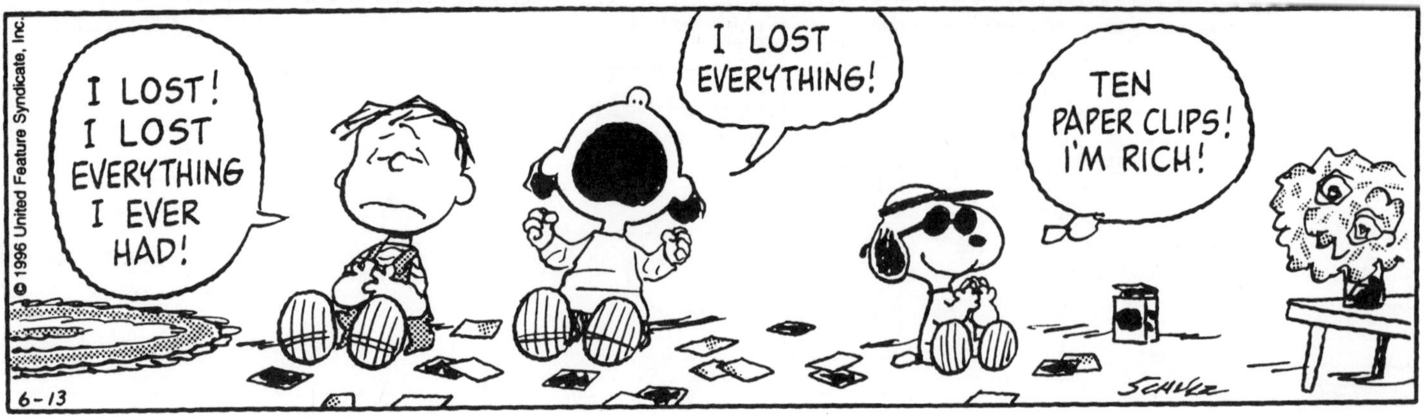
© 1996 United Feature Syndicate, Inc.
I LOST! I LOST EVERYTHING I EVER HAD!
I LOST EVERYTHING!
TEN PAPER CLIPS! I'M RICH!
6-13
SCHULZ

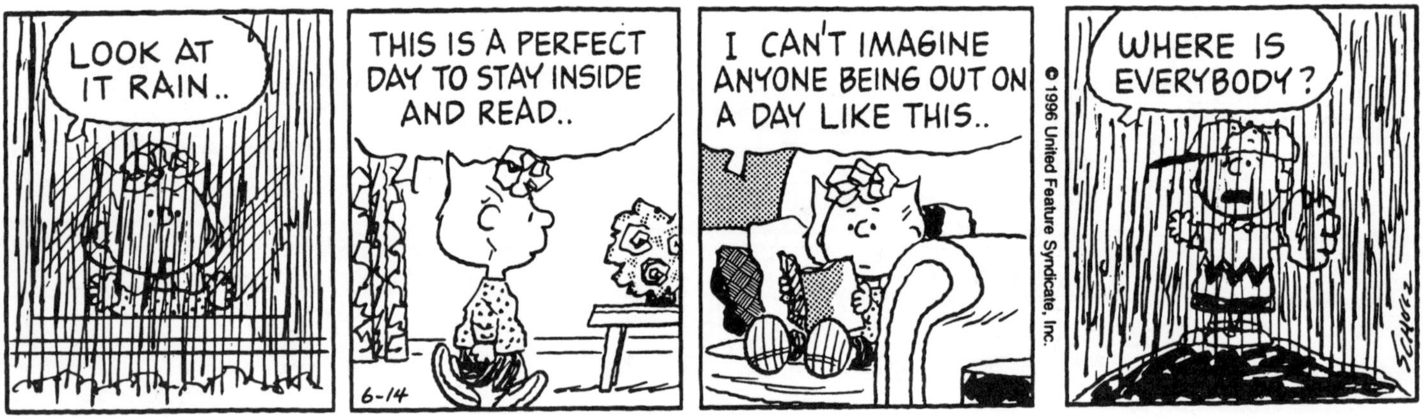
LOOK AT IT RAIN..
THIS IS A PERFECT DAY TO STAY INSIDE AND READ..
6-14
I CAN'T IMAGINE ANYONE BEING OUT ON A DAY LIKE THIS..
© 1996 United Feature Syndicate, Inc.
WHERE IS EVERYBODY?
SCHULZ

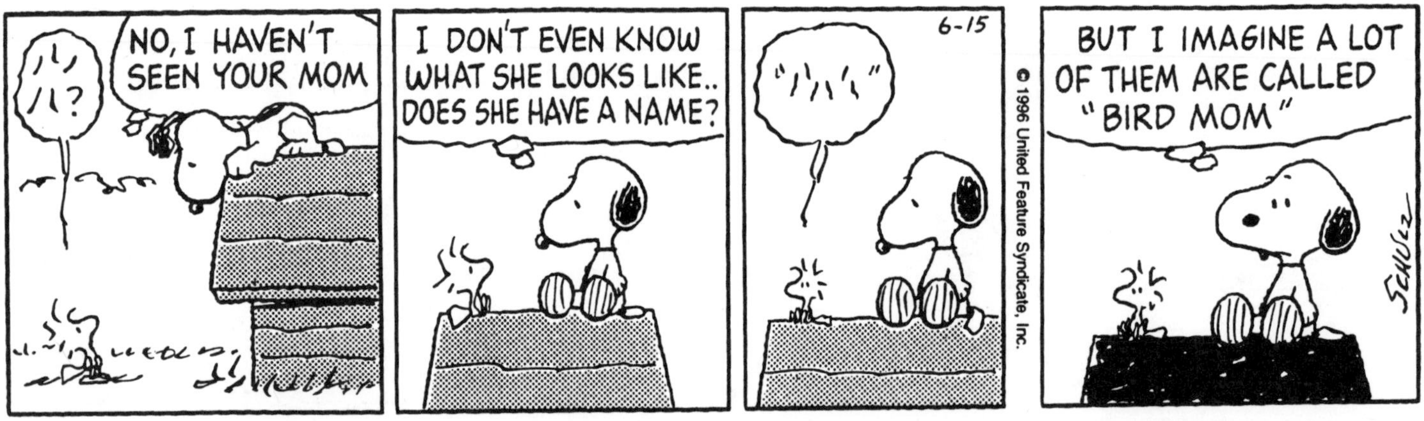
NO, I HAVEN'T SEEN YOUR MOM
I DON'T EVEN KNOW WHAT SHE LOOKS LIKE.. DOES SHE HAVE A NAME?
6-15
© 1996 United Feature Syndicate, Inc.
BUT I IMAGINE A LOT OF THEM ARE CALLED "BIRD MOM"
SCHULZ

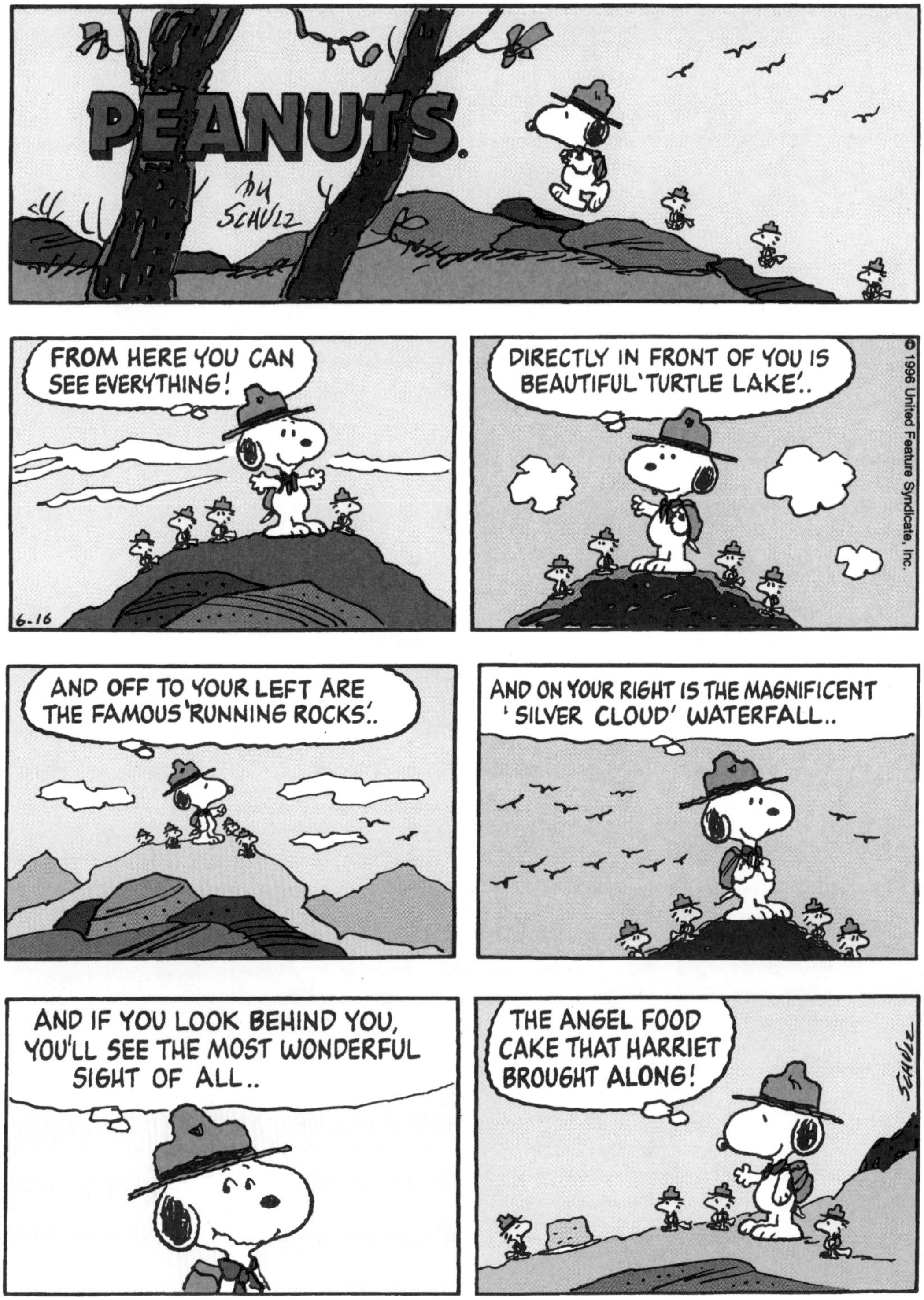
PEANUTS
by SCHULZ
FROM HERE YOU CAN SEE EVERYTHING!
6-16
DIRECTLY IN FRONT OF YOU IS BEAUTIFUL 'TURTLE LAKE'..
© 1996 United Feature Syndicate, Inc.
AND OFF TO YOUR LEFT ARE THE FAMOUS 'RUNNING ROCKS'..
AND ON YOUR RIGHT IS THE MAGNIFICENT 'SILVER CLOUD' WATERFALL..
AND IF YOU LOOK BEHIND YOU, YOU'LL SEE THE MOST WONDERFUL SIGHT OF ALL..
THE ANGEL FOOD CAKE THAT HARRIET BROUGHT ALONG!
SCHULZ

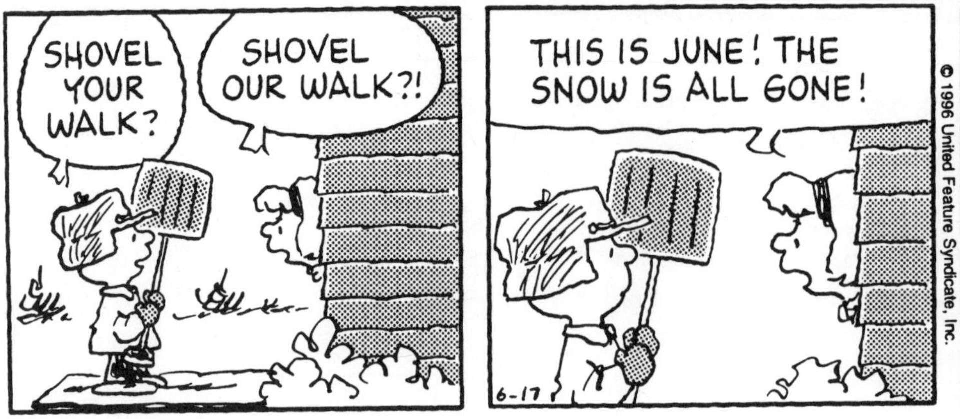
SHOVEL YOUR WALK?
SHOVEL OUR WALK?!
THIS IS JUNE! THE SNOW IS ALL GONE!
6-17
© 1996 United Feature Syndicate, Inc.
I WAS HOPING YOU HADN'T NOTICED..

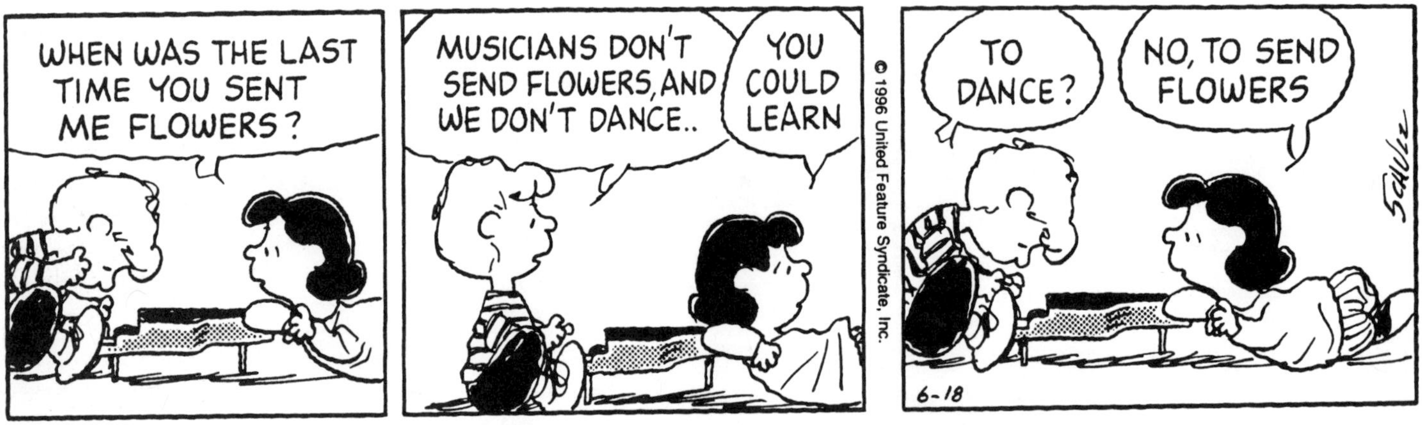
WHEN WAS THE LAST TIME YOU SENT ME FLOWERS?
MUSICIANS DON'T SEND FLOWERS, AND WE DON'T DANCE..
YOU COULD LEARN
© 1996 United Feature Syndicate, Inc.
TO DANCE?
NO, TO SEND FLOWERS
SCHULZ
6-18

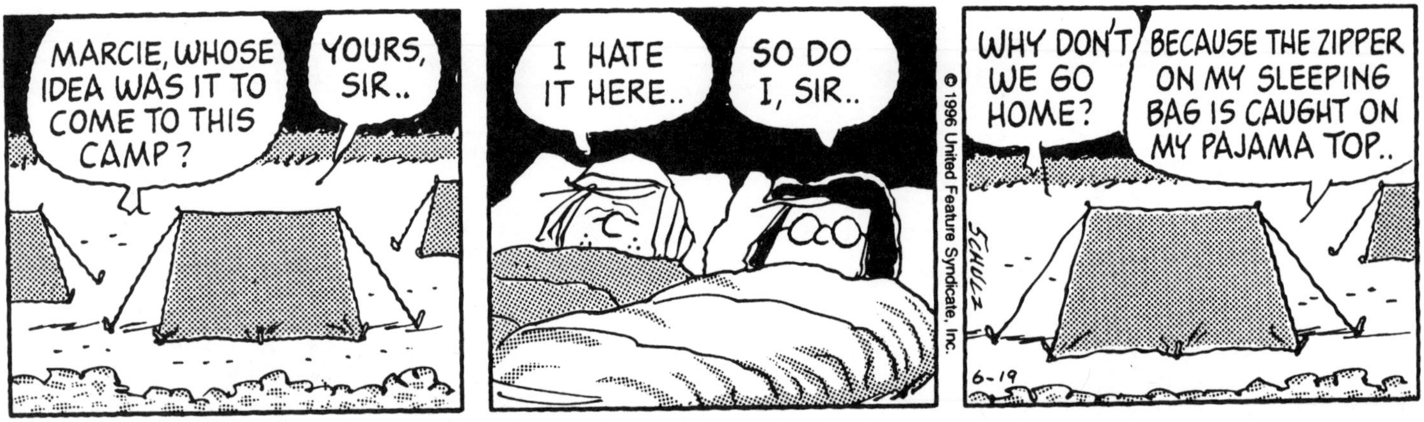
MARCIE, WHOSE IDEA WAS IT TO COME TO THIS CAMP?
YOURS, SIR..
I HATE IT HERE..
SO DO I, SIR..
© 1996 United Feature Syndicate, Inc.
SCHULZ
WHY DON'T WE GO HOME?
BECAUSE THE ZIPPER ON MY SLEEPING BAG IS CAUGHT ON MY PAJAMA TOP..
6-19

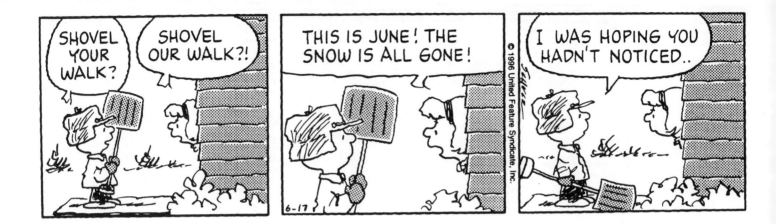

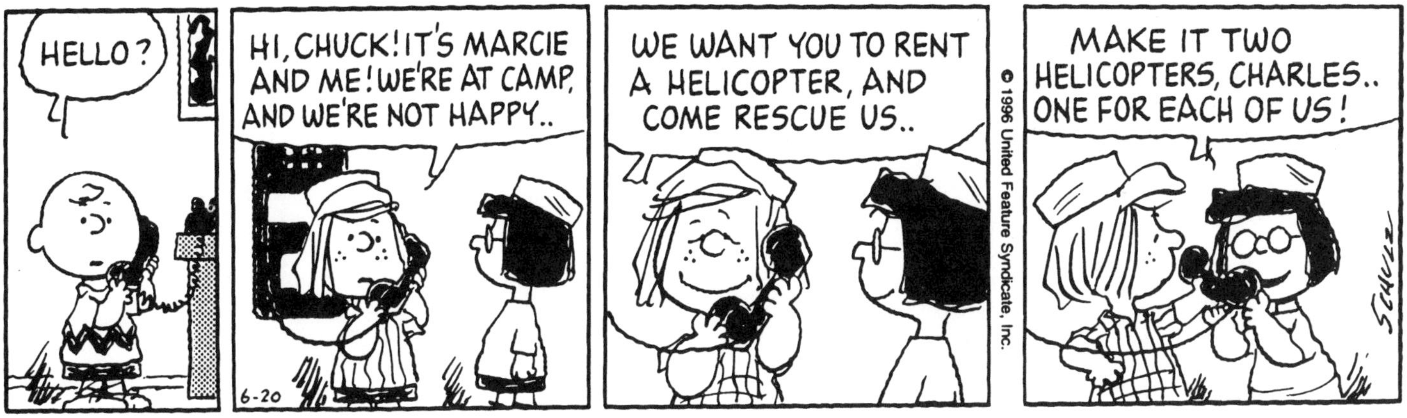
HELLO?
HI, CHUCK! IT'S MARCIE AND ME! WE'RE AT CAMP, AND WE'RE NOT HAPPY..
6-20
WE WANT YOU TO RENT A HELICOPTER, AND COME RESCUE US..
© 1996 United Feature Syndicate, Inc.
MAKE IT TWO HELICOPTERS, CHARLES.. ONE FOR EACH OF US!
SCHULZ

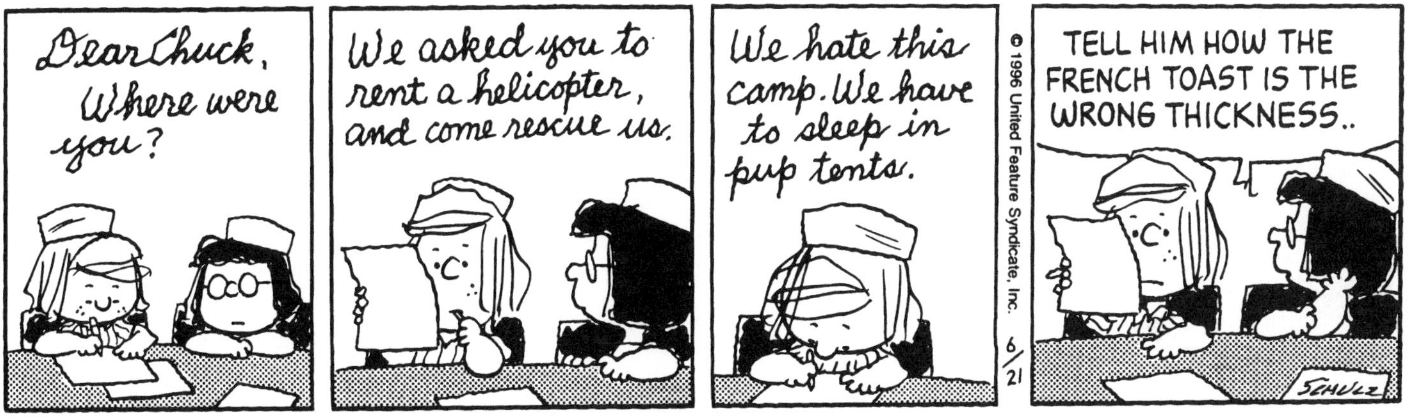
Dear Chuck, Where were you?
We asked you to rent a helicopter, and come rescue us.
We hate this camp. We have to sleep in pup tents.
© 1996 United Feature Syndicate, Inc.
6/21
TELL HIM HOW THE FRENCH TOAST IS THE WRONG THICKNESS..
SCHULZ

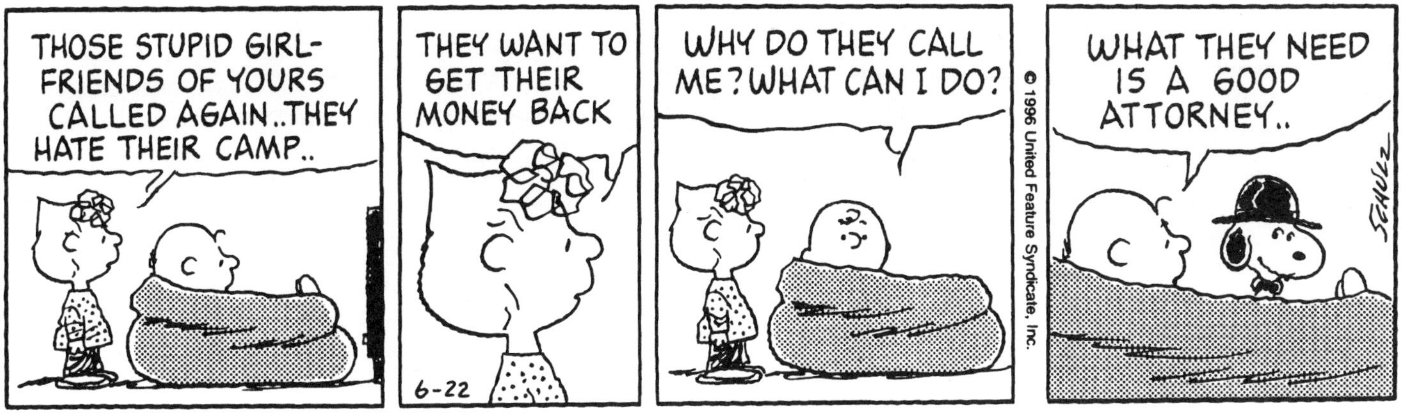
THOSE STUPID GIRL-FRIENDS OF YOURS CALLED AGAIN..THEY HATE THEIR CAMP..
THEY WANT TO GET THEIR MONEY BACK
6-22
WHY DO THEY CALL ME? WHAT CAN I DO?
© 1996 United Feature Syndicate, Inc.
WHAT THEY NEED IS A GOOD ATTORNEY..
SCHULZ

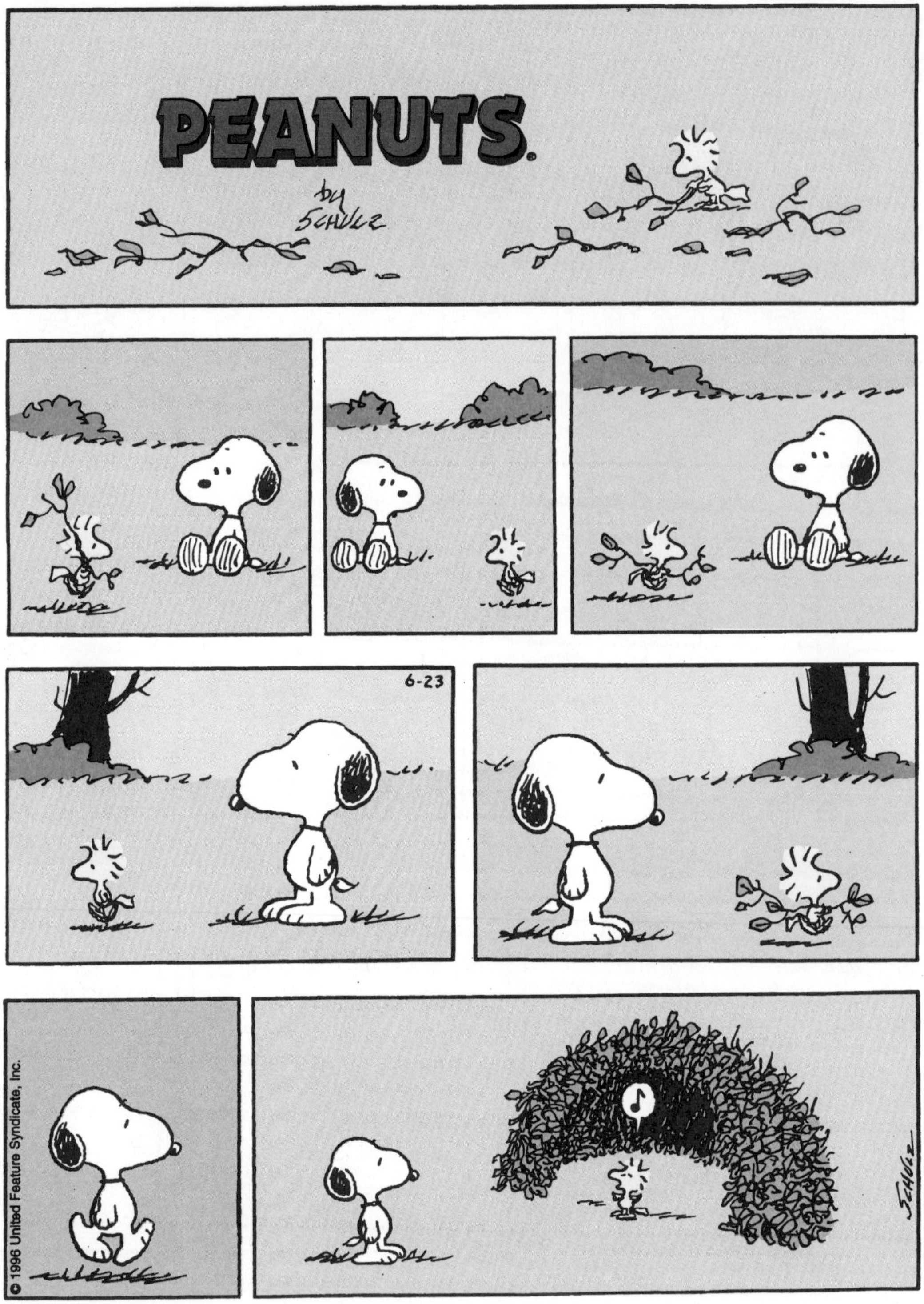
PEANUTS
by SCHULZ
6-23
© 1996 United Feature Syndicate, Inc.
SCHULZ

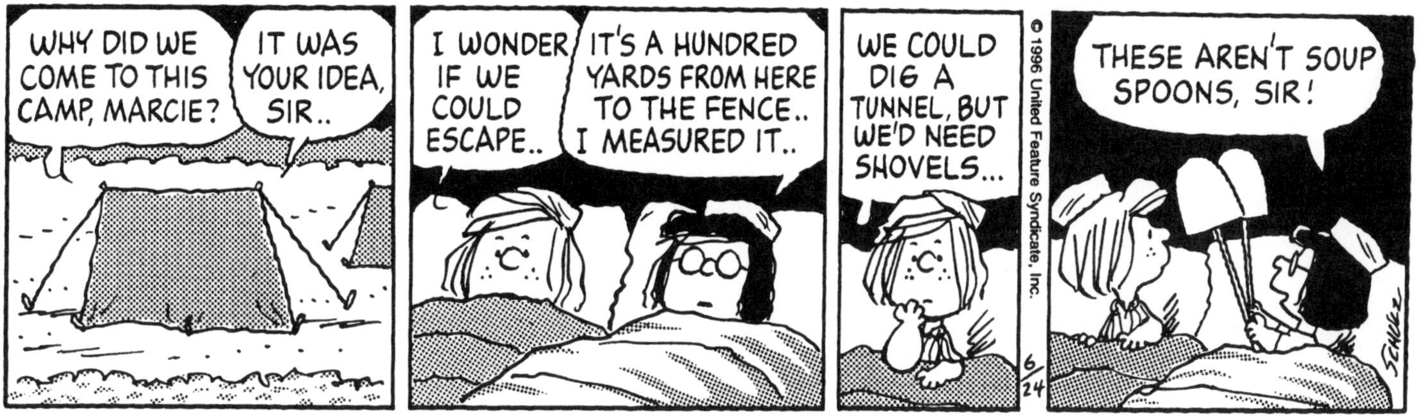
WHY DID WE COME TO THIS CAMP, MARCIE?
IT WAS YOUR IDEA, SIR..
I WONDER IF WE COULD ESCAPE..
IT'S A HUNDRED YARDS FROM HERE TO THE FENCE.. I MEASURED IT..
WE COULD DIG A TUNNEL, BUT WE'D NEED SHOVELS...
© 1996 United Feature Syndicate, Inc.
6/24
THESE AREN'T SOUP SPOONS, SIR!

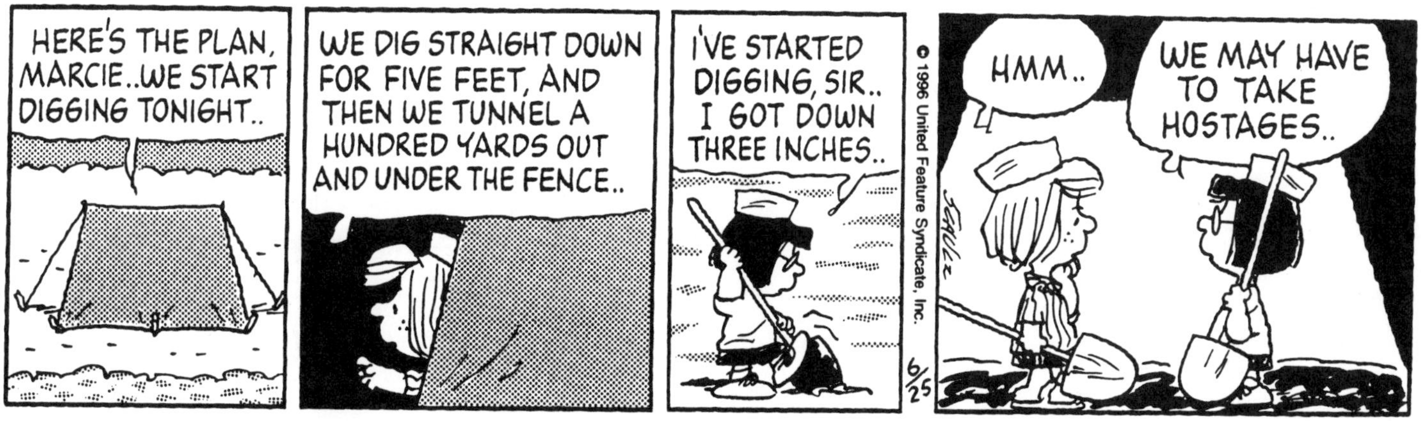
HERE'S THE PLAN, MARCIE..WE START DIGGING TONIGHT..
WE DIG STRAIGHT DOWN FOR FIVE FEET, AND THEN WE TUNNEL A HUNDRED YARDS OUT AND UNDER THE FENCE..
I'VE STARTED DIGGING, SIR.. I GOT DOWN THREE INCHES..
© 1996 United Feature Syndicate, Inc.
6/25
HMM..
WE MAY HAVE TO TAKE HOSTAGES..

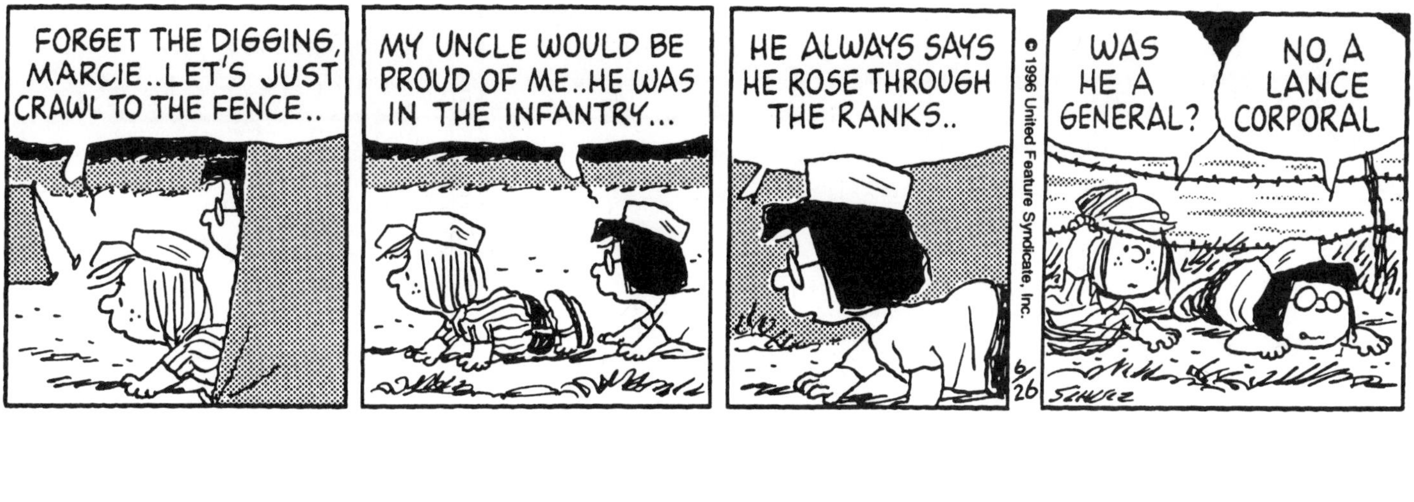
FORGET THE DIGGING, MARCIE..LET'S JUST CRAWL TO THE FENCE..
MY UNCLE WOULD BE PROUD OF ME..HE WAS IN THE INFANTRY...
HE ALWAYS SAYS HE ROSE THROUGH THE RANKS..
© 1996 United Feature Syndicate, Inc.
6/26
WAS HE A GENERAL?
NO, A LANCE CORPORAL

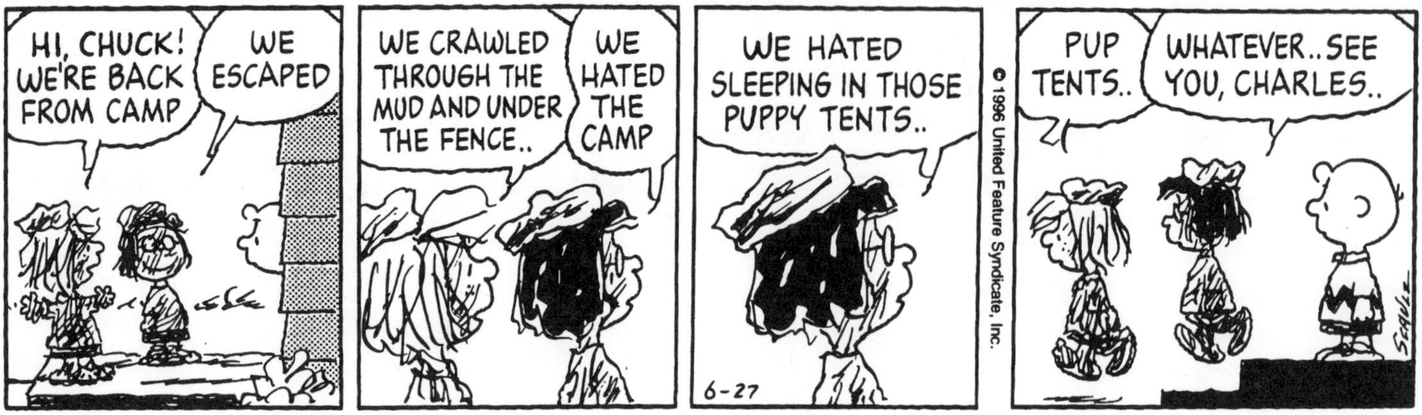
HI, CHUCK! WE'RE BACK FROM CAMP
WE ESCAPED
WE CRAWLED THROUGH THE MUD AND UNDER THE FENCE..
WE HATED THE CAMP
WE HATED SLEEPING IN THOSE PUPPY TENTS..
6-27
© 1996 United Feature Syndicate, Inc.
PUP TENTS..
WHATEVER..SEE YOU, CHARLES..
SCHULZ

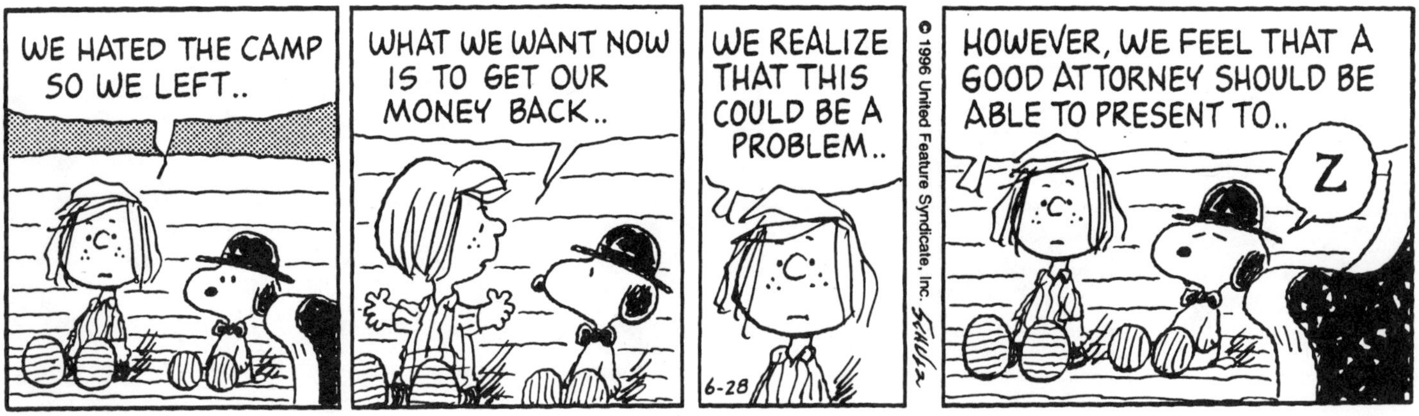
WE HATED THE CAMP SO WE LEFT..
WHAT WE WANT NOW IS TO GET OUR MONEY BACK..
WE REALIZE THAT THIS COULD BE A PROBLEM..
6-28
© 1996 United Feature Syndicate, Inc.
SCHULZ
HOWEVER, WE FEEL THAT A GOOD ATTORNEY SHOULD BE ABLE TO PRESENT TO..
Z

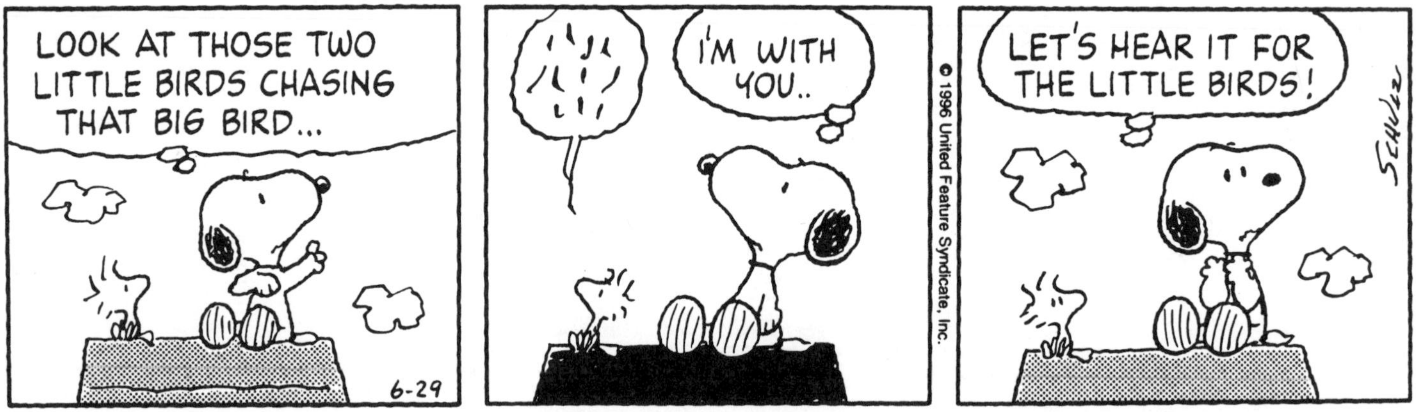
LOOK AT THOSE TWO LITTLE BIRDS CHASING THAT BIG BIRD...
6-29
I'M WITH YOU..
© 1996 United Feature Syndicate, Inc.
LET'S HEAR IT FOR THE LITTLE BIRDS!
SCHULZ

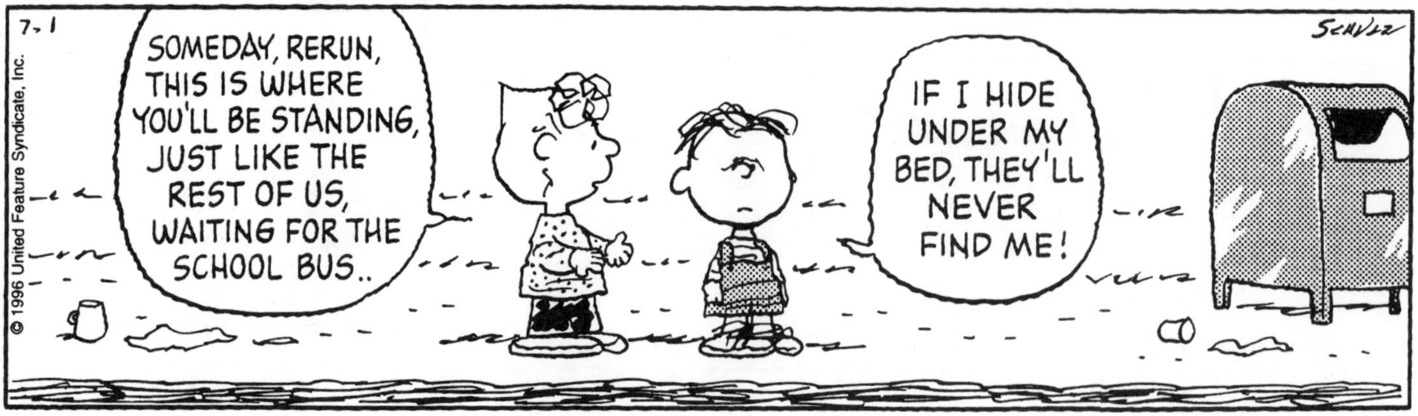
7-1
SOMEDAY, RERUN, THIS IS WHERE YOU'LL BE STANDING, JUST LIKE THE REST OF US, WAITING FOR THE SCHOOL BUS..
IF I HIDE UNDER MY BED, THEY'LL NEVER FIND ME!
© 1996 United Feature Syndicate, Inc.

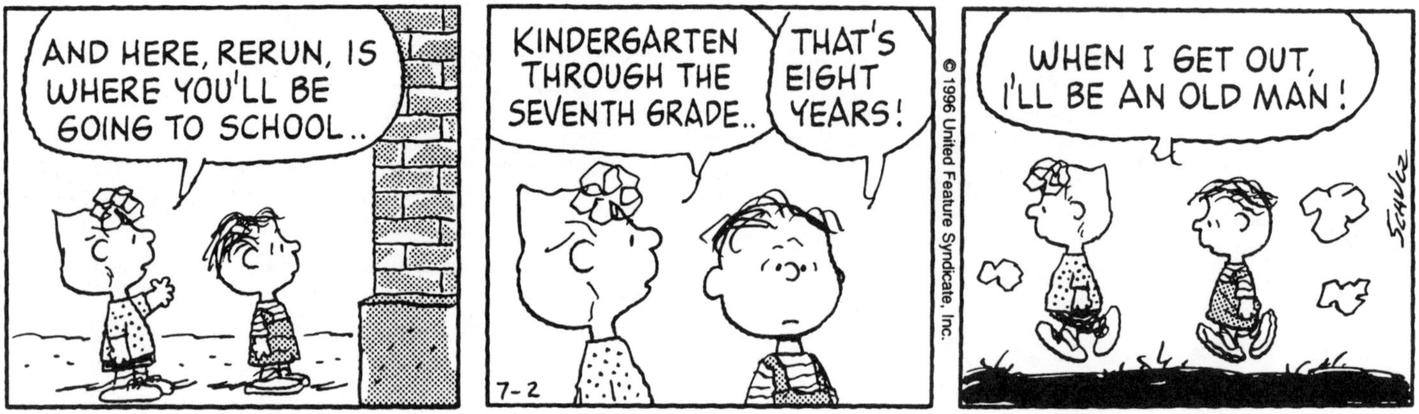
AND HERE, RERUN, IS WHERE YOU'LL BE GOING TO SCHOOL..
KINDERGARTEN THROUGH THE SEVENTH GRADE..
THAT'S EIGHT YEARS!
WHEN I GET OUT, I'LL BE AN OLD MAN!
7-2
© 1996 United Feature Syndicate, Inc.

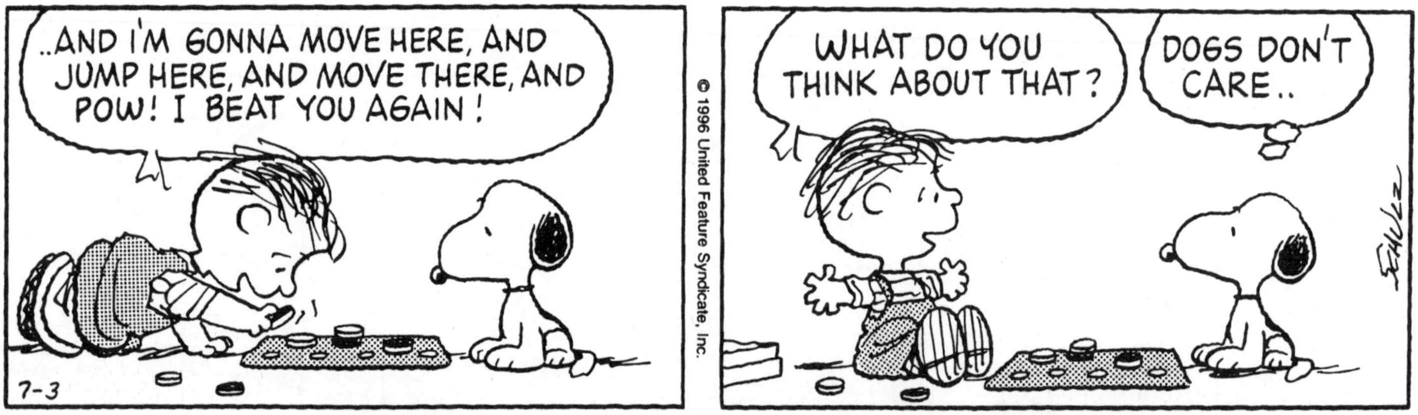
..AND I'M GONNA MOVE HERE, AND JUMP HERE, AND MOVE THERE, AND POW! I BEAT YOU AGAIN!
WHAT DO YOU THINK ABOUT THAT?
DOGS DON'T CARE..
7-3
© 1996 United Feature Syndicate, Inc.

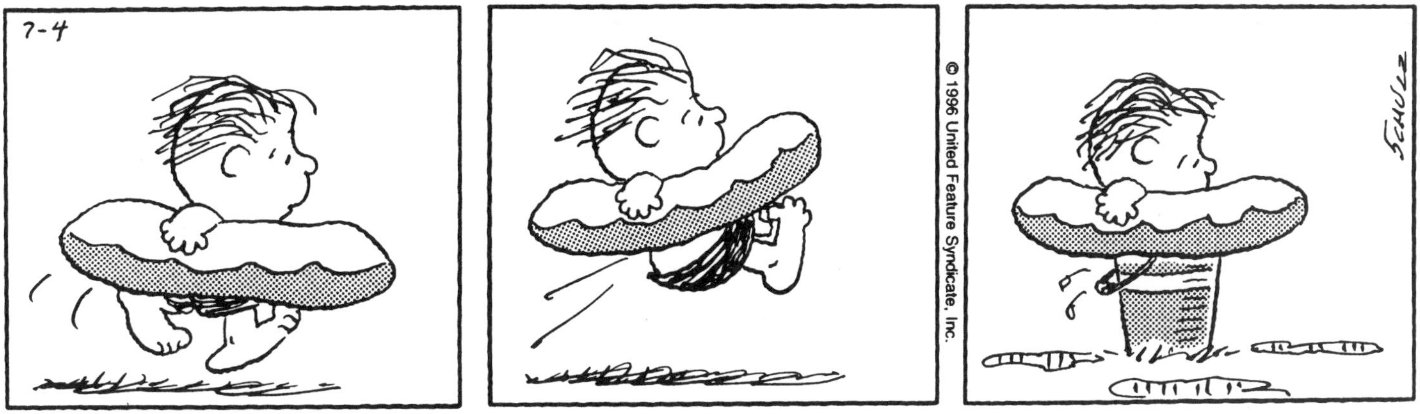
7-4
© 1996 United Feature Syndicate, Inc.
SCHULZ

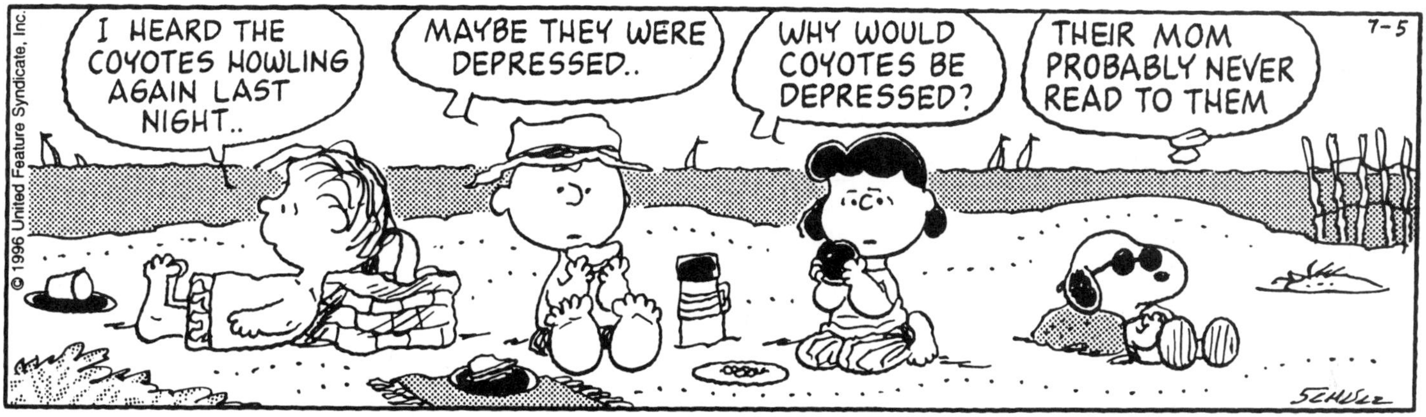
© 1996 United Feature Syndicate, Inc.
I HEARD THE COYOTES HOWLING AGAIN LAST NIGHT..
MAYBE THEY WERE DEPRESSED..
WHY WOULD COYOTES BE DEPRESSED?
7-5
THEIR MOM PROBABLY NEVER READ TO THEM
SCHULZ

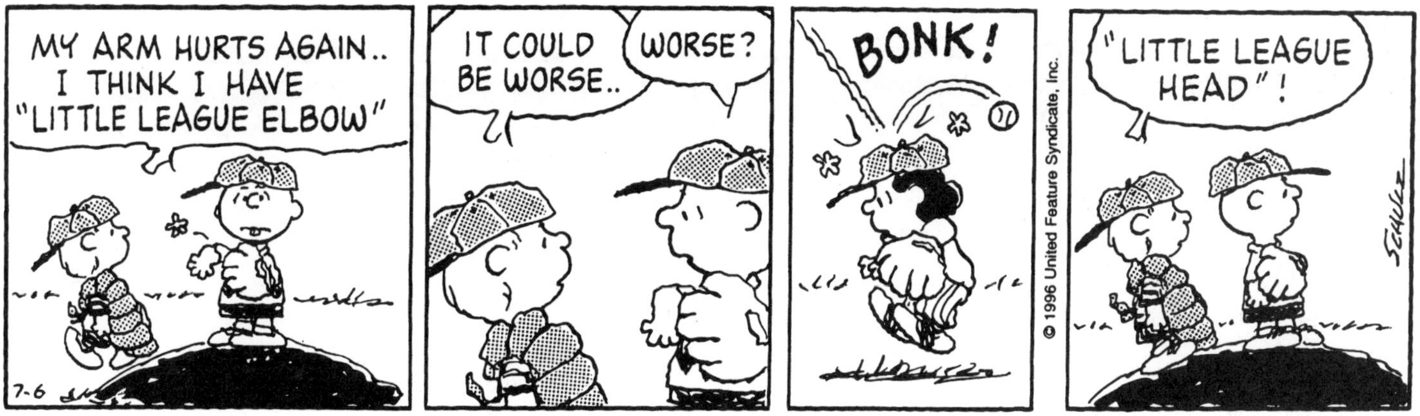
MY ARM HURTS AGAIN.. I THINK I HAVE "LITTLE LEAGUE ELBOW"
7-6
IT COULD BE WORSE..
WORSE?
BONK!
© 1996 United Feature Syndicate, Inc.
"LITTLE LEAGUE HEAD"!
SCHULZ

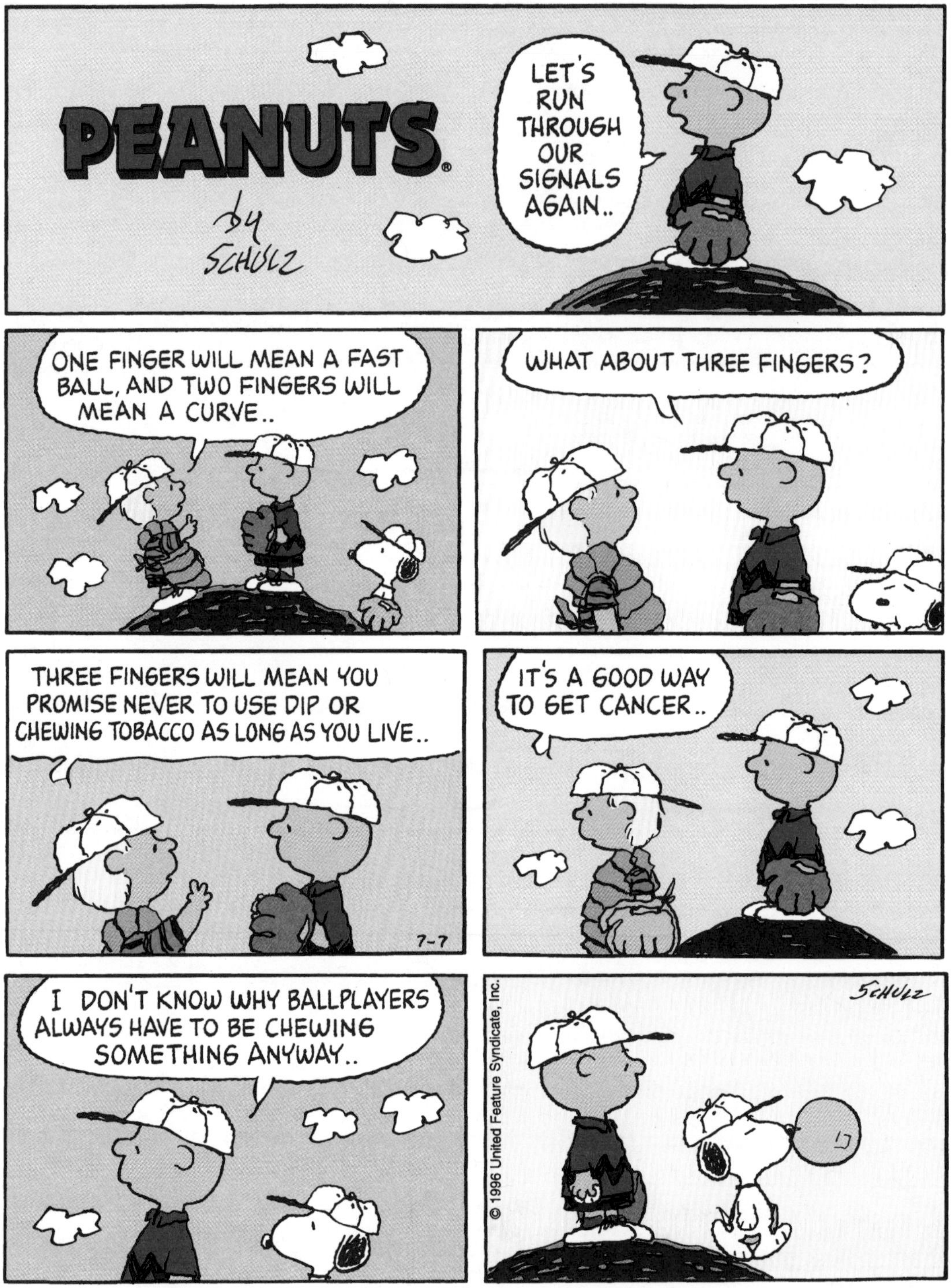
PEANUTS
by SCHULZ
LET'S RUN THROUGH OUR SIGNALS AGAIN..
ONE FINGER WILL MEAN A FAST BALL, AND TWO FINGERS WILL MEAN A CURVE..
WHAT ABOUT THREE FINGERS?
THREE FINGERS WILL MEAN YOU PROMISE NEVER TO USE DIP OR CHEWING TOBACCO AS LONG AS YOU LIVE..
7-7
IT'S A GOOD WAY TO GET CANCER..
I DON'T KNOW WHY BALLPLAYERS ALWAYS HAVE TO BE CHEWING SOMETHING ANYWAY..
SCHULZ
© 1996 United Feature Syndicate, Inc.

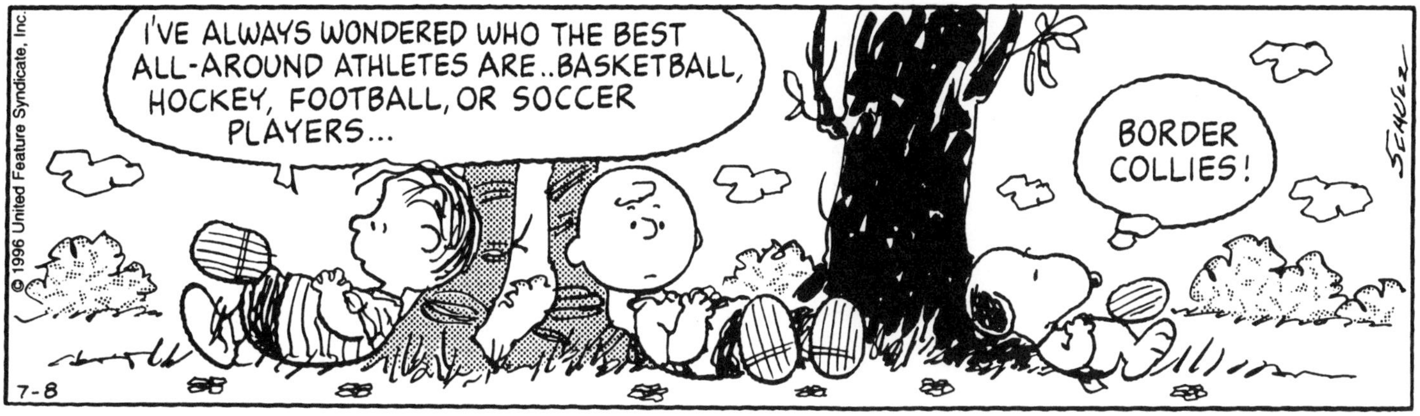
© 1996 United Feature Syndicate, Inc.
I'VE ALWAYS WONDERED WHO THE BEST ALL-AROUND ATHLETES ARE..BASKETBALL, HOCKEY, FOOTBALL, OR SOCCER PLAYERS...
BORDER COLLIES!
7-8

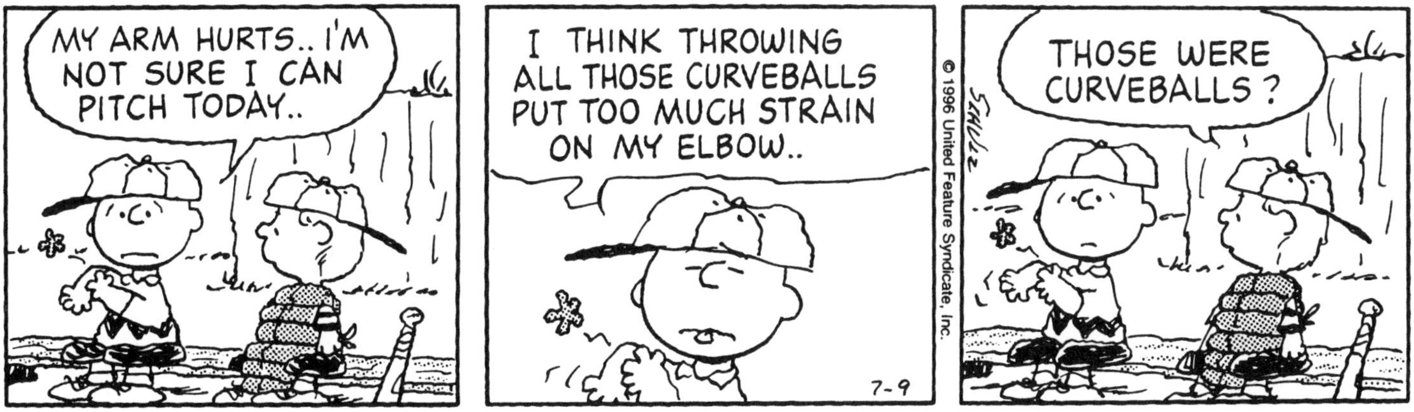
MY ARM HURTS.. I'M NOT SURE I CAN PITCH TODAY..
I THINK THROWING ALL THOSE CURVEBALLS PUT TOO MUCH STRAIN ON MY ELBOW..
© 1996 United Feature Syndicate, Inc.
7-9
THOSE WERE CURVEBALLS?

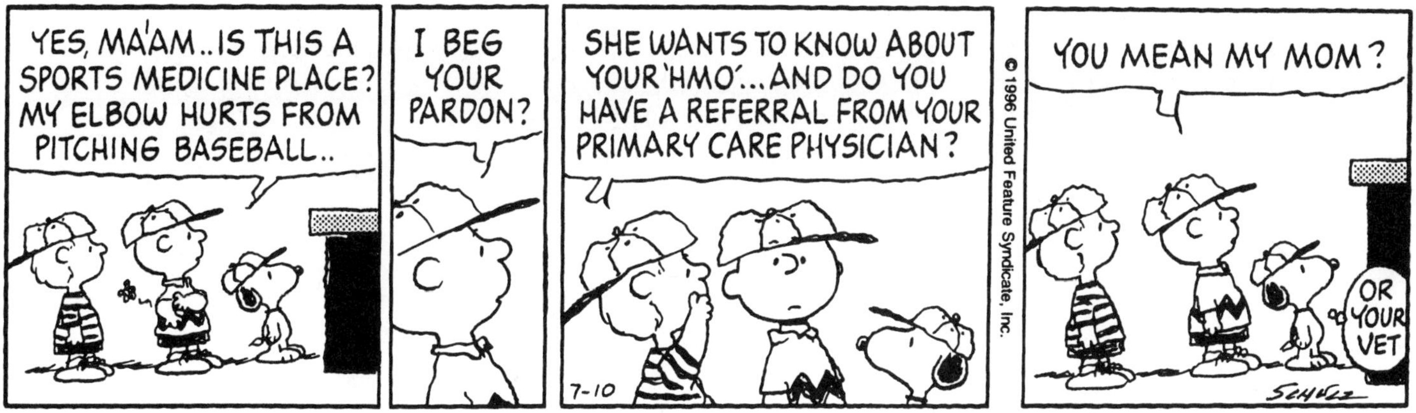
YES, MA'AM..IS THIS A SPORTS MEDICINE PLACE? MY ELBOW HURTS FROM PITCHING BASEBALL..
I BEG YOUR PARDON?
SHE WANTS TO KNOW ABOUT YOUR 'HMO'...AND DO YOU HAVE A REFERRAL FROM YOUR PRIMARY CARE PHYSICIAN?
7-10
© 1996 United Feature Syndicate, Inc.
YOU MEAN MY MOM?
OR YOUR VET

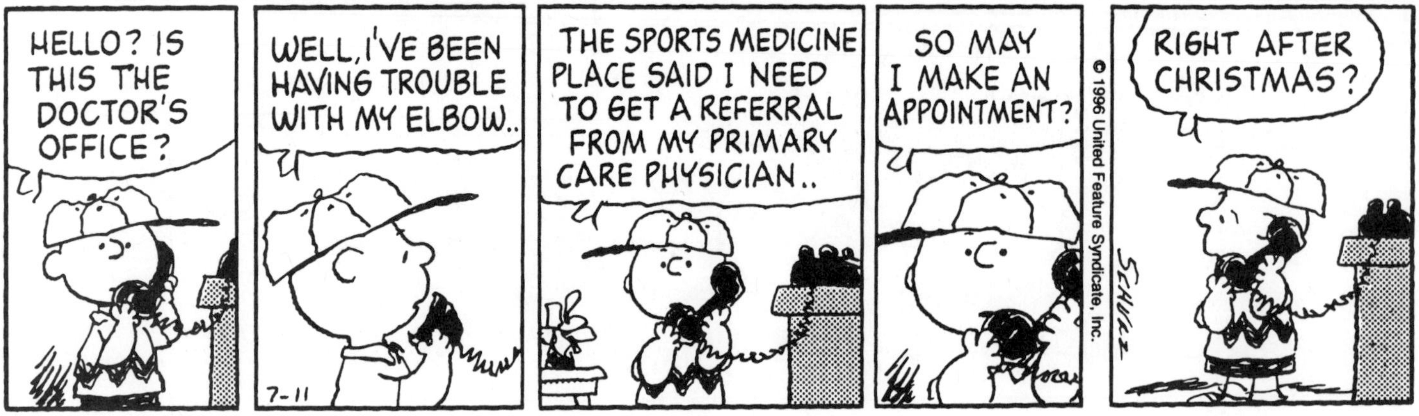
HELLO? IS THIS THE DOCTOR'S OFFICE?
WELL, I'VE BEEN HAVING TROUBLE WITH MY ELBOW..
THE SPORTS MEDICINE PLACE SAID I NEED TO GET A REFERRAL FROM MY PRIMARY CARE PHYSICIAN..
SO MAY I MAKE AN APPOINTMENT?
© 1996 United Feature Syndicate, Inc.
RIGHT AFTER CHRISTMAS?

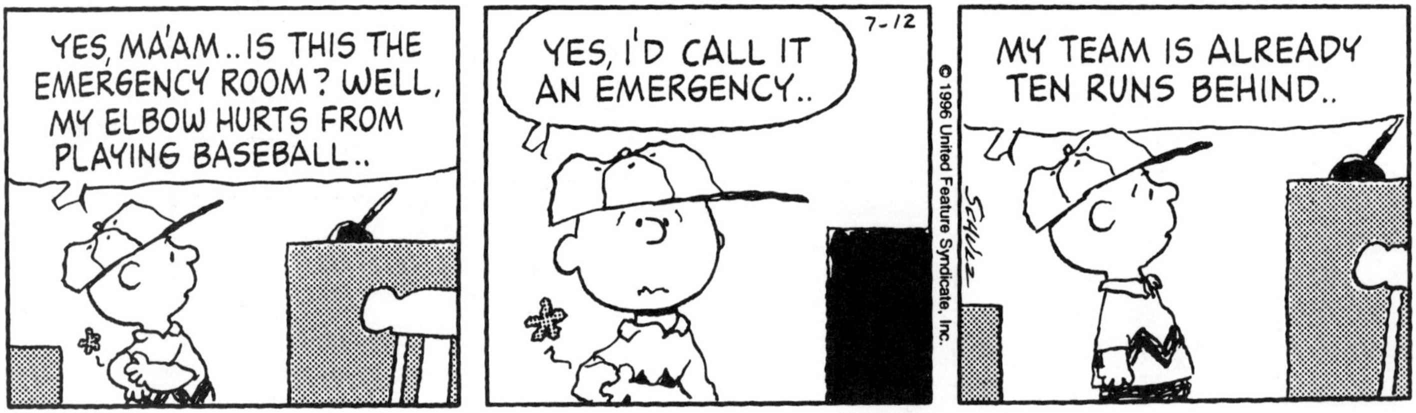
YES, MA'AM..IS THIS THE EMERGENCY ROOM? WELL, MY ELBOW HURTS FROM PLAYING BASEBALL..
YES, I'D CALL IT AN EMERGENCY..
© 1996 United Feature Syndicate, Inc.
MY TEAM IS ALREADY TEN RUNS BEHIND..

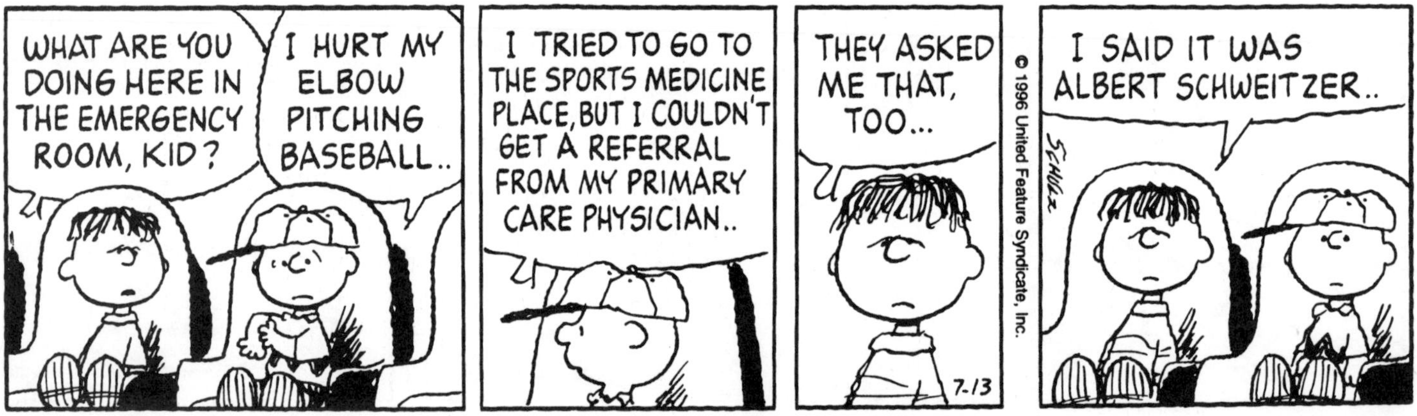
WHAT ARE YOU DOING HERE IN THE EMERGENCY ROOM, KID?
I HURT MY ELBOW PITCHING BASEBALL..
I TRIED TO GO TO THE SPORTS MEDICINE PLACE, BUT I COULDN'T GET A REFERRAL FROM MY PRIMARY CARE PHYSICIAN..
THEY ASKED ME THAT, TOO...
© 1996 United Feature Syndicate, Inc.
I SAID IT WAS ALBERT SCHWEITZER..

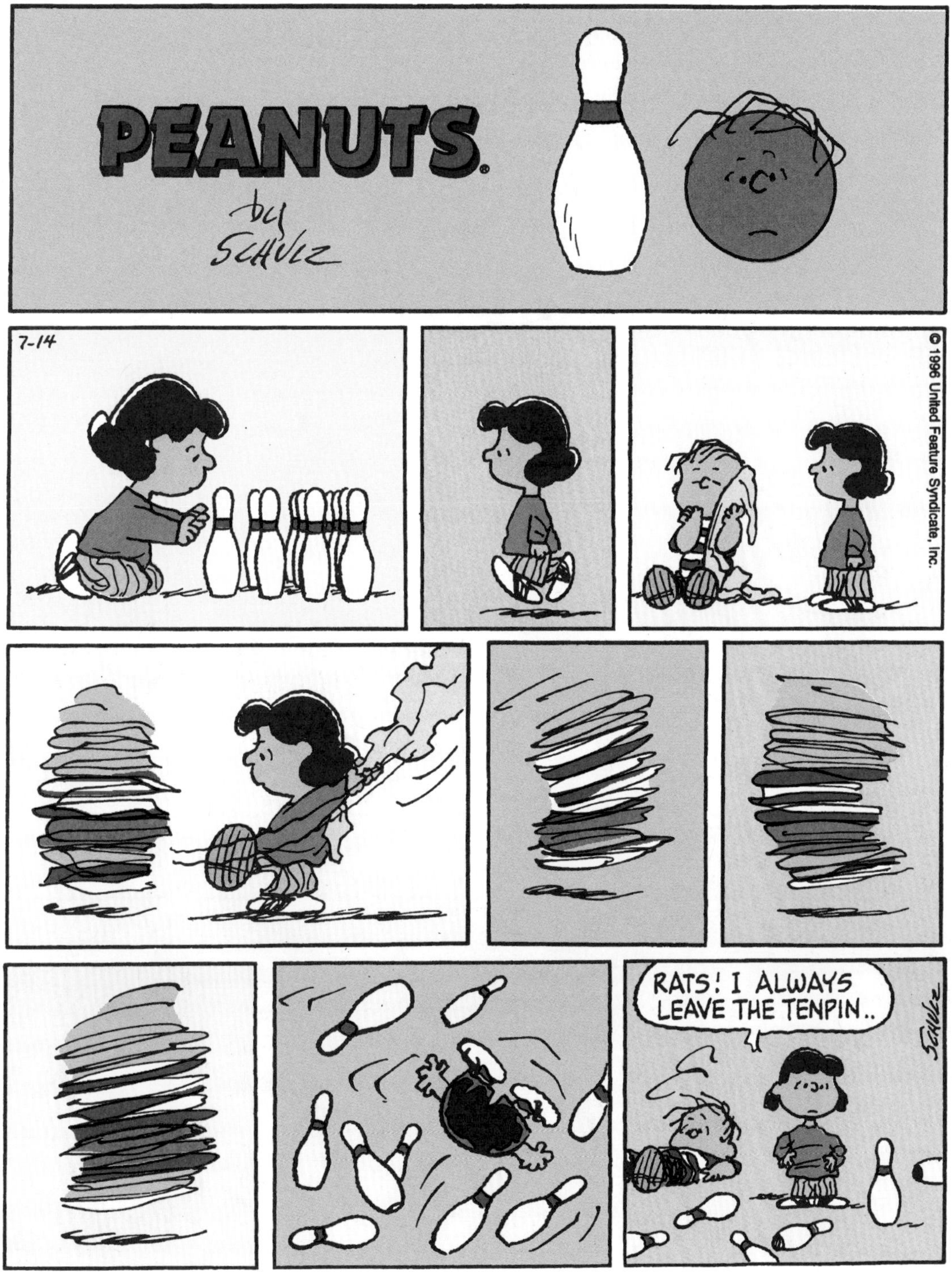
PEANUTS
by SCHULZ
7-14
© 1996 United Feature Syndicate, Inc.
RATS! I ALWAYS LEAVE THE TENPIN..
SCHULZ

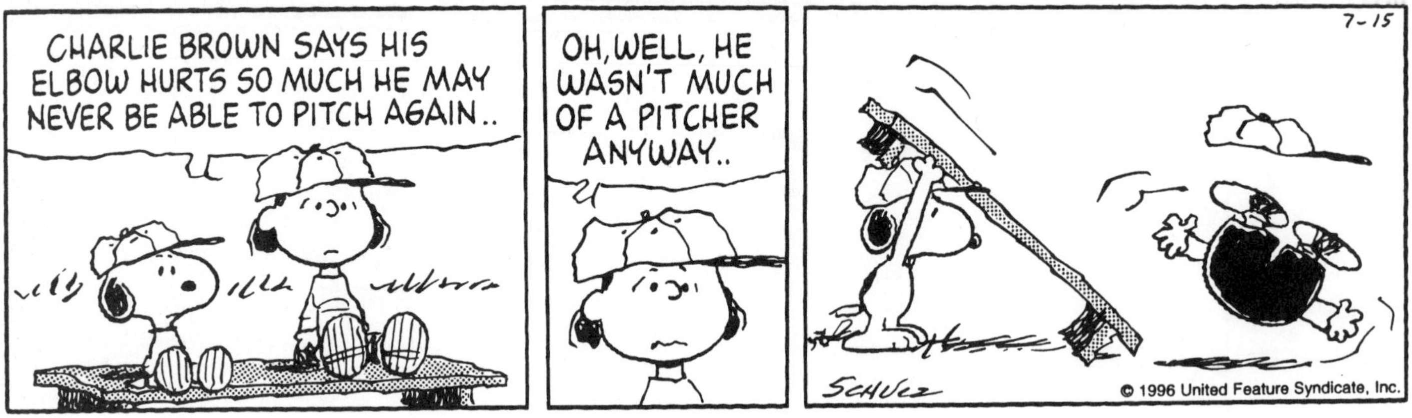
7-15
CHARLIE BROWN SAYS HIS ELBOW HURTS SO MUCH HE MAY NEVER BE ABLE TO PITCH AGAIN..
OH, WELL, HE WASN'T MUCH OF A PITCHER ANYWAY..
SCHULZ
© 1996 United Feature Syndicate, Inc.

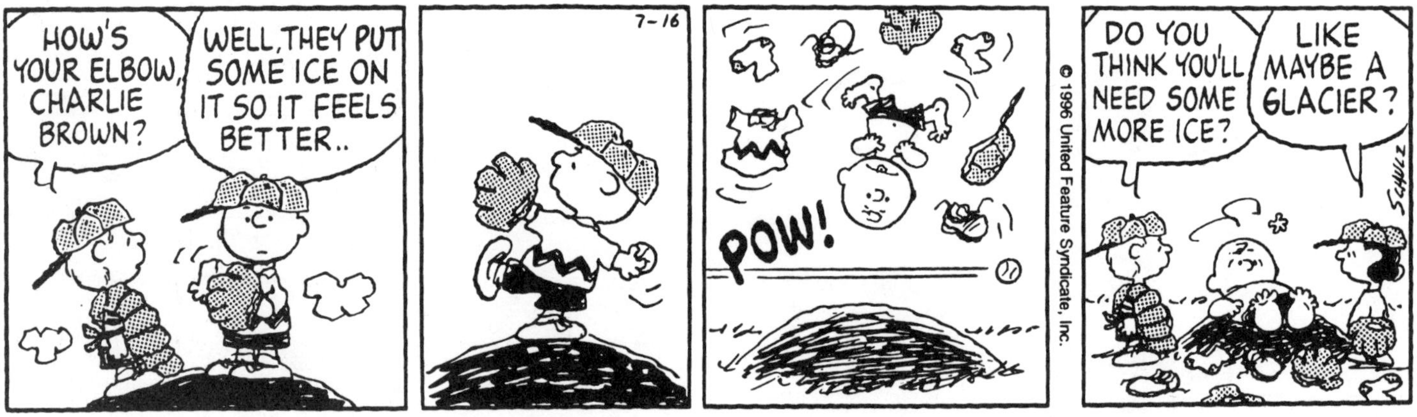
7-16
HOW'S YOUR ELBOW, CHARLIE BROWN?
WELL, THEY PUT SOME ICE ON IT SO IT FEELS BETTER..
POW!
© 1996 United Feature Syndicate, Inc.
DO YOU THINK YOU'LL NEED SOME MORE ICE?
LIKE MAYBE A GLACIER?
SCHULZ

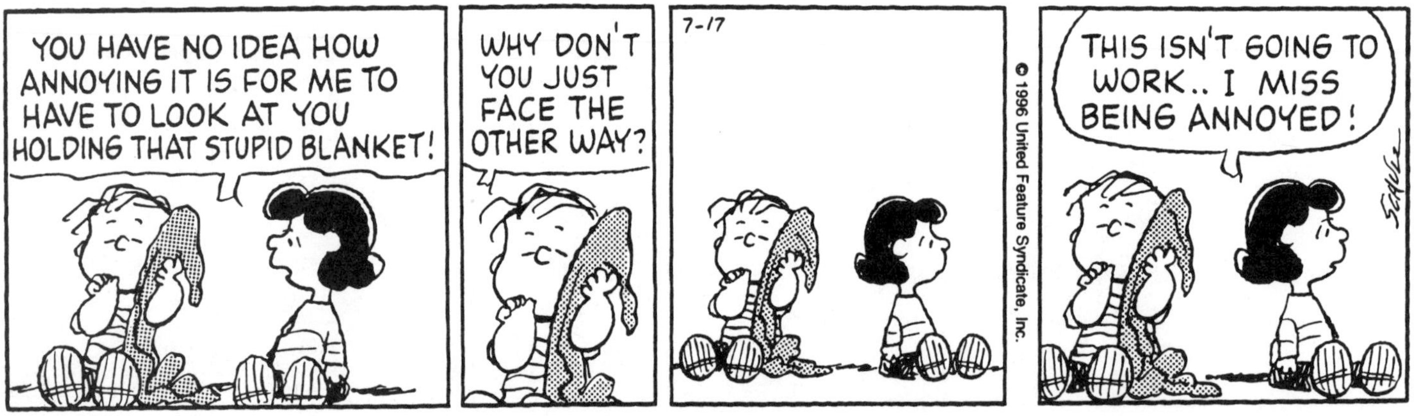
7-17
YOU HAVE NO IDEA HOW ANNOYING IT IS FOR ME TO HAVE TO LOOK AT YOU HOLDING THAT STUPID BLANKET!
WHY DON'T YOU JUST FACE THE OTHER WAY?
© 1996 United Feature Syndicate, Inc.
THIS ISN'T GOING TO WORK.. I MISS BEING ANNOYED!
SCHULZ

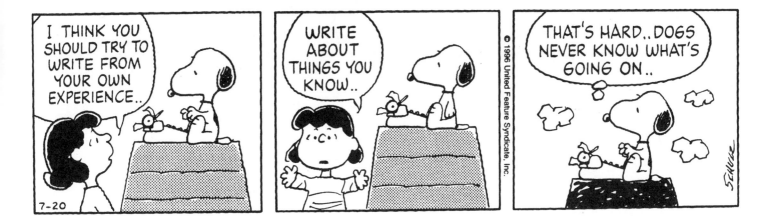

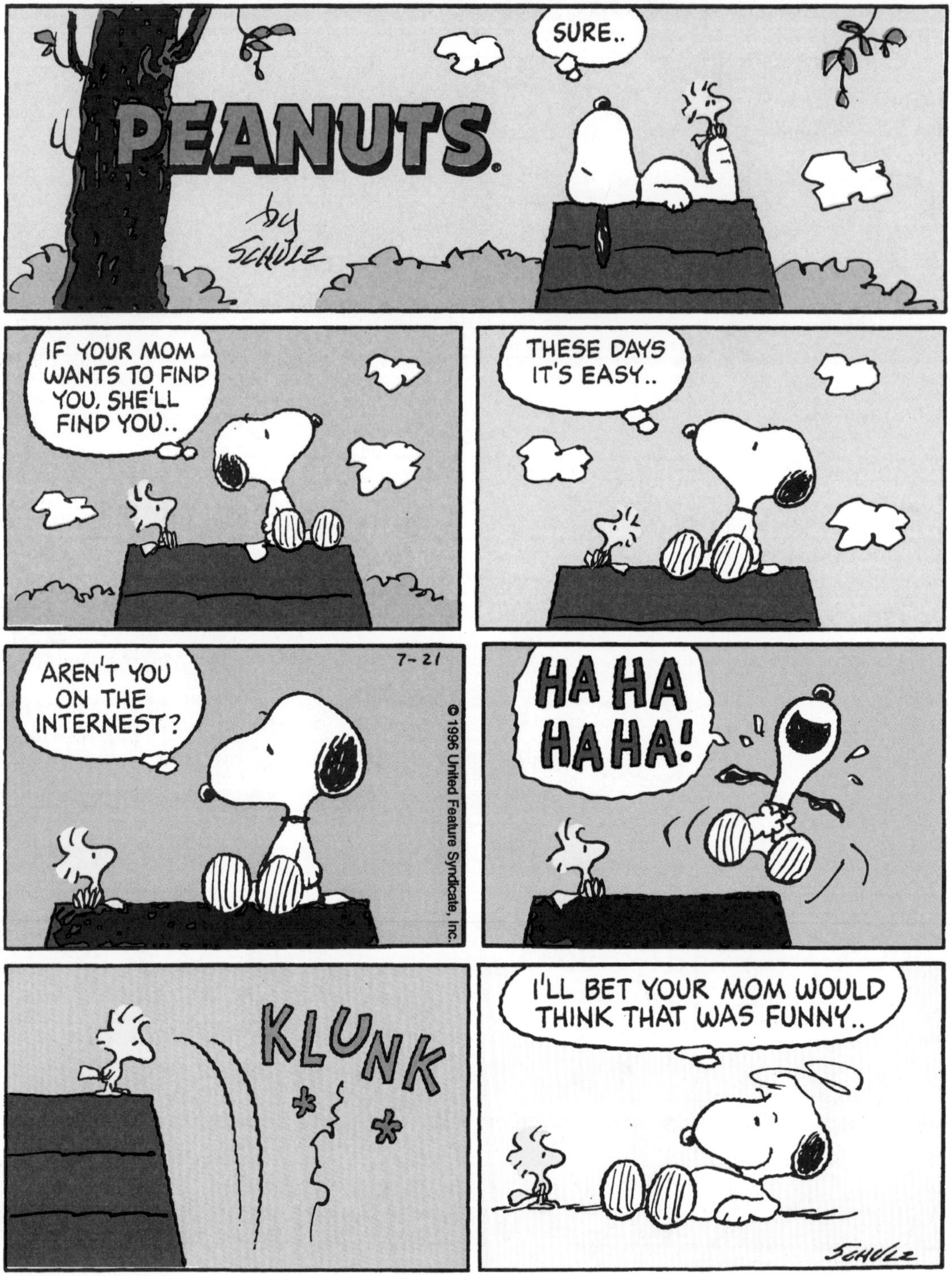
PEANUTS
by SCHULZ
SURE..
IF YOUR MOM WANTS TO FIND YOU, SHE'LL FIND YOU..
THESE DAYS IT'S EASY..
7-21
AREN'T YOU ON THE INTERNEST?
© 1996 United Feature Syndicate, Inc.
HA HA HA HA!
KLUNK
I'LL BET YOUR MOM WOULD THINK THAT WAS FUNNY..
SCHULZ

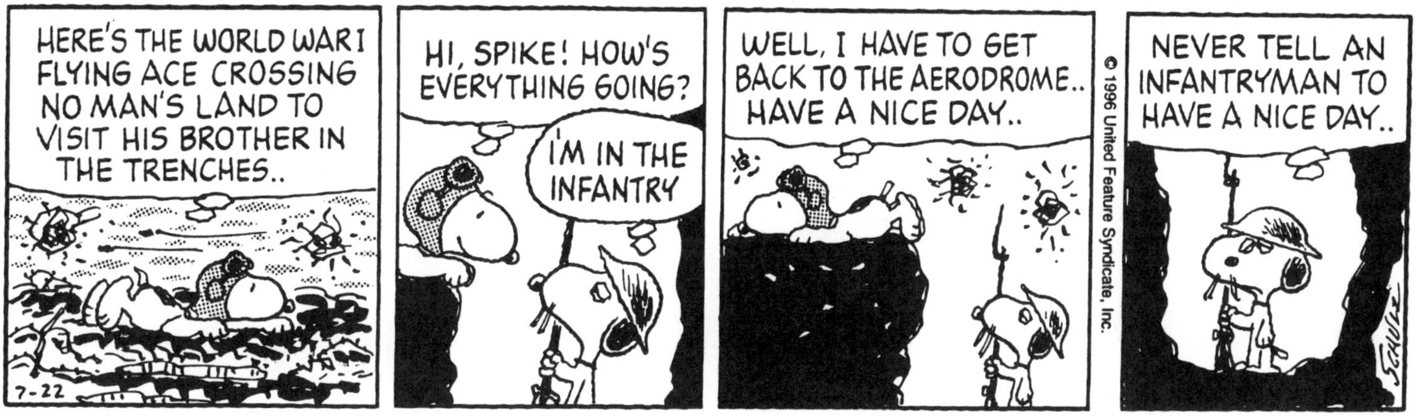
HERE'S THE WORLD WAR I FLYING ACE CROSSING NO MAN'S LAND TO VISIT HIS BROTHER IN THE TRENCHES..
7-22
HI, SPIKE! HOW'S EVERYTHING GOING?
I'M IN THE INFANTRY
WELL, I HAVE TO GET BACK TO THE AERODROME.. HAVE A NICE DAY..
© 1996 United Feature Syndicate, Inc.
NEVER TELL AN INFANTRYMAN TO HAVE A NICE DAY..
SCHULZ

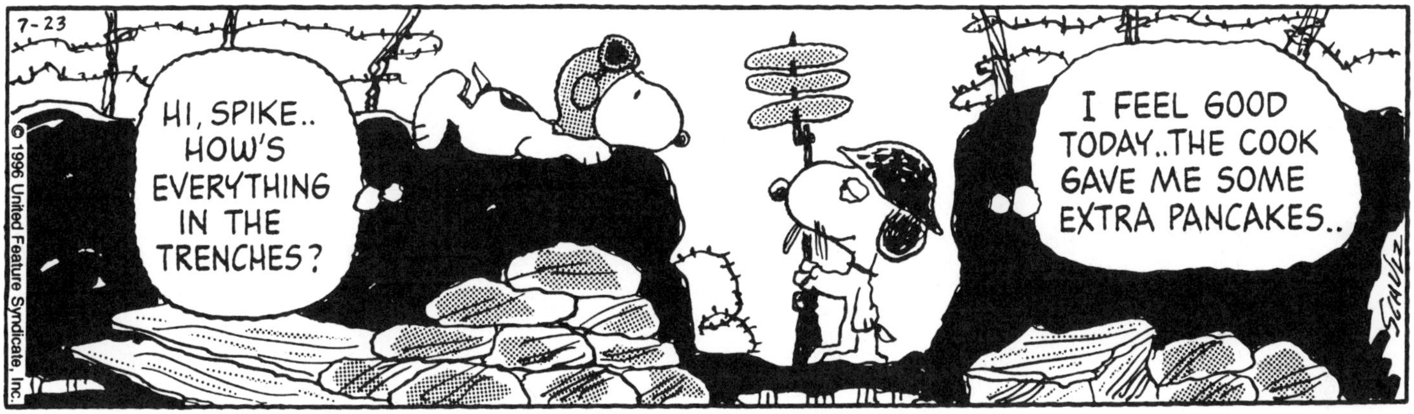
7-23
© 1996 United Feature Syndicate, Inc.
HI, SPIKE.. HOW'S EVERYTHING IN THE TRENCHES?
I FEEL GOOD TODAY..THE COOK GAVE ME SOME EXTRA PANCAKES..
SCHULZ

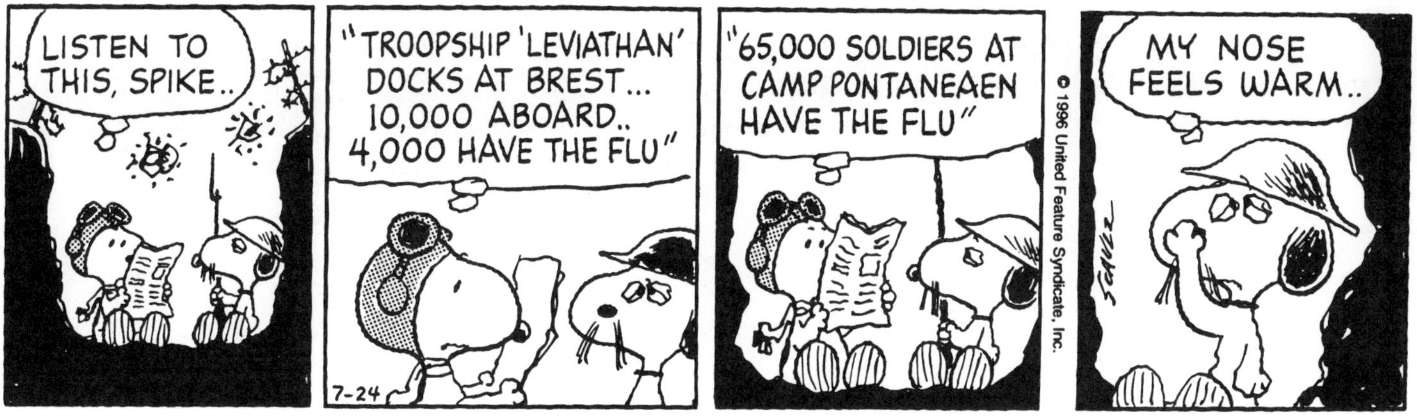
LISTEN TO THIS, SPIKE..
"TROOPSHIP 'LEVIATHAN' DOCKS AT BREST... 10,000 ABOARD.. 4,000 HAVE THE FLU"
7-24
"65,000 SOLDIERS AT CAMP PONTANEAEN HAVE THE FLU"
© 1996 United Feature Syndicate, Inc.
MY NOSE FEELS WARM..
SCHULZ

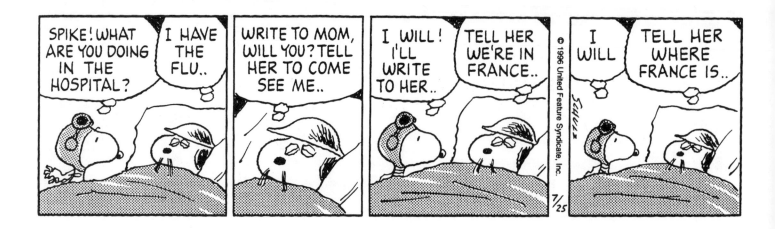

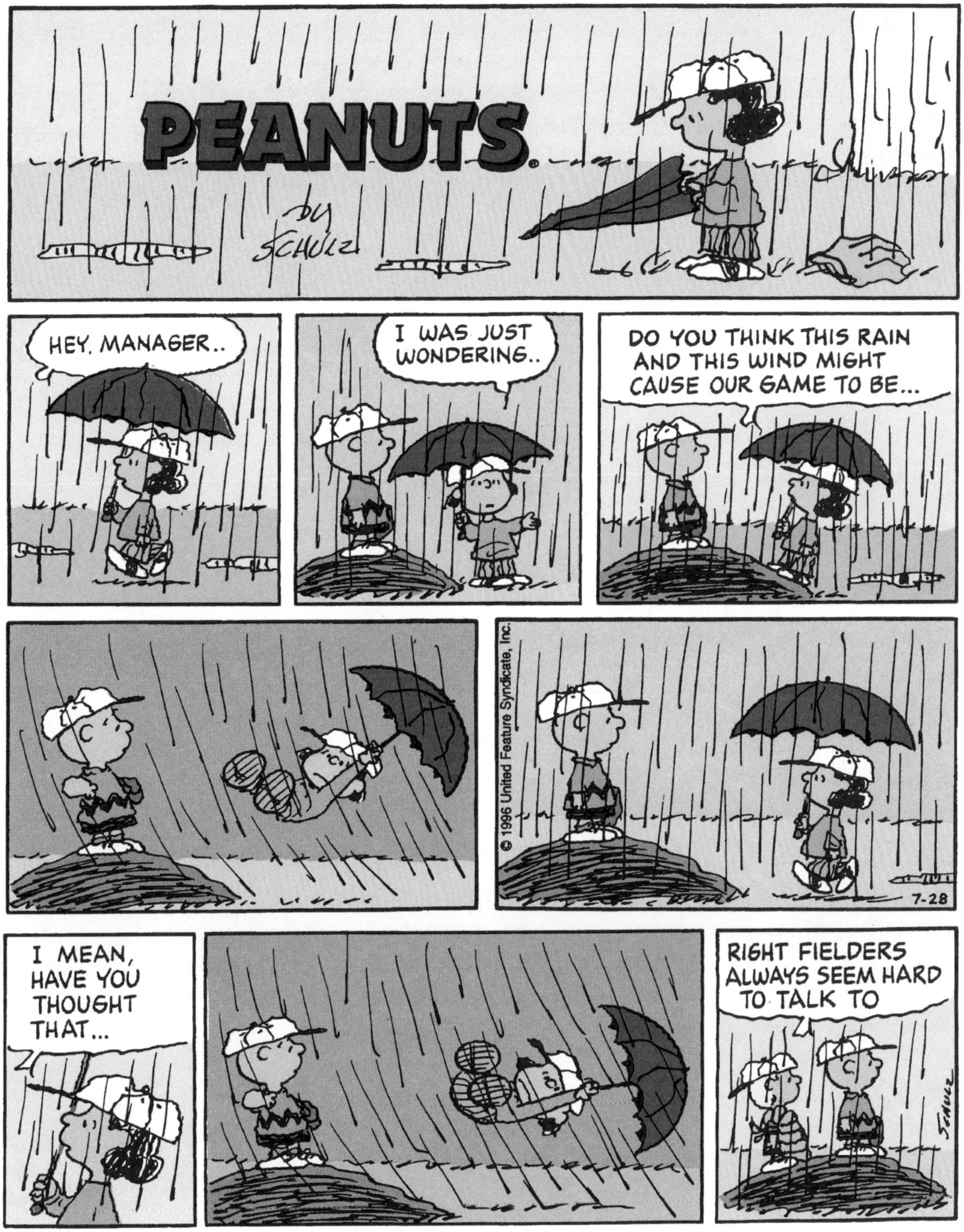
PEANUTS
by Schulz
HEY, MANAGER..
I WAS JUST WONDERING..
DO YOU THINK THIS RAIN AND THIS WIND MIGHT CAUSE OUR GAME TO BE...
© 1996 United Feature Syndicate, Inc.
7-28
I MEAN, HAVE YOU THOUGHT THAT...
RIGHT FIELDERS ALWAYS SEEM HARD TO TALK TO
Schulz

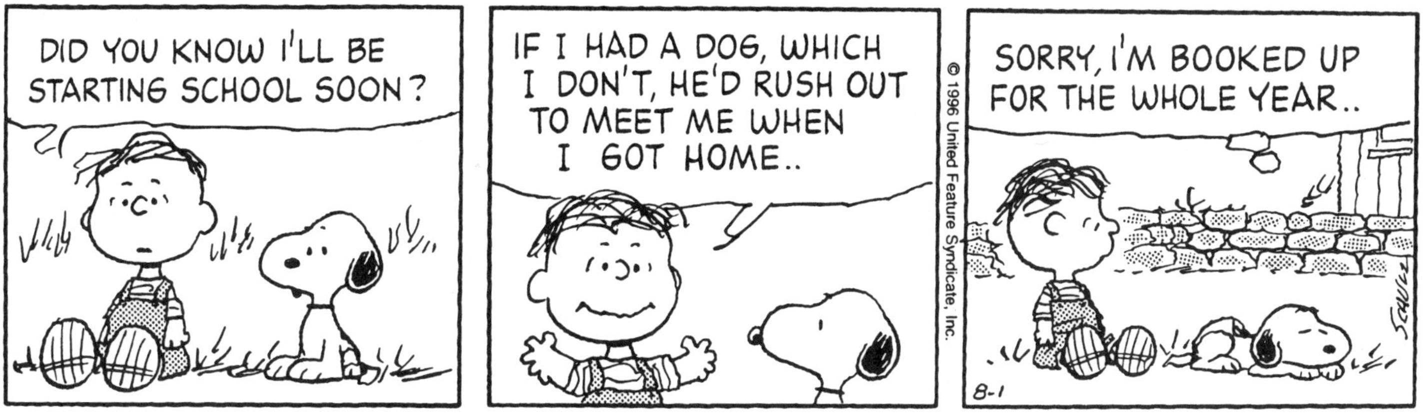
DID YOU KNOW I'LL BE STARTING SCHOOL SOON?
IF I HAD A DOG, WHICH I DON'T, HE'D RUSH OUT TO MEET ME WHEN I GOT HOME..
SORRY, I'M BOOKED UP FOR THE WHOLE YEAR..
SCHULZ
8-1

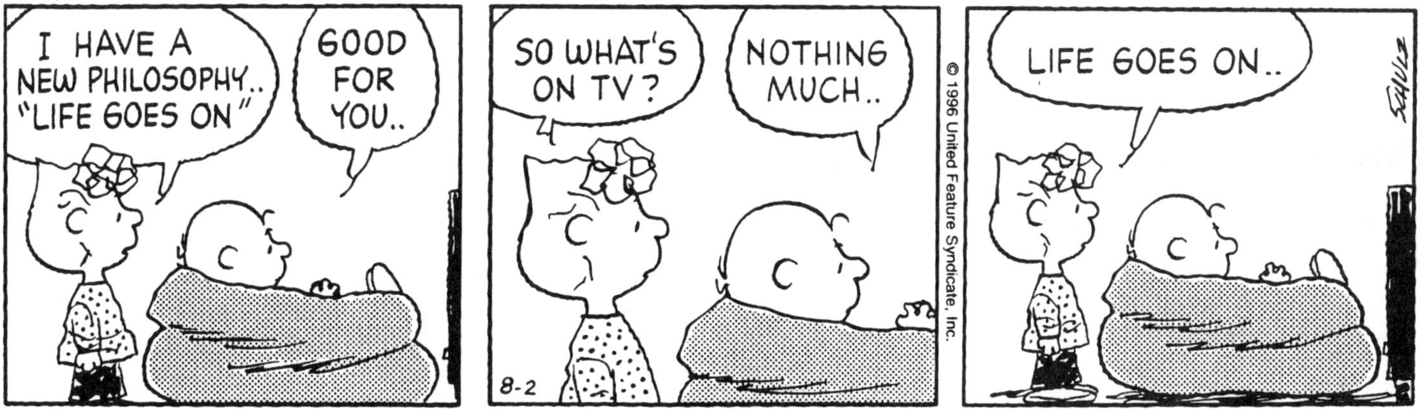
I HAVE A NEW PHILOSOPHY.. "LIFE GOES ON"
GOOD FOR YOU..
SO WHAT'S ON TV?
NOTHING MUCH..
LIFE GOES ON..
SCHULZ
8-2

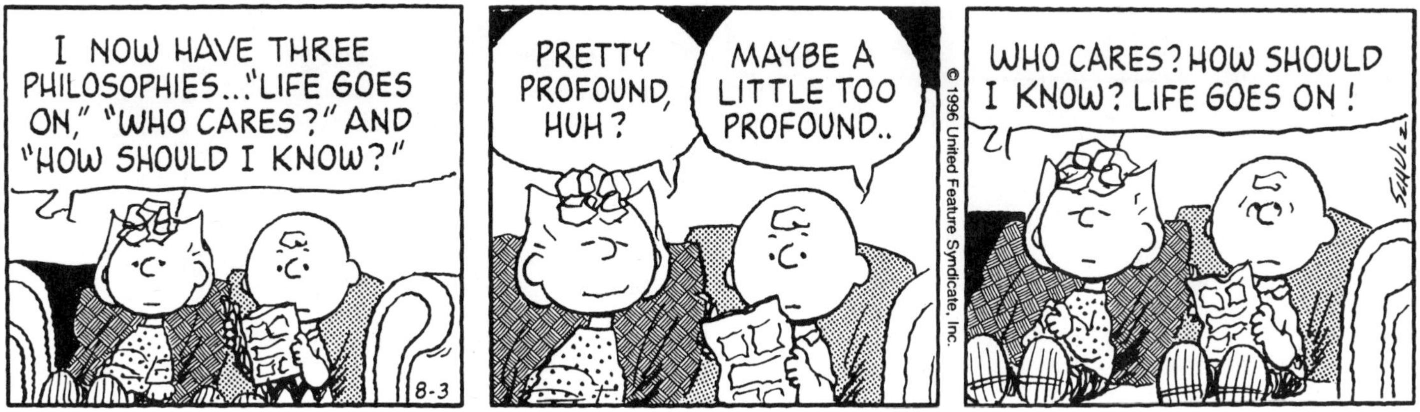
I NOW HAVE THREE PHILOSOPHIES.."LIFE GOES ON," "WHO CARES?" AND "HOW SHOULD I KNOW?"
PRETTY PROFOUND, HUH?
MAYBE A LITTLE TOO PROFOUND..
WHO CARES? HOW SHOULD I KNOW? LIFE GOES ON!
SCHULZ
8-3

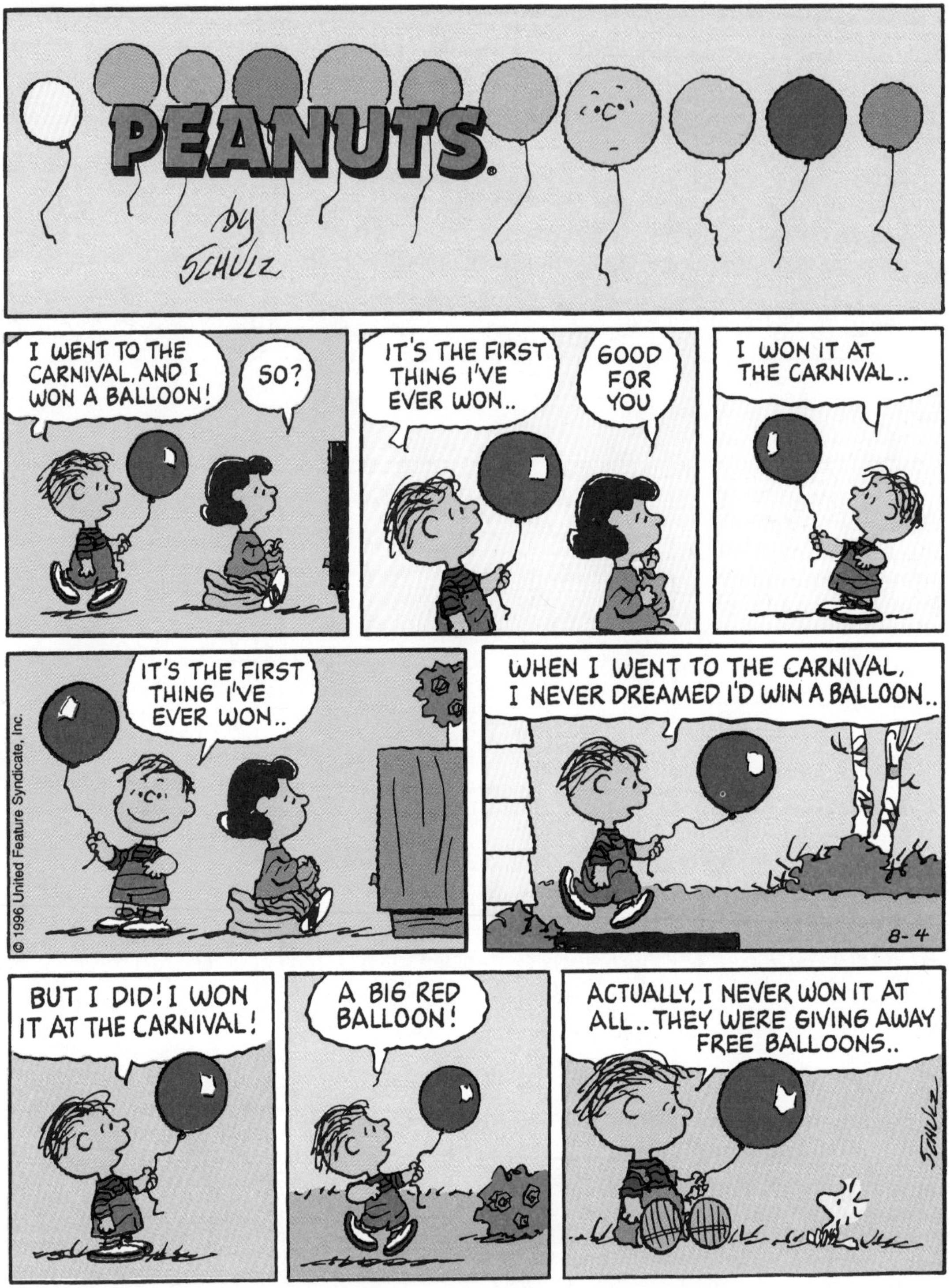
PEANUTS®
by SCHULZ
I WENT TO THE CARNIVAL, AND I WON A BALLOON!
SO?
IT'S THE FIRST THING I'VE EVER WON..
GOOD FOR YOU
I WON IT AT THE CARNIVAL..
IT'S THE FIRST THING I'VE EVER WON..
© 1996 United Feature Syndicate, Inc.
WHEN I WENT TO THE CARNIVAL, I NEVER DREAMED I'D WIN A BALLOON..
8-4
BUT I DID! I WON IT AT THE CARNIVAL!
A BIG RED BALLOON!
ACTUALLY, I NEVER WON IT AT ALL.. THEY WERE GIVING AWAY FREE BALLOONS..
SCHULZ

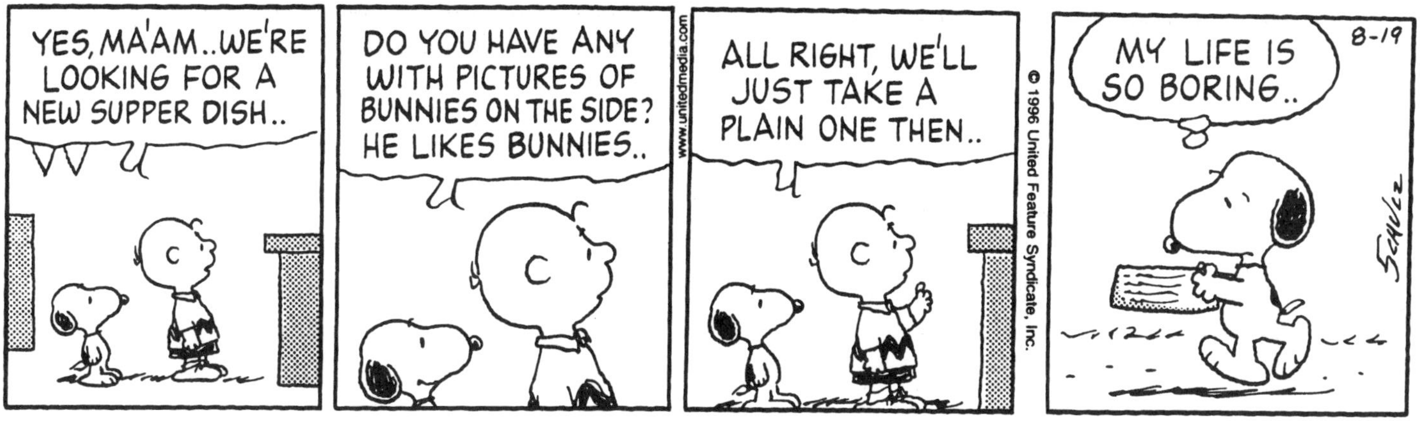
YES, MA'AM.. WE'RE LOOKING FOR A NEW SUPPER DISH..
DO YOU HAVE ANY WITH PICTURES OF BUNNIES ON THE SIDE? HE LIKES BUNNIES..
www.unitedmedia.com
ALL RIGHT, WE'LL JUST TAKE A PLAIN ONE THEN..
© 1996 United Feature Syndicate, Inc.
8-19
MY LIFE IS SO BORING..
SCHULZ

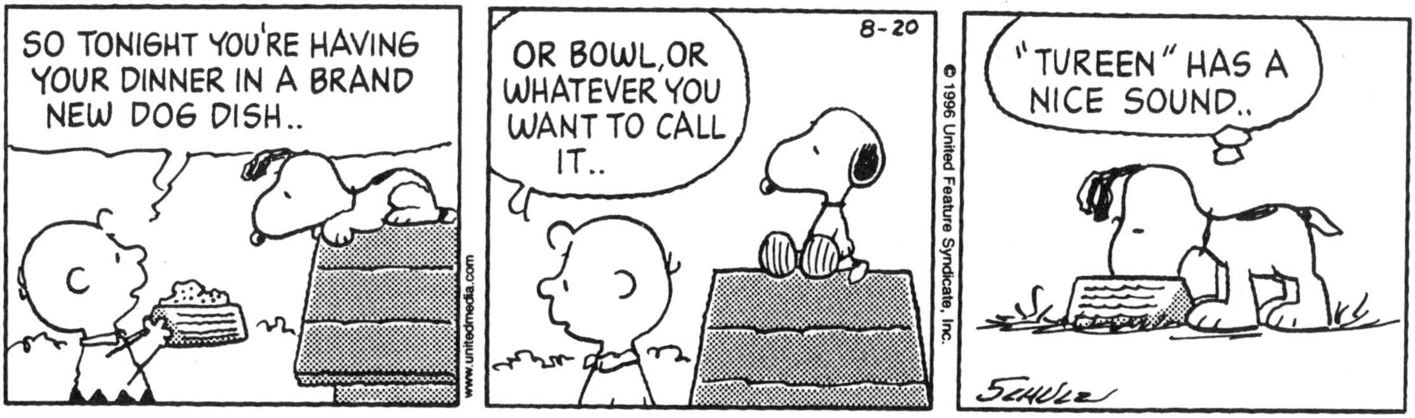
SO TONIGHT YOU'RE HAVING YOUR DINNER IN A BRAND NEW DOG DISH..
www.unitedmedia.com
8-20
OR BOWL, OR WHATEVER YOU WANT TO CALL IT..
© 1996 United Feature Syndicate, Inc.
"TUREEN" HAS A NICE SOUND..
SCHULZ

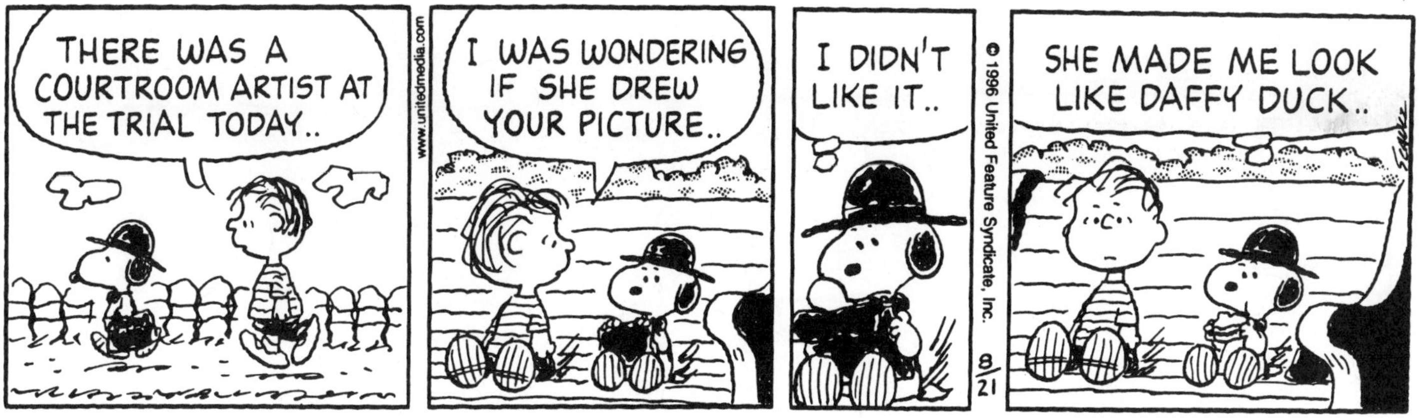
THERE WAS A COURTROOM ARTIST AT THE TRIAL TODAY..
www.unitedmedia.com
I WAS WONDERING IF SHE DREW YOUR PICTURE..
I DIDN'T LIKE IT..
© 1996 United Feature Syndicate, Inc.
8/21
SHE MADE ME LOOK LIKE DAFFY DUCK..
SCHULZ

105

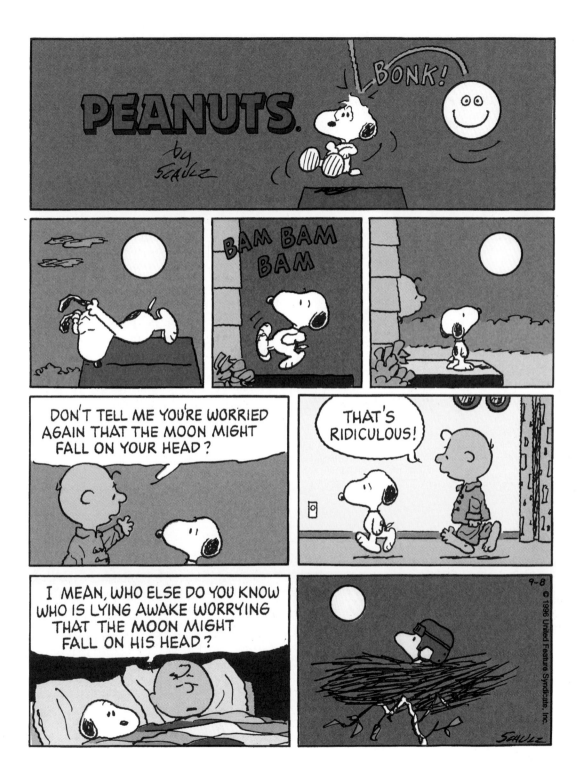

116

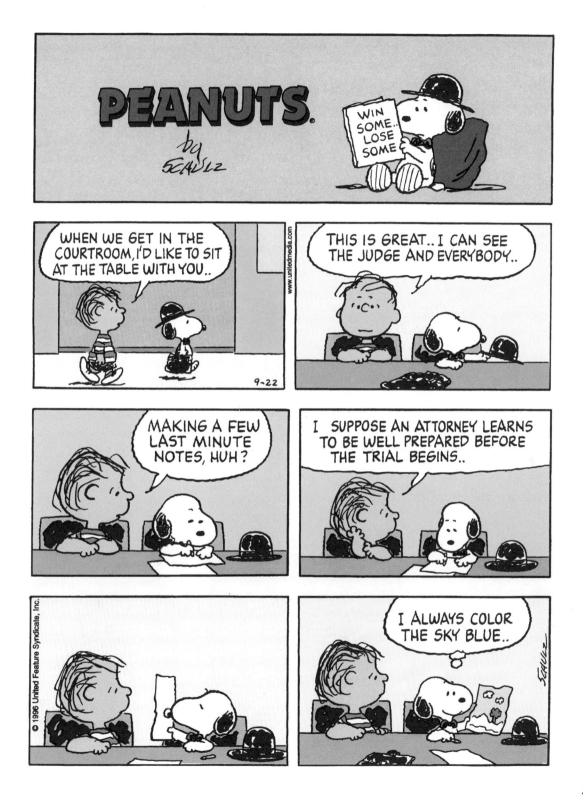

119

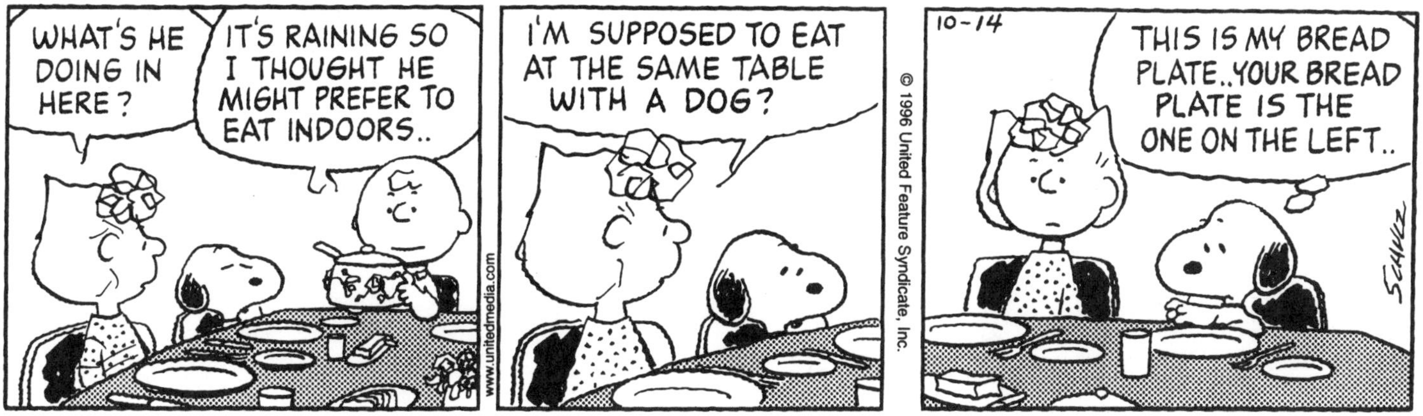
WHAT'S HE DOING IN HERE?
IT'S RAINING SO I THOUGHT HE MIGHT PREFER TO EAT INDOORS..
www.unitedmedia.com
I'M SUPPOSED TO EAT AT THE SAME TABLE WITH A DOG?
© 1996 United Feature Syndicate, Inc.
10-14
THIS IS MY BREAD PLATE..YOUR BREAD PLATE IS THE ONE ON THE LEFT..
SCHULZ

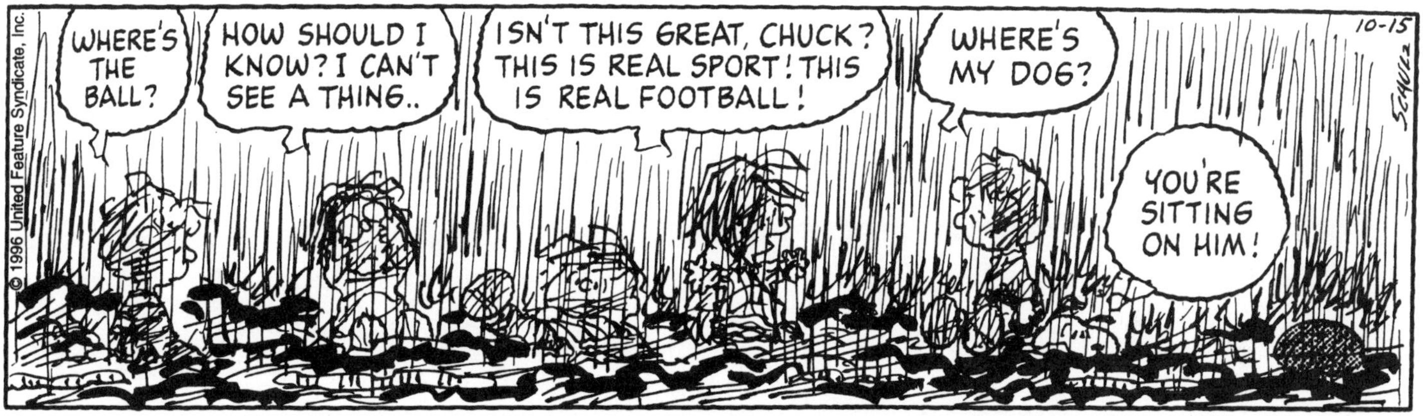
© 1996 United Feature Syndicate, Inc.
WHERE'S THE BALL?
HOW SHOULD I KNOW? I CAN'T SEE A THING..
ISN'T THIS GREAT, CHUCK? THIS IS REAL SPORT! THIS IS REAL FOOTBALL!
WHERE'S MY DOG?
10-15
SCHULZ
YOU'RE SITTING ON HIM!

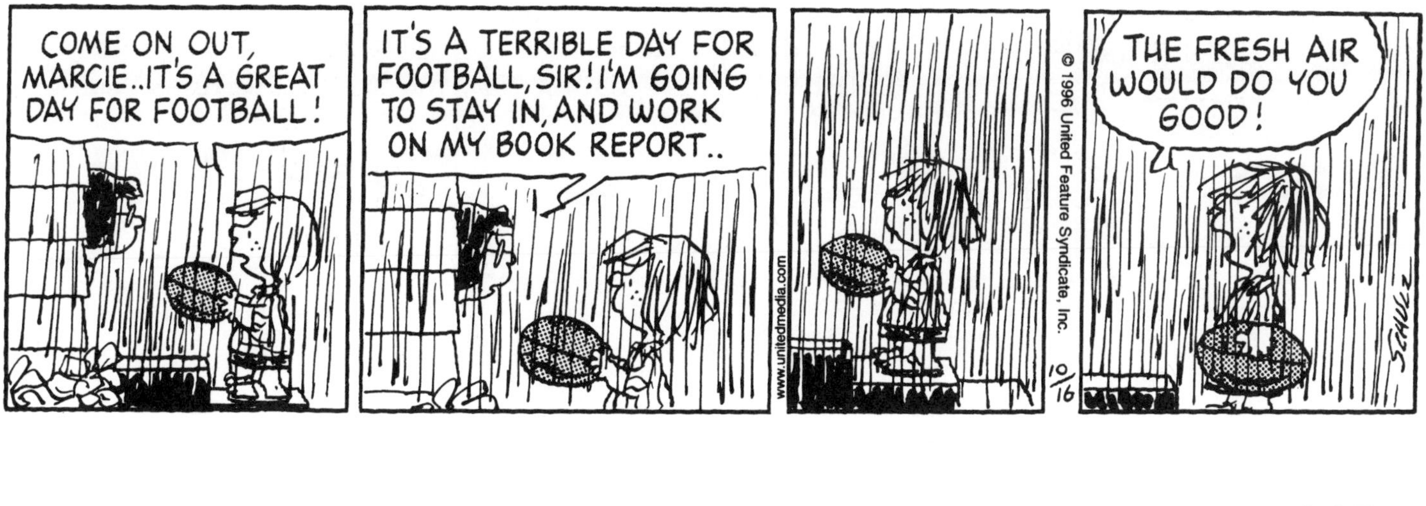
COME ON OUT, MARCIE..IT'S A GREAT DAY FOR FOOTBALL!
IT'S A TERRIBLE DAY FOR FOOTBALL, SIR! I'M GOING TO STAY IN, AND WORK ON MY BOOK REPORT..
www.unitedmedia.com
© 1996 United Feature Syndicate, Inc.
10/16
THE FRESH AIR WOULD DO YOU GOOD!
SCHULZ

128

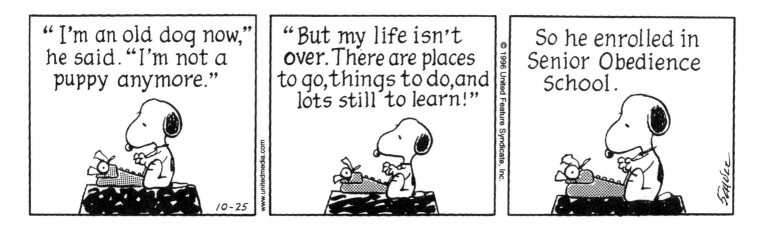

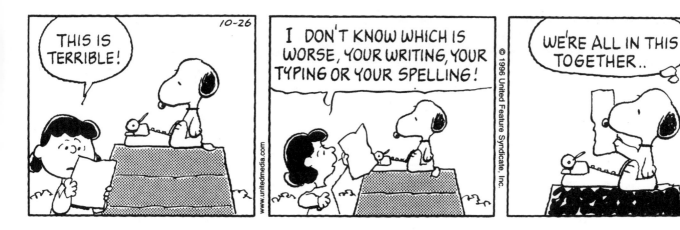

134

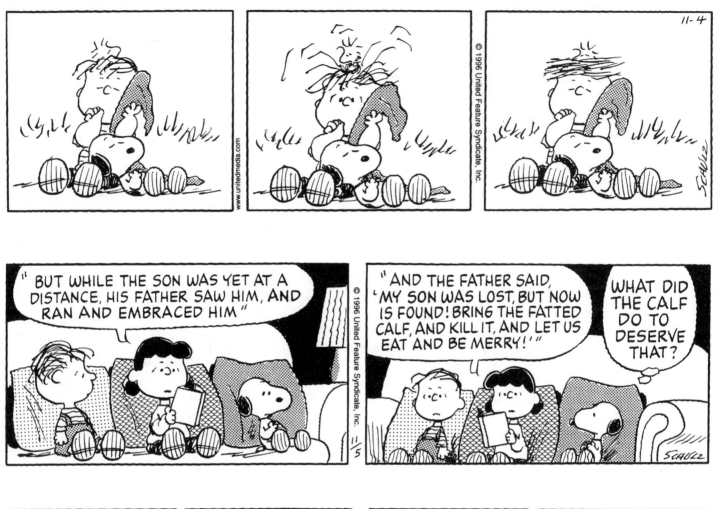

PEANUTS
by SCHULZ
WHEN IS HE COMING, MA?
HUSH, CHILD..
© 1996 United Feature Syndicate, Inc.
I THINK I SEE HIM!
SCHULZ 11-10
THANK YOU..
THANK YOU.. NICE TO SEE YOU..
THANK YOU..
NICE TO SEE YOU..
THANK YOU..
EVEN LINUS HIMSELF WAS SURPRISED AT THE HUGE CROWD THAT HAD GATHERED TO WELCOME HIM ON HIS RETURN..

139

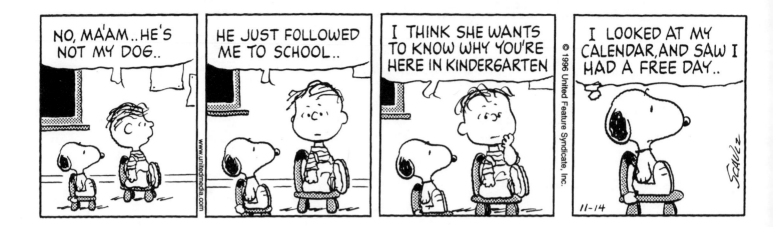

140

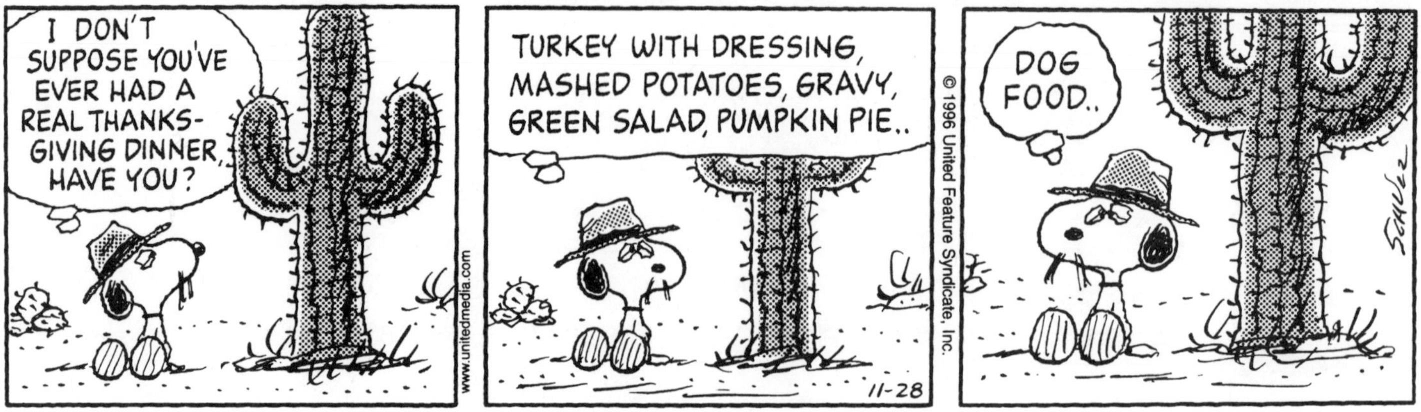
I DON'T SUPPOSE YOU'VE EVER HAD A REAL THANKSGIVING DINNER, HAVE YOU?
www.unitedmedia.com
TURKEY WITH DRESSING, MASHED POTATOES, GRAVY, GREEN SALAD, PUMPKIN PIE..
11-28
© 1996 United Feature Syndicate, Inc.
DOG FOOD..
SCHULZ

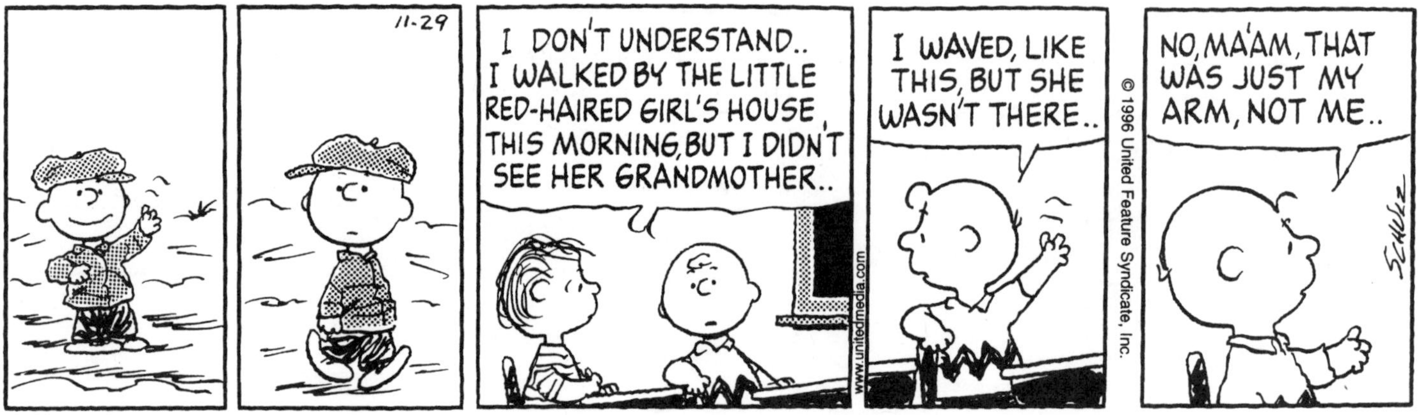
11-29
I DON'T UNDERSTAND.. I WALKED BY THE LITTLE RED-HAIRED GIRL'S HOUSE THIS MORNING, BUT I DIDN'T SEE HER GRANDMOTHER..
www.unitedmedia.com
I WAVED, LIKE THIS, BUT SHE WASN'T THERE..
© 1996 United Feature Syndicate, Inc.
NO, MA'AM, THAT WAS JUST MY ARM, NOT ME..
SCHULZ

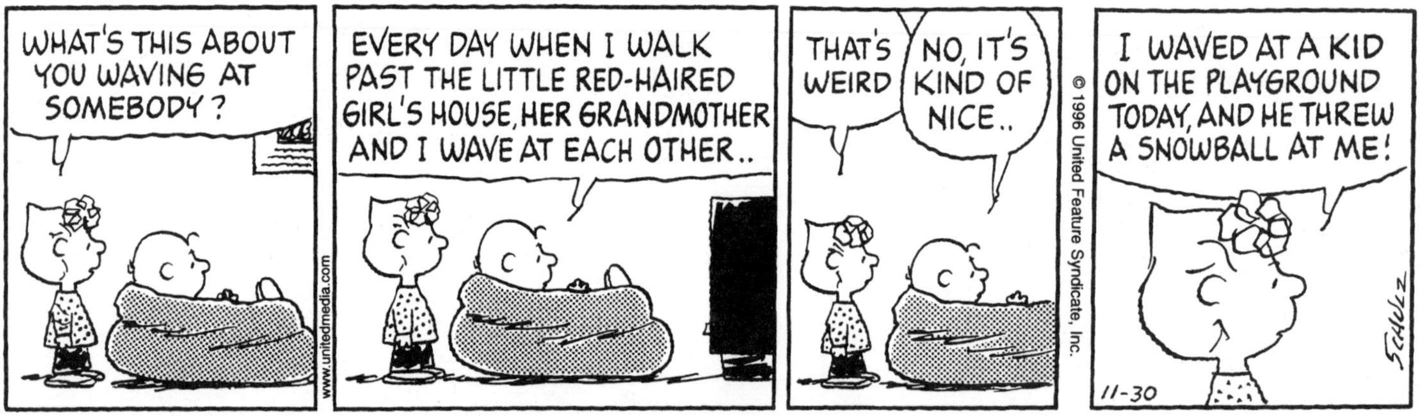
WHAT'S THIS ABOUT YOU WAVING AT SOMEBODY?
www.unitedmedia.com
EVERY DAY WHEN I WALK PAST THE LITTLE RED-HAIRED GIRL'S HOUSE, HER GRANDMOTHER AND I WAVE AT EACH OTHER..
THAT'S WEIRD
NO, IT'S KIND OF NICE..
© 1996 United Feature Syndicate, Inc.
I WAVED AT A KID ON THE PLAYGROUND TODAY, AND HE THREW A SNOWBALL AT ME!
11-30
SCHULZ

148

152

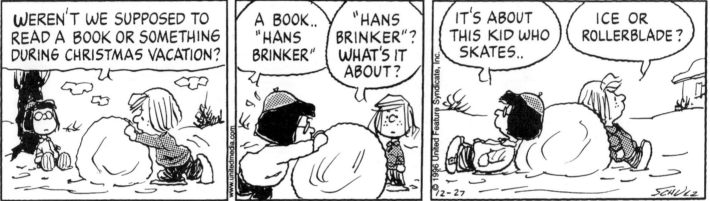

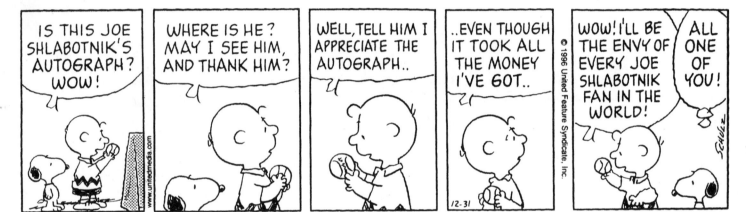